"You need to meet a good friend of mine" was a memorable request from evangelist Leonard Ravenhill many years ago. I had learned that it was rare for Leonard to endorse anyone. Follow-up came quickly, and soon his friend Mike Brown and I became the best of friends.

The depth of our relationship was enriched by spending years together in the trenches of the Brownsville Revival. We worked as a team. I gave the altar calls, and Dr. Brown did everything he could to enlist the new young warriors into Bible school. His and the other leaders' efforts paid off, as we saw thousands discipled and launched out into the whitened harvest fields. Now, years later, we remain solid friends and continue fighting side by side for the souls of men.

It is my privilege to recommend Mike's book on true, undefiled grace. His writing is of the highest quality. He is a master at defending the truth.

You, the reader, are the deciding jury. Dr. Brown is the attorney, and this book is his captivating argument. When the last word is read the verdict will be clear: God's grace will have been defined and defended.

Now, let peace reign in your heart on this most precious virtue of our loving Savior.

—Steve Hill

Evangelist and Author of *Spiritual Avalanche*

We are living in a crucial hour when deception is sweeping into the church through a distorted grace message that is quickly growing in popularity. I'm so thankful for leaders like Michael Brown who are boldly standing up for the glorious truth of the biblical grace message. Michael is a trusted scholar who writes with a voice of loving correction rather than criticism or condemnation. He rightly divides the Scriptures to shed light on the errors of the distorted grace teaching and bring us back to a place of balance and true liberty. I encourage everyone to read *Hyper-Gr*[illegible] lives and share it with as many as yo[illegible]

[illegible]ke Bickle

[illegible]f IHOPKC

God's amazing grace is both "amazing" and "gracious," and we can all thank Him for that. But Dr. Michael Brown believes that as recipients of God's good grace, it behooves us to come to terms with what Scripture reveals about the essence and substance of our amazing grace, and to offer a corrective to those who misrepresent and cheapen it. This book is a must-read.

—Dr. Jeffrey L. Seif
Distinguished Professor of Bible and Jewish Studies,
Kings University

Dr. Michael Brown is one of the key voices today on the issues that face the church and the issues that face the society as a whole. His response to the loss of standards in the church fostered by hyper-grace (nonbiblical view of grace) teaching is a powerful statement. The whole meaning of salvation is at stake. As usual, Dr. Brown's prose is passionate, powerful, and persuasive with a masterful use of the biblical text.

—Dr. Daniel Juster
Director of Tikkun International

HYPER-GRACE

MICHAEL L. BROWN, PhD

HYPER-GRACE

Most Charisma House Book Group products are available at special quantity discounts for bulk purchase for sales promotions, premiums, fund-raising, and educational needs. For details, write Charisma House Book Group, 600 Rinehart Road, Lake Mary, Florida 32746, or telephone (407) 333-0600.

Hyper-Grace by Michael L. Brown, PhD
Published by Charisma House
Charisma Media/Charisma House Book Group
600 Rinehart Road
Lake Mary, Florida 32746
www.charismahouse.com

Author's Note: All italics in Scripture quotations reflect the author's emphasis with the exception of quotations from the Complete Jewish Bible (CJB), which italicizes Hebrew terms.

Cover design by Justin Evans
Design Director: Bill Johnson

Visit the author's website at www.AskDrBrown.org.

Library of Congress Cataloging-in-Publication Data:
Hyper-grace / Michael Brown. -- First edition.
pages cm
Includes bibliographical references.
ISBN 978-1-62136-589-1 (trade paper) -- ISBN 978-1-62136-590-7 (ebook)
1. Grace (Theology) I. Title.
BT761.3.B75 2014
234--dc23

2013037431

14 15 16 17 18 — 9 8 7 6 5 4 3 2
Printed in the United States of America

CONTENTS

PREFACE

IN HIS BOOK *What's So Amazing About Grace?* author Philip Yancey relates a story about the significance of grace. He writes:

> During a British conference on comparative religions, experts from around the world debated what, if any, belief was unique to the Christian faith. They began eliminating possibilities. Incarnation? Other religions had different versions of gods' appearing in human form. Resurrection? Again, other religions had accounts of return from death. The debate went on for some time until C. S. Lewis wandered into the room. "What's the rumpus about?" he asked, and heard in reply that his colleagues were discussing Christianity's unique contribution among world religions. Lewis responded, "Oh, that's easy. It's grace."[1]

It is out of both love and jealousy for God's grace that I have written this book. Like many of you reading these pages, I have seen the destructive effects of legalism, which I define as externally imposed religion, specifically, rules without relationship, standards without a Savior, and laws without love. And I have experienced and seen the glorious, liberating impact of grace. In fact, I can't imagine living outside of God's grace even for a minute, and I would never write anything that would minimize grace or take it for granted.

But grace is often misunderstood. You see, it is not only the Lord's unmerited favor, although that is a glorious starting point, often expressed as **G**od's **R**iches **A**t **C**hrist's **E**xpense. It is also His ongoing empowerment, His continued working on our behalf—what Jesus did for us when He saved us as lost sinners and what He continues to do in, through, and for us now that we are saved. To quote A. M. Hunter, "Grace means primarily the free, forgiving love of God in Christ to sinners and the operation of that love in the lives of Christians."[2]

In the last few years, however, a wonderful message about grace has become mixed with some serious distortions and errors, claiming to be a new revelation of grace or a so-called "grace reformation" or "grace revolution." And although I have heard many wonderful testimonies from those whose lives have been changed by the truths of the message—and those truths are life-changing—because this new version of the message of grace has been distorted, it is also hurting many others, not to mention dividing churches and leading some into outright heresy.

That being said, I didn't simply decide to write this book, nor have I written it as God's policeman, sent to enforce proper doctrine in the church. (I'll talk about this more in the first few chapters.) Instead, these issues came knocking at my door, especially in the last twelve months. It seemed that everywhere I turned I ran into people presenting "grace" teachings to me in the most exaggerated, aggressive, unscriptural, pushy, and even judgmental ways, most all of them repeating the same points, often even using the same words. And from across the country, and even around the world, pastors and leaders began to contact me—people who love grace deeply—saying, "Where is this stuff coming from? Please address it!"

So I have written this book in obedience to the Lord, clearly feeling His calling to speak out in the name of grace and truth, concerned about the spiritual well-being of many brothers and sisters in the body. But I wrestled deeply over this before God, not wanting to write in a reactionary way. I wanted to write only as I sensed the life-giving flow of the Spirit. It is up to the Lord and others to decide whether I have succeeded, but I was determined to write in a way that exalted grace and built up rather than tore down. (Where I have torn down error, I have done my best to replace it with biblical truth.)

Over the course of writing I contacted a number of leaders with whom I disagreed, asking them if I rightly understood their positions or if they still held to their views. In each case they made clear to me that yes, this is where they stood. I trust I have quoted them fairly, and that's one reason for the hundreds of endnotes to this book: first, to cite sources accurately, and second, to back up the positions I have taken here and to point the reader to further resources. (I'm fully aware that not all hyper-grace teachers agree on all points, but I did my best to present representative examples from the most influential teachers.)

I want to underscore, however, that with the exception of those who have stepped into outright heresy, this is a dispute within the body, a set of strong differences among fellow-believers, men and women with whom I plan to spend eternity and, in most cases, people from whose writings and messages I have enjoyed outside of those areas where we differ. And I have sought to address things in that spirit, being both fair and gracious, straightforward and conciliatory.

Not surprisingly, some have taken exception to the fact that I and a number of others have referred to this message as "hyper-grace," but I have done so to be descriptive. On the one hand, many who preach this message say, "Yes! Amen! Grace is hyper!" And so they embrace the concept of "hyper-grace." On the other hand, from my vantage point it is clear to me that their message goes beyond true grace, hence it is "hyper" in that sense of the word. Again, you, the reader, will have to decide if the message is "hyper" in the good or the bad sense of the word.

I have also referred to this as "the modern grace" message, again in a neutral sense that will be decided by the content of the teaching. Is it a glorious message that is being preached and taught today—hence "modern" in that sense; or is it a contemporary, distorted version of the message—hence "modern" in that sense? But notice that I have not referred to it as "counterfeit grace," because I believe that wonderful grace truths are being taught by many of these leaders, which is one of the reasons so many of their books get five-star reviews from their readers who say, "I have been so blessed and set free because of this message of grace, and I am closer to the Lord than ever before!"

In light of that, I have written carefully, not wanting to steal anything from those who have been helped through the modern grace message, starting the book with a chapter that extols grace, constantly emphasizing the glories of God's grace throughout the book, and ending with a chapter on the finished work of the cross. And for those who have reacted against grace because of contemporary abuses, it is my prayer that this book will help you recover the grace of the Lord Jesus.

One last note about terminology: in recent months I have increased the call for teachers, preachers, professors, and Bible translators to stop using the name "James" in place of "Jacob" in reference to Jesus' disciple (as the Greek uses Jacob throughout the New Testament).[3] I have also been encouraging the recovery of "Judah" for "Jude" (yes, this certainly makes a difference!). So throughout this book, I use Jacob with James in parentheses and the same with Judah/Jude.

As a supplement to this book, I have put together some relevant, free resources that can be downloaded by writing to info@askdrbrown.org and using the subject "Hyper-Grace Download." You'll also find thousands of hours of free resources on a wide range of subjects as well as my blog at AskDrBrown.org. Please let us know if the book has been of benefit to you, and be assured that we are here to help you grow in the grace and knowledge of the Lord.

-1-

WHY I LOVE THE MESSAGE OF GRACE

IT WAS JOHN Newton, the former slave trader and the author of "Amazing Grace," who penned the famous words "How precious did that grace appear the hour I first believed." I can relate to that personally, and that's one reason I'm so jealous for the unadulterated grace of God—grace without mixture, grace without leaven, grace without exaggeration.

On December 17, 1971, the revelation of God's love so flooded my heart that I told the Lord I would never put a needle in my arm again, and I was free from that moment on. No more heroin. No more speed. No more hallucinogenic drugs. Jesus truly delivered me!

For the previous six weeks there had been a tremendous battle in my soul, beginning November 12, 1971, when I first believed that Jesus died for my sins. This alone was a major breakthrough for a sixteen-year-old, rebellious, proud, Jewish rock drummer! Prior to that I had mocked the message of the gospel and boasted about my sin, but as the believers in a little Italian Pentecostal church in Queens, New York, prayed for me without my knowing it, the Holy Spirit began to convict me, and I knew something was terribly wrong with my life.

Then after the light went on in my heart in November, I wrestled with God, shooting heroin one day and going to church the next, until that memorable service on December 17. As the pastor's wife played the piano and we sang the old hymns—hymns that sounded like little ditties to me compared to the Led Zeppelin and Jimi Hendrix music I listened to day and night—I became overwhelmed by the joy of the Lord and received a dramatic revelation.

In my mind's eye I saw myself filthy from head to toe, and then I saw myself washed cleaned with the blood of Jesus and clothed with beautiful white robes, only to go back and play in the mud. I was spurning God's love, a love that was poured out on me when I was a filthy, godless sinner. I was mocking the blood of Jesus, blood that was shed for me when I was stealing money from my own father and bragging about how deceitful I could be.

At that moment God's goodness exposed my badness, and I surrendered my life to the Lord and said good-bye to the life I had been living. And it was not hard to make the radical break. What a Savior!

Something else happened to me that December night. The guilt was gone. All of it! This too was a remarkable miracle.

You see, before the Spirit began to convict me of my sins, I would lie in bed at night, high on drugs and thinking about my sinful lifestyle and actions, but instead of feeling guilty, I felt proud. I thought of myself as quite an accomplished sinner! But when those believers starting praying for me, I became riddled with guilt over my sins, even though I had sinned without feeling any guilt for the previous two years. Now, when I lay in bed late at night, high on drugs and unable to sleep, the ugliness of my lifestyle would gnaw at me inside, deep under my skin, and I couldn't get rid of it. The very sins I had boasted about just weeks earlier were now a source of real shame.

But the night the Lord washed me clean and broke the addiction to drugs in my life, He did something else. He took away all the guilt, and no matter how hard I looked for it, even when I remembered some of the very worst things I had done, there was no feeling of guilt at all. God had forgiven and forgotten my sins, and He was no longer holding them against me. That is amazing grace!

There's something else I need to share that will help explain why I love God's grace so much. Some weeks after I was saved, I was sitting in the kitchen one night, talking with my Jewish dad, and he asked me a direct question: "Did you steal that money from me a few months back?"

Not only had I stolen the money—the last of several times I had committed that ugly act—but I had cut through the screen door in the back of the house to make it look as if someone had broken in. When my father came home and saw the damaged door and the money gone, I told him friends of mine had stolen it. To punish me, my dad said that none of my friends could come over to the house again, but I was sure he knew I did it.

Well, I was a believer now, and I couldn't lie to my wonderful dad, but I did. I told him I hadn't stolen the money, and with that I went upstairs to my bedroom and fell to my knees, feeling miserable. Immediately—and I mean immediately!—I was stricken with the Spirit's conviction, and I knew I couldn't lie to my father. So I told the Lord I was sorry for lying and that I would tell my dad the truth. All conviction left, and I thought to myself, "Well, maybe it was enough to tell the Lord I was sorry. Maybe I don't have to tell my dad." But like a holy dagger, conviction hit me again and I said, "All right, Lord, I'll tell him the truth."

So I went back downstairs where my father was still sitting, and I told him what I had done. And, as remarkable as this sounds, this is how my father responded (and he was not a believer in Jesus in any way at that time). He said to me, "Michael, when I saw the money missing I knew immediately you had stolen it, and I forgave you on the spot." (My eyes are tearing up as I write this more than forty-one years later.) "But what hurt me was that you had a need and didn't come to me for help." That was my earthly father!

Can you imagine what it was like to have a father like that? That's one reason I believe that for almost all my years in the Lord I have never doubted my heavenly Father's love and approval. That's also part of the reason I walk in a deep sense of security, why I find it easy to receive forgiveness when I have fallen short, and why walking in grace seems as natural to me as breathing air. But I fully understand that many other committed believers do not have this same experience, and I discovered this as a fairly young believer as well. Let me explain.

Feeling "Not Good Enough"

By the time I had been saved for one year, I was so hungry for God's Word and His presence that I would spend at least six hours alone with Him in my room every day, praying at least three hours (as a

Pentecostal, I would pray for one hour in tongues), reading the Word for two hours, and memorizing Scripture verses for one hour. (God gave me the grace to memorize twenty verses a day for about six months straight, and I could do it in one hour.) My best friend, who had helped lead me to the Lord, also spent a lot of time with the Lord every day, and we would normally compare notes in our youthful zeal, asking each other how much time was spent in prayer and the Word. (I know that might sound legalistic, but we really did love the Lord, and we loved the Word and prayer, and it was just our youthful immaturity that caused us to discuss this every day.)

One day he told me he had spent less than two hours total in prayer and the Word, whereas I had gotten in my normal six hours. When I asked him what happened, he explained that he had messed up in his thought life, giving way to lust. Because he felt miserable about it, he didn't spend as much time with the Lord. I told him the same thing had happened to me, but I still prayed and read the Word as always. When he asked me how I could sin in that way and still meet with God, I told him I confessed the sin to the Lord and was cleansed, and I went on without skipping a beat. Sadly he couldn't relate to this.

This got me wondering what was different between him and me. Later he told me about the tragic death of his father a few years earlier, and I began to put some pieces together. His dad had been at a Nathan's hot dog stand on Long Island in the early days of hallucinogenic drugs, and someone secretly spiked the mustard with LSD. His dad put the mustard on his hot dog without any clue of what happened. When he started to "trip," he thought he was losing his mind, and for many months after that he would have flashbacks, until he finally killed himself.

When I heard my friend's story, which I hadn't known before, I thought to myself, "I wonder if I can receive forgiveness more easily than he can because of the different situations with our earthly fathers?" Since then I've read about some of the most famous atheists whose lack of faith (or opposition to faith) can be traced back to the early death or abandonment of their father or to a weak father figure.[1]

Whatever the case of these atheists may be, I do understand that many fine believers have very sensitive consciences, and they are constantly guilt-ridden because they feel they are never doing enough. (I went through this for a couple of years when I started working full-time after high school and attending college and I no longer had six to seven hours to be with the Lord every day.) These individuals take God's words very literally, and if they are not loving God with their entire being every waking moment, or if they are not sacrificially loving their neighbors every day of their lives, they feel like selfish sinners.

They wonder: "Why should I be having fun with my family when there are lost sinners to reach?" "Why should I buy ice cream for my kids when there are starving children in my own country?" "Why should I relax when I'm supposed to be running my race?" As a serious, committed Christian shared with me one Sunday after I spoke on grace, "All my life as a believer I've always felt these words following me: not good enough."

That's why I'm truly thrilled to see so many believers being liberated by the modern grace message, especially those who tend to be introspective and self-condemning. I do not want to tamper with this for a moment, nor do I ever want to denigrate God's incredible mercy, even for a split second. And I am not standing on some "holier-than-thou" soapbox, judging the rest of the body. Perish the thought! In fact, I can honestly say that I have experienced more of God's grace and mercy since I have been saved than when I got saved.

God forbid that any of us would ever react *against* grace because others may teach about it in an exaggerated, distorted, or erroneous way. To the contrary, it is jealousy *for* God's grace that moves me to write this book. And, as I mentioned in the preface, it is because I have been determined to write only when I sensed the life-giving flow of the Spirit that I took a considerable amount of time to finish the book.

I also want to emphasize that those I'm differing with in this book are brothers and sisters in the Lord—at least, to the best of my knowledge—and with rare exception I find much in their writings and messages that thrills my soul and blesses me deeply. Often, as I would be reading their books, I would be shouting amen on one page, only to groan on the next page as a verse was misused or a key truth overlooked or a falsehood stated as if it were true.

And as I have read the books of men such as Joseph Prince, Clark Whitten, Steve McVey, Andrew Farley, Rob Rufus, Paul Ellis, and other modern grace teachers, I have prayed, "Father, show me what these men have that I need to hear. Give me a fresh revelation of Your grace! Show me anything I'm missing or not walking in or not faithfully communicating."

You see, I am not God's policeman, sent to keep the church straight and to enforce orthodox doctrine on every believer. All of us see in part and all of us know in part (1 Cor. 13:8–12), and while there are foundational doctrinal truths that I would die for and of which I have no doubt whatsoever, it would be the height of arrogance for me to think that everything I believe, to the last detail, is right and that anyone who differs with me in any area is wrong. What foolishness!

In 1992 I received a phone call from a nationally respected pastor at whose church I had recently begun preaching. In the previous few months I had been getting frustrated with some bad teaching in the body (not directly related to today's hyper-grace message), and rather than waiting before the Lord for His heart and insight, I began searching through the Scriptures with a frustrated attitude, trying to find ways to prove these other teachers wrong. But in the back of my mind, for some reason, I was saying to myself, "You need to do a fresh study of grace."

This highly respected pastor had sensed what was happening to me, and he called me to speak into my life—and to talk to me about grace! He explained to me how, just a couple of years earlier, God had told him that in some of his preaching he had been guilty of condemning the innocent. (See Proverbs 17:15.) (He actually shared this publicly with his whole congregation.) He said he saw that I could have the same tendency if I didn't rightly understand grace. I listened to him with rapt attention!

When I hung up the phone after our long talk, Nancy, my wonderful, faithful wife, asked me what we talked about. I broke down crying, and when she asked me why I was crying, I told her it was because God loved me enough to correct me! The divine correction made me feel specially loved. (I told you that I find it very easy to walk in the Father's love!)

I wrote to the pastor immediately, recognizing exactly what he was saying about the rut I had fallen into, and our fruitful ministry relationship continued for years after that, as he recognized that I understood and received the counsel he was giving to me. More importantly, the fresh study of grace that I undertook in 1992—in particular, focusing on the Greek word *charis*—brought me deep insights that I have preached and that I live by to this very day.[2]

Some of the modern grace teachers preach grace with these same insights, just as I preach and believe, and yet they are introducing some serious deviations as well—dangerous deviations that could lead to the kind of error that puts people in bondage rather than liberates. And that is why I have written this book. So if you love grace as I do, then by all means, keep reading.

-2-

IS THERE A NEW GRACE REFORMATION?

IS THERE A new reformation sweeping the church today, a reformation as radical and important as the Protestant Reformation that rocked the world five hundred years ago? According to a growing number of Christian leaders, the answer is emphatically yes. Some of these leaders even feel they are at the forefront of this new movement, often styled a "grace reformation."

Pastor Clark Whitten, author of *Pure Grace: The Life Changing Power of Uncontaminated Grace*, claims that, "Little has changed in the Protestant church in more than 500 years"—until now, that is. He believes that Luther and Calvin "got it right concerning justification, or how one is saved.... But they missed it on sanctification, or how one is perfected into the likeness of Christ."[1]

Whitten states that Luther and Calvin, followed by the Protestant church ever since, taught a doctrine of "saved by grace but perfected by human effort," an approach that has produced "a Church that is judgmental, angry, hopeless, helpless, dependent, fearful, uninspired, ineffective, and perpetually spiritually immature." Because of this, Whitten claims, we have failed to impact our culture and have become a laughingstock to most "casual observers." And Pastor Whitten contends that this doctrine has also brought "personal devastation" to countless believers who have consequently checked out on church (or on God Himself).[2]

This concerned pastor minces no words in his attack on what he labels "religion—not real Christianity," which, he says, "is and always has been in the behavior modification and sin management business. It is so lucrative and so firmly entrenched in the Church that it will take *a second Great Reformation and a revelation of no less importance than Luther's to correct this great and spiritually murderous lie.*"[3]

Has Whitten overstated his case? According to Alan Chambers, who led Exodus International for a number of years until its closing in 2013, the answer is emphatically no. As noted by New Testament scholar Robert Gagnon, "on March 25, 2012, [Chambers] introduced Clark's book with the words: 'God has unveiled something that has been veiled for hundreds and hundreds of years.'"[4]

John Crowder, who identifies himself as a "new mystic," goes even further, saying, "Just as there is a *new mysticism* on the rise, I believe it is coupled with a new reformation. The good news will be preached with such clarity that, even the days of Luther will seem utterly primitive in its concepts of grace and faith." Yes, "Even the reformers were not reformed enough. You will see how the cross united us to Christ, not just positionally, but effectively. It doesn't just cover our sins, but eradicates sinfulness itself from us."[5]

He goes on to proclaim:

> What I am telling you here is one of the most revolutionary principles in Christendom. I am preaching reformation clearer than it was preached 500 years ago. Martin Luther, you didn't go far enough. God didn't just cover your sins; He erased *sinfulness* from you.... The good news will be preached with such clarity that, even the days of Luther will seem utterly primitive in its concepts of grace and faith.[6]

Indeed, Crowder writes that "a clarity is coming to the preaching of the gospel like has not been heard since the days of the Apostle Paul."[7] Other modern grace teachers share similar sentiments. In his book *GRACE, the Forbidden Gospel*, Andre van der Merwe writes:

> Once again in the church there is a struggle for a theological reformation that will liberate believers to break free from the yoke of bondage that has been put on the children of God by people who may have had good intentions, but that have only taught the religious doctrines and traditions that they themselves have been taught.[8]

His prayer is that his book will "destroy the religious arguments and doctrines of demons forever,"[9] referring to whatever teaching contradicts this allegedly new revelation of grace. Strong words. That's why the full title of his book is *GRACE, the Forbidden Gospel: Jesus Tore the Veil. Religion Sewed It Back Up*. The church at large, according to this title, is apparently working against Jesus and the gospel. And even though van der Merwe is a fairly young believer who himself has been transformed through this new grace revelation, other leaders are lining up to commend his work and to second these sentiments.

Tony Ide, pastor of Freedom Life Fellowship in Perth, Australia, had this to say about van der Merwe's book:

> This is more than a few personal opinions on grace. This book stands as an excellent concise commentary on the subject that breaks misconceptions, stirs faith, builds confidence and refutes the cynical critics. There is [a] grace reformation sweeping the earth and Andre has done much to further its advance. A recommended and essential resource for all grace exponents.[10]

Pastor Steve McVey, a best-selling author and the president of Grace Walk Ministries, writes:

> The climate of the church of Jesus Christ today finds itself in a place where legalism has a debilitating effect on many people. Across the world, the focus within the church is largely on our behavior and how we need to do a better job in living the Christian life if we expect God to move on our behalf and in our midst. The result of that focus has been devastating. The only antidote to this problem is grace and that's what this book is all about.[11]

Yes, nothing less than a new reformation in the church's understanding of grace will do, as stated by Rob Rufus, pastor of City Church International in Hong Kong: "The church today does not need another spiritual revival (because revivals come and go); it needs another theological reformation as it did in the days of Martin Luther! Reformation will automatically bring about revival."[12] Pastor Rufus, of course, is speaking of the same grace reformation, or in the words of

Joseph Prince, perhaps the best-known modern grace preacher, it is a "Gospel Revolution."[13]

Clark Whitten's grace teaching has drawn high praises by well-known pastors, Christian university presidents, and internationally respected leaders, some of whom are personal friends of mine and in whose churches I have preached. One of these leaders exclaimed, "Without a doubt, [Clark Whitten] is the greatest authority on the subject of grace I know."[14]

Could it be, then, that there really is a grace reformation sweeping the body today? Could it be that the church has been so stuck in legalistic religion for the last five hundred years that nothing less than a radical reformation can get us out of the rut?

Fresh Encounters With Grace

It seems clear that many believers have been caught up in externally imposed religion (which is the essence of legalism), seeking to please God by following an endless list of "dos" and "don'ts," never being certain of the Father's love and looking first to their own efforts rather than looking first to the cross. Consequently they are always falling short and never walking in the abundant life that Jesus has for them.

Within a two-day span I heard from two women, both friends of our family and former students in our ministry school, both married with children and active in God's service. One wrote this: "I am one of many who have been changed drastically and fantastically by the 'grace message.' Judging by the amazing fruit of it in my life and my family's life as we have gone through some very hard times, it is the fruit of the true grace message."

Speaking of one well-known, modern grace teacher, she explained that while she only agreed with about 80 percent of what he taught, she said, "I feel like I have taken a bath and glimpsed the beauty of Jesus and what He did for me almost every time I hear him." This is wonderful to hear, and I do not want to tamper with something so sacred and liberating.

The other ministry school grad wrote this: "I can say for me, I sure tried, and worked, and failed. Finally, almost three years ago, I finally had a 'Grace encounter' that changed my life. Can honestly say I'm more free, more confident, and more 'sin-LESS' than I've ever been. If that makes sense."

She shared with me the struggles she'd had for years in her marriage and personal walk with the Lord, because of which she received counseling and teaching from her church. After a while, the truths of God's grace took hold:

> I get before Daddy G-d, and "be" and out of that love, the "works" happen. Out of love, and not trying. I could never explain this to another, or they might think I'm one who condones sin, or who takes Grace the wrong way. I know better, because my tree is bearing fruit!!! My love for the ones I didn't have time for is growing. Too much to write. But now I LOVE life. With all the trials, I love my life!!!! That is amazing to me!!! That is Grace!!

This is from the Lord!

Andre van der Merwe describes what his life was like before he understood God's grace, and he is certain that many other believers live just like this:

- You constantly need someone to tell you that God still loves you, and even though you know this, you don't really believe it.
- You are never really sure that if you were to die right now that you are actually going to heaven.
- You lack confidence in approaching God because of guilt about something you've done.
- You mostly feel that you are not doing enough for God to be pleased with you; etc.[15]

Personally, I can't relate to the items on this list in terms of my own walk with the Lord, since, as I said previously, I live with a 24/7 assurance of my Father's love for me. In fact, aside from a short season in the mid-1970s when I felt God was not pleased with me because I wasn't spending at least six hours a day in the Word and prayer (which had been my habit when I was eighteen years old), I have never struggled with any of these areas. But I have met many believers who struggle as Andre did, and when I hear today that through a revelation of God's grace they are now living in intimacy with the Lord and overflowing with joy at His great love for them, I am thrilled. That is truly wonderful news, and it indicates that, for many, there is a need for a fresh infusion of anointed teaching on the beauty and glory and wonder of God's amazing grace.

At the same time I constantly hear stories from believers and leaders concerned about the modern grace message, like this one: "I have seen the effects of this message on my own loved ones. It has ruined our family and caused many of them who loved the Lord to stray." And this: "We have seen this up close and personal with some of our family members. Very destructive things are going on." And this from a pastor, who said, "[Of] the three close male friends I have had in the past, all three from the grace side, two were unfaithful and then left their wives and the third just left. I have had no one close in the grace group (forgive my terms) displaying good, lasting fruit."

A woman wrote to me on Facebook in response to my teachings on hyper-grace:

> Your words pierce my hard heart and bring tears to my eyes. I can't believe how far away from my Savior I have strayed listening to "feel good" Christian teachers. Thank you for drawing me back with your word of truth. It is much needed today, as I know I am not alone in being a victim of deception in the Christian world. Thanks again and God bless you!

A man who had served with a well-known hyper-grace leader wrote to me at length, wanting me to understand just how bad things were:

> I heard more "F" and "S" words in that movement than anywhere else in my entire life. After all, you're "legalistic" if you EVER tell someone to "not" do something. (Grace only empowers us to do things, it never tells us to NOT do things—that's legalism or "do-do" Christianity as they called it. This is why Titus 2:11–12 was instrumental in leading me out of the movement.)

Is this simply a matter of a glorious truth being misunderstood and abused, or is it a matter of a glorious truth being diluted and polluted by errors, leading to backsliding, compromise, and even apostasy? Years ago Charles Spurgeon gave this strong word of caution:

> I have admitted that a few human beings have turned the grace of God into lasciviousness; but I trust no one will ever argue against any doctrine on account of the perverse use made of it by the baser sort. Cannot every truth be perverted? Is there a single doctrine of Scripture which graceless hands have not twisted into mischief? Is there not an almost infinite ingenuity in wicked men for making evil out of good? If we are to condemn a truth because of the misbehaviour of individuals who profess to believe it, we should be found condemning our Lord himself for what Judas did, and our holy faith would die at the hands of apostates and hypocrites. Let us act like rational men. We do not find fault with ropes because poor insane creatures have hanged themselves therewith; nor do we ask that the wares of Sheffield [where metal objects were made] may be destroyed because edged tools are the murderer's instruments.[16]

We hear that same response today from modern grace teachers who say, "Yes, grace will be abused, but the problem is not with the message but with the abuser."

Honestly, I wish that was the case, since I love the message of grace (which I will joyfully affirm throughout this book, even if you get tired of hearing it), and it would be a shame if pastors and leaders drew back from preaching grace because it was abused. The truth is that the modern grace message is quite mixed, combining life-changing, Jesus-exalting revelation with serious misinterpretation of Scripture, bad theology, divisive and destructive rhetoric, and even fleshly reaction. And, in all too many cases, it is being embraced by believers who are not just looking for freedom from legalism but also freedom from God's standards.

An Alarming Mixture

There is no doubt in my mind, then, that the notion of a "grace reformation" (or "grace revolution") is highly exaggerated, that some of this new grace teaching is unbalanced, overstated, at times unbiblical, and sometimes downright dangerous—and I mean dangerous to the well-being of the body of Christ. In short, I do not believe that we are witnessing a new grace reformation. I believe we are witnessing the rise of a hyper-grace movement, filled with its own brand of legalistic judgmentalism, mixing some life-giving truth from the Word with some destructive error.

Of course, I have no objection to the idea that the church today, especially in the West, is in need of massive reformation and change. One of my books says this explicitly, even in the title and subtitle: *Revolution in the Church: Challenging the Religious System With a Call for Radical Change.*[17] And I do not endorse everything the past reformers taught. To give just two examples, I do not follow John Calvin's Calvinism, and as far as baptism is concerned, I stand with the Anabaptists against Martin Luther (not to mention his late-in-life horrific anti-Semitism).[18] And I believe there are many truths in the Word that one generation sees more clearly than another generation.

So, in principle, I have no problem with the *concept* of a new grace reformation. My problems with this movement are based on what I believe to be misinterpretation of God's Word and misrepresentation of His grace. In fact, at a time when the church in the West needs an urgent wake-up call leading to a fresh encounter with Jesus, the hyper-grace message is lulling many to sleep.

Simply stated (and to use some of Pastor Whitten's words), if you teach that we are saved by God's grace through faith, and that now as believers we are called by God to walk worthy of our salvation and to pursue holiness of heart and life—in other words, to work out the ongoing process of sanctification—you are preaching "behavior modification," you are in the (lucrative!) "sin management business," you are propagating the same "spiritually murderous lie" that Luther and Calvin did, and you need to receive the great new revelation of this great new reformation, the grace revolution. That is quite an accusation!

But these modern grace teachers really believe this, to the point that they are willing to imply (or state explicitly) that every church in the world that uses the Lord's Prayer in its liturgy is reinforcing "bad news that should make us shake in our boots" (even if they all wouldn't put it in those terms).[19] Why? It is because one of the foundations of their message is that the moment you were saved, God forgave not only your past and present sins but your future sins as well.

According to them, this means that it is wrong to ask God to forgive you when you sin today, and it is very wrong to think that your forgiveness is based on your forgiving others. (We will talk more about this in chapter 5.) Yet the Lord's Prayer contains the petition "forgive us our debts [meaning sins], as we also have forgiven our debtors [meaning those who sin against us]," with Jesus then adding, "For if you forgive others their trespasses, your heavenly Father will also forgive you, but if you do not forgive others their trespasses, neither will your Father forgive your trespasses" (Matt. 6:12, 14–15).

Modern grace teachers are emphatic that this does not apply to believers today, and so the hundreds of millions of believers who have used these words in prayer are also in serious error, deeply misunderstanding God's grace. That's what the "grace revolution" would have us believe.

In the preface to his book *The Unwavering Resolve of Jonathan Edwards*, Pastor Steven J. Lawson writes:

> Living the Christian life, by all biblical accounts, necessitates the passionate pursuit of personal holiness. Sanctification is never an elective course that a believer may or may not take. Neither is it an upper-level graduate study, required for only a few disciples. Instead, it is a core class, mandated for all Christians. Godliness is a lifelong study, for no one graduates from the school of Christ this side of heaven.
>
> Progress in personal holiness is absolutely crucial. The Bible says, "Pursue...sanctification without which no one will see the Lord" (Heb. 12:14, NASB). In other words, the path that leads to heaven must lead first to holiness. Jesus said, "Blessed are the

> pure in heart, for they shall see God" (Matt. 5:8). Growth in godliness marks *all* who are on the narrow path that leads to life.[20]

Lawson then portrays Edwards as a great example of godly resolve, writing that "Edwards lived with an enlarged desire to experience personal godliness. In this pursuit, he became a model of discipline worthy of our emulation."[21]

But ideas like this are anathema to many in the modern grace camp, which claims that we are already completely sanctified by faith and that we don't need to pursue holiness, let alone be disciplined in our pursuit of holiness. (We will explore this topic at length in chapter 7.) In fact, if you try sharing such concepts among proponents of the "grace reformation," you probably will quickly be met with sharp criticism. You will be called a legalist and a law-preacher, branded a Pharisee, accused of mixing law with grace, and told that you are confusing old covenant religion with new covenant liberty (which we will discuss further in chapter 3). And you will repeatedly hear the phrases "behavior modification" and "sin management," especially if you quote sentences like this: "To be sure, this pursuit [of holiness] necessitates self-discipline."[22]

Are we really to believe this is part of a glorious grace reformation? And was someone like Jonathan Edwards, one of the greatest Christian leaders in America in the eighteenth century, guilty of pursuing and even propagating a "spiritually murderous lie" (to use Whitten's phrase again)? Or was he guilty of preaching a "pseudo-gospel" (in the words of John Crowder) or promulgating "religious arguments and doctrines of demons" (to use the words of Andre van der Merwe)?

Grace and Truth

A friend of mine recently shared with me the words of a theologian who defined heresy as "where you take a half truth and make it the whole truth." That is certainly the root of all kinds of error in the body, and it is crucial that we never forget that "grace and truth" came through Jesus the Messiah (John 1:14, 17). It is essential, then, that we preach grace with truth rather than grace alone. Otherwise we will have a spiritual crisis on our hands. In fact, we already do have one on our hands.

A pastor posted this on the *Ministry Today* website after reading my article titled "A Compromised Gospel Produces Compromised Fruit":

> Dr. Brown has nailed this issue on the head. The greasy grace message is once again leading people into sin. As a pastor for more than 20 years I can tell you this "new" version of grace is destroying people's lives. Many pastors are now coming out of the closet and declaring their homosexuality as being "okay" and even "acceptable" based on the idea of grace!

"But that's outlandish!" you say. "There's no possible way that the modern grace message could lead to such abuses." Sadly that is not so, and I can demonstrate it to you.

Tell me what you think of this quote, found in the dedication of a book where the pastor (and author of the book) is thanking his congregation for taking the journey into grace with him: "This book is dedicated to the members of New Revelation Christian Church, who have taken the difficult journey from legalism to liberty and have become a better community of believers as a result."[23]

Does it sound good to you? How glorious it is to be liberated from legalism and brought into liberty! The problem is that the pastor is a practicing homosexual, and his church embraces practicing homosexuals into membership and ordains them into ministry. And the whole purpose of his book is to demonstrate that the Bible *never* condemns loving, committed same-sex relationships. This is a perfect example of grace without truth, which is really not grace at all.

How about this series of quotes, describing how a sixteen-year-old who loved the Lord almost lost his faith after becoming involved with legalistic Christians. Thankfully, we are told, he was delivered from that false teaching, which emphasized Old Testament, Levitical laws as if binding for today. Now he is enjoying the liberty of grace.

The author of this particular book writes about this young man with passion and conviction, telling us: "It was not until he was sixteen that he finally met the *wrong* people who, although calling themselves 'born-again Christians,' were nothing more than the self-righteous stumbling blocks of religion that Christ spoke of on many occasions."[24]

Who were these "self-righteous stumbling blocks of religion that Christ spoke of on many occasions"? It sounds like the very people the modern grace teachers are opposing today. Speaking of Jesus, the author writes:

> It is he who has saved—once and for all—those who put their trust on him *through a childlike and sincere faith alone* without exceptions, preconditions, or stipulations—thus nullifying and doing away with such things as religious law and tradition from the Law and the Prophets (the Old Testament law) that had imposed temporary rules on the Hebrew people for a short and specific time in history.[25]

This certainly sounds like it is taken right out of one of the many modern grace books, doesn't it? The author continues:

> Again, the aforementioned six-hundred and thirteen Old Testament Torah-based "Holiness Code" laws are all sweepingly done away with through Christ's separating mankind from the religiosity of religious law by his finished work for all on the cross, to where a relationship with God is now formed by our sincerely turning to Him by faith alone and simply asking Him—as a child would ask a parent for comfort and safety through a child-like faith—to become part of our lives, and believing (putting our trust) on Him who He has sent—and *not* by such frivolous works of obedience to *man's* rules and traditions—*nor* through being "religious," pious, and enchained to the noose of religious rule of *any* kind.[26]

There you have it. We are saved once and for all by childlike faith alone, "without exceptions, preconditions, or stipulations," and "not by such frivolous works of obedience to man's rules and traditions."

To repeat: these sound like quotes from any number of modern grace teachers, and there is some truth to them. The problem, quite sadly, is that these quotes are from another practicing homosexual who zealously argues against Christians who claim that the Bible is against loving, committed, same-sex practices, and the young man he spoke of here was a practicing homosexual "Christian." And the author accuses those who differ with him of being self-righteous, Pharisaical legalists.

This is what can happen when we preach grace without truth, and I'm afraid that many modern grace teachers, in their zeal to safeguard the glories of grace, preach their message without fundamental aspects of biblical truth. These would include: 1) God requires holy living from His people; 2) our sins do have an impact on our relationship with God; 3) you can preach grace and preach against sin at the same time; 4) there is much in the Old Testament that remains of foundational relevance to believers under grace. (And much more.)

But the stakes are higher still. According to John Crowder, "The gospel is simply too good to be true. If the message you've heard is not too good to be true, then it probably isn't. The gospel is too easy. Too marvelous. Too extraordinary. Too scandalously good to be true."[27]

Well, how far does that go? If you still believe that millions of people will suffer the judgment of hell, perhaps you haven't taken grace far enough. This is what Philip Gulley and James Mulholland argue in their book, *If Grace Is True: Why God Will Save Every Person.*[28] So, according to these authors, who believe that all human beings will ultimately be saved, John Crowder's message of grace doesn't go far enough! His message isn't "too good to be true."

But why stop with the salvation of all human beings? Why not believe that even the demons and Satan himself will be saved? This is exactly what one modern grace website suggested, proposing that even the devil and his angels could be transformed by the love and goodness of God. The website even suggested that Jerusalem would not have been destroyed if Jesus had spent more time blessing people than pronouncing judgment on the Jewish leaders!

Does this sound absolutely heretical? Of course it is, but that's what can happen when you divorce grace from truth and reject the clear teaching of Scripture, as recognized by generations of committed believers, and then label these foundational truths "religious" and "legalistic." Without a doubt, the stakes are very high.

How then do we sort this out? Modern grace adherents accuse me of mixing law with grace, while I believe they are guilty of mixing grace with error. Yet all of us believe that we should preach grace with truth. So my proposal is simple. Let's look at the major teachings put forth by the adherents of the "grace reformation," let's prayerfully compare those teachings with God's Word, let's follow God's truth wherever it leads, and let's do it with grace. Fair enough?

-3-

NAME-CALLING, JUDGMENTALISM, AND DIVISIVENESS IN THE NAME OF GRACE

ONE OF THE most disturbing elements of the hyper-grace movement is the way it judges and vilifies those outside of its camp. If you haven't received the revelation about the new grace reformation, you are called a Pharisee, a legalist, and a law-keeper (meant as an insult); you are "under works," you are in bondage—and worse. One woman sent me this testimony:

> I have seen firsthand the changes that come with people who embrace this message.
>
> I joined a small group 3 years ago that went from having regular prayer meetings and living holy connected lives together to stating "prayer is a work and denies grace" and "sin allows grace to do its great work." All of our prayer meetings and Bible studies were traded in for game-nights and nights out at the bar to "witness" where many from the group got plastered...all in the name of "grace."
>
> My heart has been so broken for my dear friends who I walked so closely with. As a group, they have embraced sin as not only acceptable, but justified and desirable. I have been completely ostracized and mocked for my stand in holiness. They don't even call me by my name anymore—they call me "Pharisee." Unfortunately, I have had to step completely away from these loved ones and am spending my life in prayer for them.

The wife of a pastor in California told me how her family had become divided by the hyper-grace message, explaining that her recent discussions with loved ones who had embraced the message had been "vicious." But what else could we expect when some hyper-grace leaders denigrate those who disagree with them in the strongest of terms, even claiming that some are trying to keep people in bondage for financial gain?

I do understand that the sheep often take things farther than their shepherds; long after John Wesley and George Whitefield had reconciled, their followers were still divided. And I'm fully aware that from all sides of almost every doctrinal divide, there is name-calling. That's one reason I do my best not to demonize those in the modern grace camp, recognizing them as fellow workers in the Lord (unless, of course, they have totally fallen into deception, which can happen in any group), and that's why I'm careful to quote their teachings in context and with fairness.

In this case, however, hyper-grace leaders are directly to blame for much of the ugly rhetoric, setting the tone with their own judgmental comments. Here's a sampling from some popular hyper-grace teachers.

According to Pastor Rob Rufus, who has many fine things to say about grace, "I cannot teach on the grace of God without addressing those who oppose grace. Grace is awesome in its power to change lives. But radical change encounters radical opposition. It is therefore not surprising that we have to deal with the grace haters."[1]

Who exactly are these "grace haters"?

> Grace haters are the legalists who will try to intimidate, manipulate and dominate people with a spirit of witchcraft. The religious spirit in them wants everyone stereotyped and conformed to their own bondage. They are parrots and puppets, no longer voices for God, but echoes, not pursuing God but pursuing opportunities for position and prestige. They are cloned to act the same, dress the same and speak in the same religious tones. You know, where everyone looks the same you can be sure a religious spirit is operating!
>
> If you try to live in the grace of God, I guarantee Satan will send his agent across your path to try to intimidate you and insinuate that you ought not to be living the way you are, that your freedom is not freedom but licentiousness. If you haven't experienced this sort of thing it's probably because you have never lived in grace.[2]

The implication, then, is that if you don't embrace Pastor Rufus's version of grace, you are a "grace hater" and you want to "intimidate, manipulate and dominate people with a spirit of witchcraft." You have a "religious spirit," and you are a person who "wants everyone stereotyped and conformed to their own bondage." Yes, you are nothing more than a "parrot and puppet" who is "not pursuing God but pursuing opportunities for position and prestige." All this in a book about grace! And even if Pastor Rufus has some extremely legalistic, controlling believers in mind, the fact is if you differ with his interpretation of grace, his followers may brand you a "grace hater."

But it is not just the name-calling that is troubling. It is the judging of people's motives (read Pastor Rufus's words again and note how motives are being judged), which is something you encounter time and again in these modern grace books. Why must it be that everyone who differs with the message of hyper-grace has ulterior motives? What provokes this kind of thinking?

Clark Whitten also has a lot to say about those who differ with his grace message:

> The rock throwing legalists who fill modern Christian churches and spawn the pharisaical preachers they listen to each Sunday seem to be more dimwitted than the Pharisees of Jesus' day. They, at least, walked away without saying a word [in John 8:9] and had sense enough to keep their mouths shut, which is more than can be said of the mean-spirited Pharisees of our day.[3]

Am I the only one who finds it ironic that Pastor Whitten uses such strong language to attack those he calls "mean-spirited"? Is this really helpful?

The bottom line, though, is that if you don't agree with Pastor Whitten's version of the grace message, you may be identified as a rock-throwing, legalistic, mean-spirited, dimwitted, Pharisee. And that's just what he says in two sentences. In fact, "Pharisees" (in the most negative sense of the word)[4] are referenced throughout Whitten's *Pure Grace* book. For example:

- God "knows something the Pharisees among us don't."[5]
- "The Holy Spirit's role in convicting believers of sin is presented by legalists and modern Pharisees as if there are many biblical references to support this concept."[6]
- "To all you Pharisees out there, good luck finding your way out of the maze."[7]
- "Pharisees are never happy about the liberty and freedom that union with Christ brings to our lives."[8]

Remarkably, in a book less than two hundred pages long, the word *legalist* (or some related form like *legalistic*, etc.) occurs *more than eighty times*. That's almost once every two pages, beginning with the acknowledgements, continuing in the endorsements, and then throughout the book.

In chapter 2 I made reference to this statement in *Pure Grace*: "Legalistic Christianity is in the sin management business full-time and failing miserably at the job. While sin management may be lucrative, it is entirely ineffective."[9]

The implication is that if you preach and teach against sin (just as Jesus and all the New Testament writers did), if you help people in practical ways to overcome sin, if you encourage a change of behavior through the gospel, then you are a legalist into "sin management." Worse still, you might well be doing it for profit. So you are not only a legalist, but you are also a mercenary!

I hate legalism too, but since Pastor Whitten offers little or no definition of the term in *Pure Grace*, the impression you get as a reader is simple: if you don't agree with the contents of the book, you are a legalist, and that is something bad—very bad! As for those who have been "liberated" by the grace message and then left their old churches, the implication is clear: their former pastors were probably pharisaical hypocrites who may even be out to make money by keeping their congregants in bondage. Can you see how problematic this kind of rhetoric is?

Pastor Rob Rufus writes that one of the signs of legalism in people is that "they are insecure, jealous, competitive, threatened—they take everything personally. People under law are bound by a spirit of rejection and they try to tie up others in Pharisaical bondage. They're touchy and competitive—they hate to see other people succeed, because that threatens them."[10]

Should we conclude, then, that it's actually hyper-grace believers and leaders who are the legalists, since they often seem to react in this very way? Once again, even if these descriptions are meant to help—without a doubt, Pastor Rufus has many great, liberating insights in his teachings—they actually cut both ways.

Pastor Whitten writes:

> There is a coming Great Awakening to the Body of Christ that will be *resisted fiercely by the legalistic establishment which has so much invested in the sin management model of discipleship*, but it will be embraced with joy and great enthusiasm by the mass of deeply dissatisfied, spiritually tormented, and tired of playing the game believers *who make up the majority of the Protestant church.*[11]

It is because of accusations like these that hyper-grace adherents, when defending the message, make comments like this:

> Many of the critics of the "so-called hyper-grace teaching" want to keep us in bondage and control so they can steal our tithes and offerings to make a name for themselves. I am into salvation by grace thru faith in Jesus. If you are not, then you not saved or born again. Tares and wheat are together until the end of the world. Examine yourself now![12]

Pastor Whitten actually claims that if you oppose this new "grace reformation," you are part of the "religious establishment"[13] and you "will, by and large, resist with gnashing of teeth.... There is a party being hosted by our heavenly Father in honor of those of us who have come to our senses in the *pig pen of legalism* and decided to come home to be with Him."[14]

To be sure, when Pastor Whitten speaks about legalists and the religious establishment, he may be speaking about people in his own circles who really do oppose the gospel. But again, he doesn't define who these alleged gospel enemies are, and, more importantly, the way his argument is cast; if you oppose his message, you are one of "them"—one of those modern-day, mean-spirited, pigpen-dwelling, legalistic Pharisees. In the end, it is almost impossible to challenge his position without being categorized by his readers as an enemy of sorts. This is grace?

Shooting the Messenger

And as I stated above, it is also all too common for hyper-grace leaders to judge the motives of those who differ with their message. The wife of a pastor in New Zealand posted on Facebook:

> Grace is extremely threatening to the law preachers because they stand to lose so much when people get grace. And they are threatened right now. That's why people like Michael Brown are speaking out about "hyper grace"—they are losing ground big time, people are getting the revelation of the finished work of the cross in their thousands. They are desperately pulling out the "licence to sin" stuff, and the "great end time deception" stuff to falsely portray what we are preaching, but it is sadly not working. Expect them to continue to bleat, but it's all for nothing. We aren't going anywhere! We intend to increase our efforts and take as many as we can from the clutches of religion! There ain't a thing they can do about it!

One of her Facebook friends added his sarcastic opinion: "We must restore the TRUTH of the trinity to the Church: Money, Bible and Minister. We will lose our hold over people and our private jets if we don't."

Isn't this remarkable? The amount of judgmentalism—all of it completely false—is really sad to see, not to mention the derogatory comments ("law preachers," "bleating"), but it is all too typical from hyper-grace leaders.

Another pastor wrote this to one of my ministry school graduates:

> I've seen pastors and young itinerants back-pedal from the Message faster than you can say "honorarium." And always in the name of "balance." Grace is not balanced. Grace is not

> convenient if your idol is ministry building and soliciting church invites. Grace invalidates your self-effort, it doesn't peddle outpourings or dependence on ministers for spiritual additives. Religion builds an industry on the concept of separation from God. Grace is the utter abolition from the shackles of religion—continual, effortless union and outpouring from the finished work of the cross.

There is it again: it's all about the money! Should we then say that Joseph Prince preaches grace in order to make money, since he himself testifies to the great blessings that have come his way, including financial blessings, since he began preaching the modern grace message? Wouldn't that be terribly judgmental?

May I be permitted, then, to ask some simple questions? Could it be that I love grace (and am not a "law preacher"), but I see error in the hyper-grace teaching? And could it be that I'm not threatened by grace (that's like saying I'm threatened by God's goodness!), that I'm not losing ground, and that I'm not desperately pulling out anything, but rather as a servant of the Lord and a lover of God's people, I'm speaking out because it is right?

I'm sure there are hyper-grace preachers who hold to their doctrine because of sin in their lives, just as there are holiness preachers who preach holiness to cover up the sin in their lives. Corruption and hypocrisy are everywhere to be found. But I believe that most, if not all, of the modern grace preachers hold to their message because they sincerely believe it is true and they are convinced it is the message the church needs. Why must my motives and the motives of those who differ with the hyper-grace message be judged in such a harsh way? Is this grace?

A woman on Facebook responding to a hyper-grace teacher's post, had this to say:

> I personally think it has all to do with $$$$$. True grace teaches freedom...freedom to think for yourself and hear from Him yourself...those who attack the grace message realize they will lose control of their congregations if they can think for themselves...ie: which means they will lose the ability to control funds...so sad! When people learn the true grace message they

> become very confident in who they are...(righteousness consciousness instead of sin consciousness). The sin consciousness is a direct path to feeling like you then have to "give" something to make yourself feel better OR to make God happy! Which in turn supports these big non grace ministries. That is the new name for them...NON-GRACE movement! I think I would rather be with the HYPER GRACERS!!!!

What an utterly graceless, judgmental post, but by now you can see that this is a common theme: "It's about control and it's about money. That's the only reason leaders reject the hyper-grace message." Do these ugly, judgmental attitudes appear out of the blue, or are some hyper-grace leaders directly responsible for planting these kinds of thoughts in people's minds?

And if you dare make a break with the modern grace folks, don't expect much grace there either. A former leader in this camp posted a carefully worded, open appeal to his friends after he left the movement. He explains what happened as a result.

> I have been labeled a "mixed preacher," a "Pharisee," a "Law mongerer," the "Christian thought police," and was told multiple times to "get a life." I will say that we must draw distinctions between extremes in the movement. Some accepted my article and said they would prayerfully consider it. However, there ARE cultic tendencies in this movement when we reach those who REALLY take the teachings as seriously as they are preached. I heard popular speakers say things like "Once you get back home, burn all your books that aren't 'Finished Works' (meaning their books and a handful of others)." And also "Once you get the grace revelation, you just can't sit in your old Law church any more. Run from those Pharisees!" This spirit of division treats membership and faithfulness to the local church community as optional, and anyone who disagrees is simply preaching "Law." I don't throw around the term cultic lightly...but it is only fitting here.[15]

If I wasn't hearing this time and time again (and being accused of the same things), and if I wasn't running into a stone wall with many modern grace adherents when I have tried to interact with them graciously through the Scriptures, I would take an account like this with a grain of salt. But given what I have seen firsthand, I see no reason to doubt this brother's testimony.

In his book *The Gospel in Ten Words*, Dr. Paul Ellis does encourage his readers not to "shoot the messengers," referring to those who do not preach his version of the grace message, and I commend him for doing so. He writes, "As someone who used to preach a counterfeit gospel I have nothing but grace for those who still do. Most of them love the Lord just as much as you or I. So love them but don't listen to them—not if they're leading you away from grace."[16]

Unfortunately, that gracious statement follows this comment, just a few lines earlier, "A counterfeit gospel will teach you to fear authority making you a target for tyrants and manipulators."[17] Who are these "tyrants and manipulators"? He doesn't tell us exactly, but they sure sound like leaders who don't preach the modern grace message.

Think of telling a room full of young people, "I know your moms and dads mean well, and you should be nice to them, even though they don't understand your needs. But remember there are some really crazy parents out there—they might actually come into your rooms to steal money out of your wallets or, worse still, secretly drug and abuse you—so be very careful!" This is similar to warning believers to watch out for non-hyper-grace authority figures who are "tyrants and manipulators."

And you can be assured that the stakes really are high. Sixteen times in his book Dr. Ellis makes reference to this "counterfeit gospel"—one that he says he once preached—in contrast with the hyper-grace gospel. For example, "A counterfeit gospel is what you have when someone tells you God won't accept you or bless you unless you first do something for him.... A counterfeit gospel glorifies the flesh—your willpower, your own resources, and understanding.... A counterfeit gospel will make a great show of being opposed to sin but will only drive sin underground.... A counterfeit gospel promotes mask-wearing dishonesty and fills churches with phonies."[18]

Of course, there is some truth to the points he is making, but must he brand this a "counterfeit gospel"? Does a "counterfeit gospel" even save? How can it if it is counterfeit? And if so many pastors and leaders are preaching a "counterfeit gospel," are they not preaching a counterfeit Christ? And didn't Paul say that those who preached a counterfeit gospel ("a different gospel—not that there is another one," Gal. 1:6–7) should be accursed, perhaps even meaning eternally condemned?

A gentleman who commented on my *Ministry Today* article titled "A Compromised Gospel Produces Compromised Fruit" came dangerously close to accusing me of preaching a gospel deserving eternal condemnation. He wrote:

> I like Dr. Brown. But, he doesn't understand "grace" and has co-mingled law with grace, which is no grace at all. We can't have it both ways. Galatians, Romans, Ephesians, 1 & 2 Corinthians, and in fact all of Paul's teaching in the epistles reveals that there can be no law mingled with grace. Also, Dr. Brown doesn't understand new creation realities or the consequence of being a new creature in Christ and what that means about who we are as Christians and that reality is more than a positional truth. The hard facts stand out. Either we have grace, or we have law. Paul teaches we have grace. And he calls the mixture, the law and a "false gospel." Dr. Brown needs to decide whether he believes the gospel of Jesus Christ and the Kingdom, or another gospel, which is law and a contraction of what Jesus Christ purchased for believers.[19]

Responses like this are typical, claiming that if you don't embrace the modern grace message, you don't understand grace, you are ignorant of "new creation realities" or of what it really means to be born again, and you are preaching a false gospel, a counterfeit gospel, "another gospel"—and a damnable one at that. Don't people like this man see how dangerously judgmental and over-the-top their accusations are?

That's one reason I did not title this book *Counterfeit Grace*. The hyper-grace teachers are still preaching God's grace through Jesus, even though they are mixing the message of biblical grace with distortions, exaggerations, and dangerous misinterpretations. Yet Dr. Ellis brands the non-hyper-grace gospel a counterfeit, with a strong warning about falling into the hands of "tyrants and manipulators." Is it any wonder, then, that the hyper-grace message is proving to be so divisive among people who love the Lord?

The division is consistently between those who have been "enlightened" and those who have not, between those who have received the new grace "revelation" and those who are still living in the religious Stone Age. That's why Pastor Steve McVey, who often writes with humility and self-effacement, can still speak of "those who've been ambushed by legalistic religion" (and this in the context of a book titled *52 Lies Heard in Church Every Sunday*, not exactly a unity-building title).[20] Yes, those legalistic, non-grace people are out to ambush you!

Joseph Prince affirms this, adding further critical comments about the motives of those who reject the hyper-grace message:

> Notice that there was one group of people that was very unhappy with what Paul was preaching—the Pharisees or what I call the "religious mafia"... These religious keepers of the law are still around today. The law blinds them.... When they see believers impacted by grace, they become "filled with envy" because they have worked so hard and depended on their own efforts to achieve their own sense of self-righteousness.[21]

One young hyper-grace leader put it this way, placing himself and modern grace teachers in the camp of Luther and Paul, while those who oppose the message are part of the man-made, pharisaical, religious camp destined to crumble:

> There will always be a Martin Luther out there, who refuses to "balance" his message of radical Grace with a little bit of Law. There will always be a Paul out there who refuses to mix Pharisaical religion with a Heaven born Gospel. The truth will always rise to the top, and the monolith of man made [sic] religion will always crumble eventually.[22]

Another woman made this comment on a hyper-grace website:

> So, the fight that is stirring in America regarding this "hyper-grace, false security" is not a surprise. The battle Jesus faced with the Pharisees is a clue to the ferociousness of religious people and their fight to "be obedient and keep the law" as the way to become holy and christ-like. They will tear you up with misunderstood scriptures to protect man's traditions. Scripture

> whipping by zealots will become more and more public. I am educating myself now to defend the true Gospel.[23]

I could repeat similar rhetoric like this almost endlessly. David Fish, who once worked closely with some hyper-grace leaders, wrote "An Open Letter to the 'Finished Works' Movement" in which he described the close-mindedness and divisiveness he often witnessed.

> I remember a student sitting in a room with other ministry school students listening to a teaching from a missionary who had devoted her life to the gospel. In the middle of the teaching, the student pulled out her iPod, put in her headphones, and pressed play on a track that read "THE PURE GOSPEL: JOHN CROWDER." I leaned over and tapped the student on the shoulder and said, "Why are you listening to that in the middle of this woman's teaching?"
>
> I was met with the all-too-familiar reply: "Well I don't listen to grace mixed with Law. I mean look at how Jesus spoke to the Pharisees."
>
> Once again: **we** are grace, **they** are Law. Are you catching the irony here?[24]

In keeping with this mentality, John Crowder posted this comment on his Facebook page on March 23, 2013: "Call me 'unloving' for pointing out the obvious. Polish it up all you want...or let's just call it what it is. Regarding religious people: 'As it is written: "God gave them a spirit of stupidity, eyes that could not see and ears that could not hear, to this very day"' (Rom. 11:8)."[25] And just who are these "religious" people? Obviously, those who reject his message.

Hyper-Grace Persecution?

To be sure, there is plenty of "garbage" being taught from the pulpit in the name of holiness (among many other doctrines), and by all means we should carefully and prayerfully evaluate what we hear. So biblical discernment isn't the issue. Rather, it is the wholesale rejection and repudiation of anything that isn't "hyper-grace" that is so dangerous. In fact, this reminds me of extremes in the Word of Faith camp. If you don't use their terminology and say it their way, and if you don't hold to their exact emphasis and doctrine, you're not preaching the Word. (Has anyone ever asked you if you to go a "Word church"? They mean a Word of Faith church, as if all other churches base their faith on the phone book rather than the Bible.)

But there's more. Being rejected for the hyper-grace message is a sign that you're preaching the truth. Andre van der Merwe put it this way, "If Paul, the champion apostle of the New Testament, had to defend the gospel of grace against these accusations and was persecuted by the legalists for preaching this gospel, then we should be considering that perhaps something is wrong if our gospel is not making the legalists of our day rise up against us."[26]

To be sure, modern grace preachers are not the first to make statements like this. In fact, D. Martyn Lloyd–Jones, the respected theologian and pastor of Westminster Chapel, said this many years ago:

> The true preaching of the gospel of grace always leads to the possibility of this charge being brought against it. There is no better test as to whether a man is really preaching the New Testament gospel of salvation than this, that some people misunderstand it and misinterpret it to mean that it really amounts to this, that because you are saved by grace alone it does not matter at all what you do; you can go on sinning as much as you like....
>
> If my preaching and presentation of the gospel of salvation does not expose it to that misunderstanding, then it is not the gospel....I would say to all preachers: If your preaching of salvation has not been misunderstood in that way, then you had better examine your sermons again, and you had better make sure that you are really preaching the salvation that is offered in the New Testament...there is this kind of dangerous element about the true presentation of the gospel of salvation.[27]

The difference is that Lloyd-Jones was not just a grace preacher. He was also a holiness preacher (in other words, he preached grace and truth), and he did not believe in the unique aspects of the modern, hyper-grace message. He believed that the Holy Spirit convicts us of sin as we walk with the Lord. He believed that we should confess our sins to God. He believed in progressive sanctification. He believed that the Sermon on the Mount applied to believers today. In fact, modern grace adherents listening to Dr. Lloyd-Jones would probably call him a legalist and a law-preacher![28]

And that's the whole problem in a nutshell. The way modern grace teachers frame their message, all those who differ with them are legalists who are out to put them back in bondage. That means the moment you question their beliefs, they go on red alert, armed to the teeth with grace verses and grace statements, ready to accuse you of being a legalistic persecutor. Even if this is not what these leaders intended, it is the constant reality. And the truth be told, the expressions many of them use only exacerbate the division and misunderstanding.

One of my colleagues, a New Testament professor, explained the correct meaning of 1 John 1:9 on his Facebook page. (For the full discussion of this verse, see chapter 5.) In response, one young man posted, "People like you only care about tying people up with the Law, not freeing them with Christ's TRUE message of forgiveness and NO CONDEMNATION!!"[29]

I have experienced this many times when seeking to reason with hyper-grace believers, all the while affirming God's grace and pointing to the Word alone as our guide as I interact with them. In response, I have been branded an "Ishmael" (born of the flesh) who is opposing "Isaac" (who was born of the Spirit). Here is a comment posted on my Facebook page and addressing me:

> Ishmael will always mock Isaac and the persecution will get even more intense as grace is poured out and thus overtakes law-living. It's coming and I'm ready in Him. I will be John (God's grace) and take in more of His love for me as the law-living folks attempt to self-sanctify and focus on their love for Him like Peter (stone). I don't expect "law-abiding" folk to get this post any more than they got my last one. Law-living folk are confounded by sin even today as the Pharisee's were back in Jesus's day. Jesus, however, was confounded by your unbelief, that will never change.

Incredible! So, in the eyes of this hyper-grace adherent, when I share Scripture with him and challenge his positions, I am mocking him. And when I reject his unbiblical teachings, I am persecuting him (and note that the perceived persecution he is experiencing "will get even more intense"). Note also that I am "law-living" and "law-abiding" (which, of course, is intended to mean something very negative; see chapter 12 for more on this). To them, I am attempting to "self-sanctify," and I am guilty of focusing on my love for the Lord (like Peter, the stone!) rather than on God's grace (so even Peter has become a bad guy!). And Jesus is "confounded" by my "unbelief."

Everywhere I turn I'm encountering similar rhetoric from the hyper-grace camp. This is some of the fruit of the so-called "grace reformation."

To his credit, Andre van der Merwe also stated: "This is not to say that we should purposely set out to provoke people, but if nobody ever opposes or questions us, it is a sure sign that our beliefs are most likely not in line with the truth of the New Covenant."[30] Unfortunately, many hyper-grace teachers seem to go out of their way to make statements that will provoke their theological opponents—the so-called Pharisees and legalists—since these radical statements, they tell us, are part of the grace revelation. And when you couple this with so much immaturity in the body, along with the fact that almost anyone can become an authority on the Internet today, this mentality of "the more people oppose me, the more right I must be" can be a formula for disaster.

So the more bad fruit the hyper-grace message produces, the more it must be true. And the more people point out serious concerns with the message, the more it must be Pauline, since Paul was criticized too. Do you see how alarming this kind of thinking can be?

Joseph Prince reinforces this mind-set with comments like this:

> The devil's strategy is to surround the truths of God with controversies. To prevent God's people from benefiting from the fullness of God's promises, he erects controversies as fences around these truths. *You can always tell how powerful a truth is by the number of controversies the devil surrounds it with!*[31]

But often it is not the message of grace sparking the controversies; it is the misrepresentation of the grace message that is causing the controversies.

I could list passage after passage in hyper-grace books that are clearly meant to provoke and are so overstated that they can only draw a reaction, but two examples from John Crowder's *Mystical Union* will suffice. He writes, "When you think of the cross, do you think of *fun*? If the answer is 'no' then you have not been taught the cross aright."[32] This is absolutely outrageous, not to mention terribly divisive, since Crowder claims that unless you have been taught to think of "fun" when you think of Jesus dying an agonizing death on the cross as the price for our sins, "you have not been taught the cross aright."

Then there is this: "I want to warn you here from the start that much of your existing theology is going to be flushed down the toilet as you read. Areas where you assumed to be an expert on the 'basics' of the faith may prove to be areas of borderline apostasy in your theological suitcase."[33] So most everyone else is wrong—borderline apostates, in fact—and John Crowder and his followers are right. Consequently, when you oppose their message based on the truth of the gospel, that is proof to them that they are preaching grace as Paul did.

I'm aware that some hyper-grace teachers will point to the way Paul attacked the legalists in his day, calling them dogs and mutilators of the flesh and wishing that those who preached circumcision would go all the way and emasculate themselves! (See Galatians 5:12 and chapter 4 for more on this claim.) There are two problems with this position: first, today's hyper-grace teachers are not Paul (neither am I). Second, he wasn't combatting different perspectives in the message of grace; he was combatting Jewish followers of Jesus who were telling Gentile followers of Jesus that unless they were circumcised and obeyed the Law of Moses, they could not be saved. Paul even called these particular Jewish men "false brothers," meaning they weren't even true believers (Gal. 2:4).

That is a far cry from today, when those of us who teach progressive sanctification (see chapter 7), or who believe that it's healthy to confess our sins to God (see chapter 5), or who believe that New Testament repentance includes turning away from sins (see chapter 6), or who quote the words of Jesus as our authority (see chapter 13) are branded pharisaical legalists who are into "sin management."

This chapter could easily be a book by itself, with ugly quote after ugly quote from hyper-grace teachers and their followers, but enough has been said to make the point. Where is the grace in the hyper-grace camp? Where is the gentleness of spirit, the kindness of heart, the deep security that is not easily offended, the Christlike attitude that refuses to retaliate, the merciful mind-set from those who have received mercy? Where is the grace?

Here's a good verse for all of us who want to please the Lord, starting with me and with you: "Let your speech always be gracious, seasoned with salt, so that you may know how you ought to answer each person" (Col. 4:6). Can we seek to model that?

Throughout the rest of this book, as I lay out differences with my modern grace colleagues, I will do my best to underscore the very real errors in their theology, especially when those errors are spiritually dangerous. But I will do my best to do so in a way that remembers that we have been washed by the same blood and forgiven by the same God, and that we will live together in the same family forever. Our differences may be sharp, but with the exception of those who have completely apostatized (or were never truly saved from the start), they are all "in-house" differences. Can we remember that?

-4-

HAS GOD ALREADY FORGIVEN OUR FUTURE SINS?

ONE OF THE foundations of the hyper-grace message is that God has already forgiven all of our sins, meaning past sins, present sins, and future sins. In fact, we are told that God doesn't even see the sins we commit since He sees us as completely sanctified and holy in His Son. (For more on the question of sanctification, see chapter 7.)

As grace teacher Ryan Rufus, son of Pastor Rob Rufus, explained, "You haven't been partially forgiven; you have been totally and completely and utterly and fully and absolutely forgiven of all your sins—past, present, and future!"[1] In the words of Joseph Prince, "His grace is cheapened when you think that He has only forgiven you of your sins up to the time you got saved, and after that point, you have to depend on your confession of sins to be forgiven. God's forgiveness is not given in installments."[2] He also wrote, "My friend, this is the assurance you can have today: The day you received Christ, you confessed all your sins once and for all."[3]

Ryan Rufus put it like this in one of his sermons:

> Most Christians don't have any trouble believing that Jesus forgives them of all their past sins. But many Christians have trouble believing that Jesus has already forgiven them of all of their future sins. They struggle with that. So they feel, they have this need that if they sin then they've got to confess the sin and repent of the sin and be cleansed of the sin, and they enter into all of these dead works, faithless works, because they don't have a revelation of total forgiveness.[4]

And just to be sure that his audience got the message, Pastor Rufus emphasized, "I want to declare to you today—all of your future sins are already forgiven!"[5] Yes, he proclaims:

> All my sins have been dealt with. All my sins have been forgiven. And so if you do sin—oh, heaven forbid!—but if you do sin...Sometimes I sin. Sorry to burst your bubble. But sometimes we do sin, OK? We're not running out wanting to sin or even preaching license to sin. I don't know any grace preachers that are preaching a license to sin—not one! But even after *if* we sin, don't start asking God for forgiveness. Don't try to confess that sin. Don't repent of that sin. Get your eyes up on Jesus. Keep your faith in Jesus. Keep walking in the Spirit covenant. Keep walking in the grace covenant. Keep declaring your absolute forgiveness.[6]

To back this position up, modern grace teachers commonly quote the words of the new covenant prophecy spoken in Jeremiah 31:31–34 and repeated in full in Hebrews 8:8–12, culminating with these words: "For I will be merciful toward their iniquities, and *I will remember their sins no more.*" This is quoted again in Hebrews 10:17—"I will remember their sins and their lawless deeds no more"—followed by an important observation in verse 18 for the Jewish believers reading the letter: "Where there is forgiveness of these, there is no longer any offering for sin."[7] In other words, because Jesus the Messiah died for all our sins, bringing us forgiveness, there is no longer a need to offer animal sacrifices for sin, nor would those sacrifices procure forgiveness. The work has been done once for all!

Once again, there is some powerful truth in the modern grace message, since on the cross Jesus paid for every sin we ever committed or ever will commit. And the moment we come to the Lord and receive His saving grace, He declares us righteous and "forgets" the sins we have committed until that moment.

Did you commit adultery before you were a believer? Did you rob and steal before you were saved? Did you mock God's name before you knew Him? When you came to Him and turned from those sins, asking for forgiveness in Jesus' name, He washed you clean and made you a new creation, and He has forgiven and forgotten the adultery, the stealing, and the mocking. He said, "I will remember their sins and their lawless deeds no more." Praise God!

And it is true that when Jesus died for us, our sins were still future since we had not even been born. So, yes, He died and paid for our future sins as well as our past and present sins. What we must realize, however, is that *the transaction of forgiveness* takes place at different points in time.[8] In other words, Jesus died for you and me sometime around AD 30, and the moment He breathed His last breath, He had paid for the sins of every human who would ever live on the earth. But were we forgiven at that point in time? Absolutely not!

Paul explains that before we knew Him, we were dead in our sins and by nature objects of wrath (Eph. 2:1–2; Col. 2:13), guilty in God's sight, and "alienated and hostile in mind, doing evil deeds" (Col. 1:21). This means that even though Jesus paid for our sins, until we turned to Him for salvation, our sins were still counted against us, separating us from God.[9] That's why, throughout the Book of Acts, the apostles urged their listeners to turn from their sins and be saved.

In other words, although Jesus had already paid for their sins, they were not yet forgiven because they had not yet appropriated forgiveness through faith. I think virtually every born-again believer agrees with the simple truth that we are not saved and forgiven until we put our trust in Jesus, even though He already paid the price for our salvation.

Then what happens when we get saved? God forgives us for all the sins *we have committed until that time*, as stated in Colossians 2:13–14: "And you, who were dead in your trespasses and the uncircumcision of your flesh, God made alive together with him, having forgiven us all our trespasses, by canceling the record of debt that stood against us with its legal demands. This he set aside, nailing it to the cross."

We had a massive debt in God's sight, a tremendous record of guilt that we could never remove in a thousand lifetimes, yet the Lord in His mercy canceled that debt and wiped away our guilt in a moment of time, making us as white as snow. That is amazing grace! So, Jesus died for our sins on the cross, but forgiveness for our sins was not transacted until the day we repented and believed. And what sins were forgiven at that point in time? The sins we had already committed.

How it could be otherwise? That was the debt we owed—the sins we had committed, not the sins we had not yet committed.

Before I demonstrate this from the Word of God, stop and think about this for a moment. When you first came to the Lord, what happened between you and the Lord? What was going on in your heart and mind?

In my case, I remember clearly the spiritual battle I was fighting, first to believe that Jesus really died for my sins—after all, as a Jew, I was raised without any faith in Jesus at all—and then, once I believed that He really was the Savior, the battle for me was to turn from my sins. I loved my sin and wanted to continue shooting heroin, using LSD, indulging the flesh, living in prideful rebellion, and pursuing my dream of being a rock star drummer. But when God's love and conviction won the day, I asked the Lord to forgive me and surrendered my life to Him.

In a moment of time I was clean! The guilt was totally gone, and even when I looked for it, I couldn't find it. I was forgiven! God remembered my sins no more!

What about sins I hadn't committed yet? The question never crossed my mind, not a single time. And I imagine it was the same thing with you. Why in the world would we be thinking about future sins? And who in their right mind would say, "Praise God! I am forgiven for all the wicked things I did, and I am already forgiven for all the wicked things I will do from here on for the rest of my life." Who would ever think like this? Honestly, in all my years in the Lord, and having seen many people come to the Lord, I have never once met anyone who thought along these lines when they got saved.

We may have wondered if we would be able to stay faithful, asking out loud, "But what if I fall?" And friends may have told us, "Don't worry. Just put your trust in Jesus, and if you mess up, just get back up and keep going. You're a child of God!" And we might have asked if God would forgive us if we sinned again in the future. But we certainly didn't think, "Praise God! I'm already forgiven for the rest of my life." And if you look at the preaching in Acts and the teaching in the Epistles, you will see that the focus was always on the sins *people had already committed or were continuing to commit*, not the sins they would commit in the future.

And so, in Acts 3, Peter urged the Jewish crowd to turn from their sins, saying to them, "Repent therefore, and turn back, that your sins may be blotted out" (Acts 3:19). Which sins? The sins they had committed until that point, as the context makes clear, focusing on their rejection of Yeshua as Messiah. And when Peter preached to the Jewish crowd along similar lines in Acts 2, he said, "Repent and be baptized every one of you in the name of Jesus Christ for the forgiveness of your sins" (Acts 2:38). Which sins? Clearly, the sins they had already committed.

That's why the Jewish crowds coming to John the Immerser to go through his baptism of repentance confessed their sins—meaning, the sins they had committed and the sins they were living in.[10] They certainly were not confessing their future sins! And that's why John urged the religious leaders to "bear fruit in keeping with repentance" (Matt. 3:8), meaning, demonstrate that your repentance is genuine by leaving the old behind and living a new life.

Simply stated, *there is not a single verse anywhere in the Bible that pronounces us already forgiven for our future sins* (meaning, sins we have not yet committed). Not one verse. Nowhere. Not even a hint of such a concept. All the promises of forgiveness have to do with sins we have already committed, since God is dealing with us in space and time, and He only forgives us for what we have actually done. It's as if you have a debit card with a prepaid amount of one million dollars, but the account is not charged until you go out and use it. In the same way, the forgiveness of all of our sins has been prepaid, but that forgiveness is not applied in advance. It is applied as needed.

Already Righteous

The good news is that God has already put us in the "righteous" column. He has already pronounced us "Not guilty!" and has brought us into His family, and if we sin as believers, forgiveness is transacted when we ask for it through the blood of Jesus. (We will discuss this further in chapter 5, "Should Believers Confess Their Sins to God?")

Forgiveness is as certain as the cross is certain: "My little children, I am writing these things to you so that you may not sin. But if anyone does sin, we have an advocate with the Father, Jesus Christ the righteous. He is the propitiation for our sins, and not for ours only but also for the sins of the whole world" (1 John 2:1–2).

This is not just common sense truth; it is truth that is crystal clear throughout the entire New Testament, from Matthew to Revelation. Jesus taught it in the Lord's Prayer, instructing us to pray, "Give us each day our daily bread, and forgive us our sins, for we ourselves forgive everyone who is indebted to us" (Luke 11:3–4). He also taught this in another prayer context, stating, "And whenever you stand praying, forgive, if you have anything against anyone, so that your Father also who is in heaven may forgive you your trespasses" (Mark 11:25). (I'm aware that many hyper-grace teachers claim these words don't apply to us today; I'll take that up in the next chapter and in chapter 13.)

If God already forgave all our sins, past, present, and future, why is Jesus talking about being forgiven on an ongoing basis? It's clear that our present sins need present forgiveness, not for the purpose of salvation but as part of our relationship with the Father. Again, this is presupposed throughout the entire New Testament.

That's why Paul often deals with sin issues when writing to the different congregations, urging them to live lives worthy of the Lord and giving instructions on how to deal with sin in their midst, as in 1 Corinthians 5. How foolish it would be to argue that Paul saw the sins of these believers and was grieved over this and addressed it, but God didn't see their sins because He had already forgiven them and saw the Corinthian church members only as perfectly righteous. Where is this taught in the New Testament?

More importantly, there were consequences to these sins, as Paul explained to the believers in Corinth, who were guilty of partaking of the Lord's Supper in an unworthy manner:

> Whoever, therefore, eats the bread or drinks the cup of the Lord in an unworthy manner will be guilty concerning the body and blood of the Lord. [Notice that Paul did not say, "But, of course, your sins have already been forgiven and God doesn't even see them." Not at all!] Let a person examine himself, then, and so

> eat of the bread and drink of the cup. For anyone who eats and drinks without discerning the body eats and drinks judgment on himself. That is why many of you are weak and ill, and some have died. But if we judged ourselves truly, we would not be judged. But when we are judged by the Lord, we are disciplined so that we may not be condemned along with the world.
>
> —1 Corinthians 11:27–32

Had there been hyper-grace believers in Corinth, they might have said to Paul, "Why are you bringing up our sins? They don't exist anymore. We are saints—after all, you called us saints in this very letter! We are blameless before the Lord, and nothing we do can possibly affect our relationship with Him. And when you make the harsh accusation that some of us are sick or some of us have died because we partook of the Lord's Table in an unworthy manner, you are speaking like a legalistic Pharisee. You are condemning us, Paul, and that is not from the Lord. All our sins are already forgiven!"

I have received similar responses from hyper-grace Christians the moment I talk with them about the negative effects of sin, even in the lives of believers. "I have already been forgiven and God does not see my sins," they tell me. "Plus, if anything I did on a daily basis had any effect on my relationship with God, that would be salvation by works." Have you heard this too?

What's ironic is that hyper-grace believers will often quote Hebrews 10:17, where God says He will no longer remember our sins, but they fail to deal with the rest of the chapter (let alone the rest of the book), where this strong warning is given to the very believers addressed in verse 17 (the context makes it clear that the author is writing to believers):

> For if we go on sinning deliberately after receiving the knowledge of the truth, there no longer remains a sacrifice for sins, but a fearful expectation of judgment, and a fury of fire that will consume the adversaries. Anyone who has set aside the law of Moses dies without mercy on the evidence of two or three witnesses. How much worse punishment, do you think, will be deserved by the one who has trampled underfoot the Son of God, and has profaned the blood of the covenant by which he was

> sanctified, and has outraged the Spirit of grace? For we know him who said, "Vengeance is mine; I will repay." And again, "The Lord will judge his people." It is a fearful thing to fall into the hands of the living God.
>
> —HEBREWS 10:26–31

I repeat: the author of Hebrews is writing to believers here, those who have already been forgiven, those whose sins God no longer remembers, those who have already received the knowledge of the truth and have already been sanctified by the blood of Jesus. (Stop for a moment and continue reading Hebrews 10:32–39, and then go right into Hebrews 11. There is not the slightest doubt about who is being addressed. It is believers!) Our past sins have been forgiven, but if we turn our back on the Lord or go back to a system of man-made religion or choose our sin rather than the Savior, "there no longer remains a sacrifice for sins, but a fearful expectation of judgment, and a fury of fire that will consume the adversaries."

How then do we understand Hebrews 10:1–3, often cited by modern grace teachers? Doesn't that refute the point that I am making here? Doesn't it say that as believers, we should no longer be conscious of our sins? The text states:

> For since the law has but a shadow of the good things to come instead of the true form of these realities, it can never, by the same sacrifices that are continually offered every year, make perfect those who draw near. Otherwise, would they not have ceased to be offered, since the worshipers, having once been cleansed, would no longer have any consciousness of sins? But in these sacrifices there is a reminder of sins every year.
>
> —HEBREWS 10:1–3

Speaking of the new covenant promises, Hebrews 10:17 states that God said, "I will remember their sins and their lawless deeds no more." Yet, as we have noted, He was talking about sins we already committed, not future sins. But Hebrews 10:1–3 seems to imply that we shouldn't ever be conscious of sin, because God forgave us once for all at the cross.

Once more we have to ask, if this is the case, why do Paul and

Peter and Jacob (commonly, but wrongly, called James) and other New Testament writers remind their readers about sins in their midst? If God doesn't want us to be conscious of sin, then why did His servants keep bringing the issue up? Why did Jacob (James) write things like this? "You adulterous people! Do you not know that friendship with the world is enmity with God? Therefore whoever wishes to be a friend of the world makes himself an enemy of God....Cleanse your hands, you sinners, and purify your hearts, you double-minded" (Jacob [James] 4:4, 8).

And why did Jesus Himself, speaking by the Spirit, expose the sins of His people in Revelation 2–3, telling the believers in Ephesus they had left their first love, rebuking the believers in Pergamum for holding to teaching that encouraged idolatry and immorality, calling the believers in Thyatira to account for tolerating the teaching of Jezebel, telling the believers in Sardis that they were dead, and rebuking the believers in Laodicea for their lukewarm, self-deceived, proud state? And He called each of them to repentance, offering them grace if they repented and giving them warnings if they refused.

Why do this if their sins were already forgiven and if God no longer wanted them to have any consciousness of sin? You would have to say that Jesus didn't understand the message of grace![11]

No Consciousness of Sin?

It looks like Paul didn't have the grace revelation either. Why else would he write things like, "I fear that when I come again my God may humble me before you, and I may have to mourn over many of those who sinned earlier and have not repented of the impurity, sexual immorality, and sensuality that they have practiced" (2 Cor. 12:21)? If the Corinthians were not to have any consciousness of their sins, what business did Paul have bringing them up again?

And what do we make of Jacob (James) 5:14–15? "Is anyone among you sick? Let him call for the elders of the church, and let them pray over him, anointing him with oil in the name of the Lord. And the prayer of faith will save the one who is sick, and the Lord will raise him up. *And if he has committed sins, he will be forgiven.*"

How can the Word be any clearer? If, in fact, the man's sickness was related to sin in his life, which is sometimes the case, when the elders pray for him God will heal him and forgive him, as the text says "he *will be* forgiven." If his future sins were already forgiven—in terms of the transaction of that forgiveness—this verse would have no meaning at all. And it obviously would be totally out of place if, as believers, we were never to have any consciousness of sin. The Word says that *at that time*, when God heals him, He will forgive him, which obviously means the sick man's sins still needed to be forgiven. The hyper-grace teachers are simply wrong when they claim that all our future sins are forgiven the moment we are saved.

Not only so, but Jacob (James) 5:16 would also be meaningless if the hyper-grace message was true, as Jacob turns from the subject of receiving forgiveness from God in verse 15 to the subject of receiving forgiveness from one another: "Therefore," he writes, recognizing the damaging effects of sin and the connection that sometimes exists between sin and sickness, "confess your sins to one another and pray for one another, that you may be healed."

Why in the world would we confess our sins to each other if we are no longer conscious of sin? Really, *how* in the world *could* we do this if we are not conscious of our sins? What would we confess? And how utterly ludicrous to think that it's fine for us to confess our sins to each other but not to God.[12]

And then there is Hebrews 12:1–4, a passage that becomes completely meaningless if we are supposed to have no consciousness of our sins:

> Therefore, since we are surrounded by so great a cloud of witnesses, let us also lay aside every weight, *and sin which clings so closely,* and let us run with endurance the race that is set before us, looking to Jesus, the founder and perfecter of our faith, who for the joy that was set before him endured the cross, despising the shame, and is seated at the right hand of the throne of God. Consider him who endured from sinners such hostility against himself, so that you may not grow weary or fainthearted. *In your struggle against sin you have not yet resisted to the point of shedding your blood.*[13]

How then do we understand Hebrews 10:1–3? Hebrews scholar William Lane explains:

> Under the old covenant worshipers never experienced a definitive cleansing.... Even on the occasion of the awesome ceremonies associated with the ritual of the Day of Atonement worshipers continued to have a "consciousness of sins" [he's quoting the Greek text here]. This expression connotes the Hebrew sense of a burdened, smitten heart, which became most pronounced on the Day of Atonement when it was necessary to confront the holiness of God.... As long as this sense of sin and transgression with respect to God remained, there could be no effective service of God. A decisive cleansing of the conscience is a prerequisite for unhindered access to God (10:22), and this has been achieved only through the sacrifice of Christ.[14]

In fact, Lane makes this observation about the most important day on the biblical calendar for ancient Israel, the Day of Atonement, *the day* in the year designated for forgiveness of sins. "What impressed the writer of Hebrews was that a remembrance of sins, which constituted a barrier to worship, was confirmed and renewed... 'year after year,' by the annual Day of Atonement ritual."[15] This is what is also written in Hebrews 9:13–14: "For if the blood of goats and bulls, and the sprinkling of defiled persons with the ashes of a heifer, sanctify for the purification of the flesh, how much more will the blood of Christ, who through the eternal Spirit offered himself without blemish to God, purify our conscience from dead works to serve the living God."

So, the point is not that we are never to be conscious of sin in our life, which is an impossible concept based on the clear testimony of the entire New Testament. The point is that the work of forgiveness was accomplished once and for all at the cross by Jesus, wiping away our guilt and pronouncing us righteous and holy, with no need for another sacrifice or an annual Day of Atonement to bring us cleansing. So we live as forgiven people, and rather than having to bring an annual (or daily or weekly or monthly) sacrifice of atonement, we look back to the cross, celebrating the forgiveness we have received. And if we do sin, we confess our sins to God and leave them behind, rejoicing in the fact that the payment has already been made. (See the next chapter for more on this.)

As expressed beautifully in just seven Hebrew words in Proverbs 28:13, "The one who covers his transgressions will not prosper, but whoever confesses them and forsakes them will find mercy" (NET). And if we ever doubt that mercy, we need just look to Jesus. As the old hymn proclaims:

> Jesus paid it all,
> All to Him I owe;
> Sin had left a crimson stain,
> He washed it white as snow.[16]

-5-

SHOULD BELIEVERS CONFESS THEIR SINS TO GOD?

SINCE HYPER-GRACE TEACHERS believe that the moment we are saved, God pronounces all our sins forgiven—meaning, past, present, and future sins—they also believe that there is no need for us to confess our sins to God as believers or to ask for forgiveness. As expressed by Paul Ellis, "Forgiveness seems to be a blind spot for many people. We just can't get it into our heads that God has forgiven us completely and for all time."[1]

Naturally, the verse that comes to mind is 1 John 1:9: "If we confess our sins, he is faithful and just to forgive us our sins and to cleanse us from all unrighteousness." That seems to settle the issue, doesn't it? John is writing to us, to believers, and we are told that we should confess our sins to God, and He will forgive us and cleanse us when we do.

Hyper-grace teachers reject this interpretation, telling us that this verse was written for unbelievers in the congregation John was addressing (specifically, Gnostic unbelievers), and so it does *not* apply to believers. In fact, we are told it *cannot* apply to us since we already have been forgiven. According to Ryan Rufus:

> Many Christians when they sin feel unrighteous, dirty, unholy—they feel they have let God down and that God is no longer pleased with them. They feel they need to do "something." So guilt drives them to want to do something to get rid of the sin, or get rid of the guilt of their sin. That guilt wants to lead them to get rid. So they say; "God, I have got to confess my sins and I have got to repent of these terrible sins and get cleansed of these sins. I have got to promise I will never do this sin again."[2]

Rufus rejects this mind-set emphatically, as do virtually all hyper-grace preachers:

> I want to tell you, know that there is no scripture in the new covenant for new covenant believers that tells you, you have got to continually confess your sins and repent of your sins and ask forgiveness for all your sins. Why? Because *one* sacrifice for *all* time for *all* of your sins has already dealt with *every* single one of your sins![3]

What does this mean on a practical level? To quote Ryan Rufus again, it means "we are not called to confess our sins—we are called to confess our righteousness in Jesus Christ!"[4] Put another way by Andre Rabe (but equally incorrect in terms of 1 John 1:9), "Confession of sin is not the act in which we tell God about our sin, but the act in which we tell sin about our God."[5]

But Rufus goes further: "As a new covenant born-again believer, to now go and ask forgiveness after you have sinned is a sin. It is the sin of unbelief. You don't believe in the finished work of the cross. You are trying to do something and don't realize it is already done!"[6]

It is a sin to ask God for forgiveness after you sin? Then what, exactly, should you say if you sin? "Father, thank You that even that sin has been dealt with and I am still perfectly righteous"?

Yes, according to Pastor Rufus:

> You may have sinned and feel a bit guilty and want to say sorry to God and to ask for forgiveness now. The heart is not wrong. That is not bad! The heart is right, but the full revelation of the finished work of the cross is not in the heart. It is OK to say; "God, I'm sorry. I did not want to do that. That's not part of my new creation nature. You know what, God, though? I am not going to get all morbid and introspective and sorrowful and guilty! You don't want that. You want me to lift up my head, get in the Spirit and stay in the Spirit, and thank You for the free gift of righteousness and total forgiveness. And I fix my eyes on Jesus who has forgiven me of all my sins. I thank You that I am the righteousness of God in Christ Jesus."[7]

I mean no offense in saying this, but aside from being extremely similar to some well-meaning Word of Faith extremes where you have to "say it" just right to get the right results, this strikes me as extremely legalistic—and really quite odd for a child of the Father. I can say I'm sorry, but I can't say, "Forgive me, Abba," otherwise I'm committing the sin of unbelief? This is grace? This is an intimate, personal relationship with God?[8]

I certainly affirm so much of what Pastor Rufus is saying, specifically that we have been made righteous by God, that God forgives and forgets, that we should keep our eyes focused on Jesus, that we should take hold of the reality that we are new creations in Him, and that we should not get morbid or hopeless. But is it true that God has already forgiven our future sins? Is it true that we should not confess our sins and ask for forgiveness? Absolutely not.

This is the typical hyper-grace understanding of 1 John 1:9: the verse is not written to believers but to nonbelievers, and it is telling them they need to confess their sins to God in order to be saved. John is inviting the unbelievers mixed into his congregations to come to the saving knowledge of the Lord, just as he and the other believers have.[9]

Consistently, modern grace teachers tell us John is specifically addressing Gnostic unbelievers who had infiltrated John's congregations. This statement by Andrew Farley is representative:

> John is not correcting believers in his opening statement. He's addressing Gnostics who had infiltrated the early church and were teaching false doctrines.... Verse 9 is a remedy for unbelievers who have been influenced by Gnostic peer pressure and are now claiming sinless perfection. John is essentially asking, "Instead of claiming that you have no sin, will you consider changing your mind? Instead of claiming you've never sinned, how about agreeing with God?" He's inviting Gnostics to rethink their point of view. If they'll admit their sinfulness, then God can do a saving work in their lives.[10]

Similarly, Andre van der Merwe writes, "This verse [1 John 1:9] has to be read in the context of the rest of the book of John—written to a group of believers whose ranks had previously been infiltrated by teachers of Gnosticism."[11] This is something taught by Joseph Prince, who wrote, "John was not writing to believers in that chapter. He was addressing the Gnostics who had infiltrated the early church. Gnostics are heretics who do not believe in the existence of sin."[12] Echoing this is Chuck Crisco: "In John's epistle the beginning chapter is written to Gnostics not Christians."[13] And on and it goes. (Just try raising 1 John 1:9 on Facebook among your hyper-grace friends, and watch how many of them tell you that this was written to Gnostics!)

Now, as someone trained in biblical scholarship, I have to admit that I'm immediately suspicious when everyone in a particular camp happens to "know" something about a particular text when the world's top scholars don't even agree on it. In other words, how is it that everyone I speak to in the hyper-grace camp—from the most educated in the Word to the least educated in the Word—seems to know that 1 John was written to combat Gnostic heresy and that John was addressing (Gnostic) unbelievers in chapter 1 verse 9? How did they all happen to know this?

The leading commentators on the Epistles of John, men and women who have spent decades meticulously researching the text, often praying over it for years as well, studying all available background material so as to put 1 John in its original context, do not universally agree that John was combatting Gnostic heresy in his letters. In fact, one of the leading authorities on the writings of John, Professor Rudolph Schnackenburg, said this: "The heresy which occasioned 1 and 2 John cannot be parallel with any other manifestation of heresy known from that era. Yet it has affinities with more than one such movement."[14] Not only so, but most scholars agree that Gnosticism didn't even exist until the second century AD—in other words, *after* 1 John was written! At best, it was the seeds of Gnosticism that were being addressed rather than a clearly defined, full-blown heretical system.

The New Bible Commentary notes, "There is dispute about how early Gnosticism appeared. It is very probable that it was much later than the time when this letter was written, but it did not spring out of empty air. Many of the teachings later included in the fully developed Gnostic systems were in circulation in the first century."[15] So, some of the ideas may have been there already, but it is wrong to speak of the "Gnostic" background to 1 John, and it is almost certainly wrong to say that John was addressing Gnostics here. Professor Stephen Smalley, author of a 425-page commentary on 1–3 John, wrote, "It is important to recall that in the NT period the climate of thought which was eventually known as 'Gnosticism' was unsystematized; so that it is more accurately described in the first century AD as the espousal of 'gnostic *tendencies*,' or as 'pre-gnosticism.'"[16]

This means that it is certainly *possible* that John was addressing some pre-Gnostic developing heresies, but that is open for debate. Without a doubt, though, this position is quite overstated by hyper-grace teachers, not to mention wrongly applied (with reference to 1 John 1:9). Yet hyper-grace believers tell us with confidence that this was the case, for the most part just repeating what they have heard from their teachers.

If you hold to this view, can I ask you some honest questions? Do you know who the Gnostics were? Did they exist before the time of Jesus? Were there "Christian" Gnostics as well as "Jewish" Gnostics? What were the main teachings that they believed? Can you tell me what Docetism is? What other books (or verses) in the New Testament seem to be addressing Gnosticism? How long did the church combat Gnostic heresy? Finally, what is the evidence, textually, archeologically, linguistically, or theologically, that demonstrates that 1 John is addressing Gnosticism?[17]

I ask these questions not to embarrass anyone but rather to reveal that many have simply repeated what they heard about the background to 1 John 1:9 without studying the issues for themselves. I even wonder how many hyper-grace teachers have carefully researched the matter as opposed to parroting what they heard from another colleague whom they respect. Is this a responsible thing for teachers of the Word to do? (See Jacob [James] 3:1.)

Who Was John Addressing?

New Testament scholar and Bible background expert Craig Keener suggests that any of the following scenarios might explain the issues being addressed in 1 John: John was encouraging Jewish believers who had been expelled from the synagogues; he was addressing the pressure the believers faced to compromise and commit idolatry or to listen to false prophets; he was addressing "a community like Ephesus, where the church had expelled the false teachers but needed love for one another (Rev. 2:2–4).... On the other hand, the issue might be one of the heresies that was developing toward full-blown Gnosticism."[18]

But let's say that 1 John *was* written to combat growing Gnostic heresy. That does not mean that 1 John 1:9 was addressed to unbelievers who were intermingled in John's congregations. In fact, both the context and the original Greek make such a view impossible to the point that when I shared the hyper-grace interpretation with one of my friends—a humble, Jesus-loving, Spirit-filled New Testament scholar who has written thousands upon thousands of pages of commentaries on New Testament books—he actually cringed.

First John is addressing believers, not unbelievers. In fact, Professor Keener notes, "One point is beyond dispute: the primary troublemakers are clearly 'secessionists,' people who had been part of the Christian community John addresses but *who had withdrawn from that community*."[19] The nonbelievers were no longer in the midst of these congregations, so it's "beyond dispute" that John is not addressing them in this letter. He is writing to believers about these heresies, but he is *never* addressing the heretics themselves.

Look carefully at the usage of the words *we*, *us*, and *our* in 1 John 1:1–10.

> That which was from the beginning, which *we* have heard, which *we* have seen with *our* eyes, which *we* looked upon and have touched with *our* hands, concerning the word of life—the life was made manifest, and *we* have seen it, and testify to it and proclaim to you the eternal life, which was with the Father and was made manifest to *us*—that which *we* have seen and heard *we* proclaim also to you, so that you too may have fellowship with *us*; and indeed *our* fellowship is with the Father and with his Son Jesus Christ. And *we* are writing these things so that *our* joy may be complete.
>
> This is the message *we* have heard from him and proclaim to

> you, that God is light, and in him is no darkness at all. If *we* say *we* have fellowship with him while *we* walk in darkness, *we* lie and do not practice the truth. But if *we* walk in the light, as he is in the light, *we* have fellowship with one another, and the blood of Jesus his Son cleanses *us* from all sin. If *we* say *we* have no sin, *we* deceive ourselves, and the truth is not in *us*. If *we* confess *our* sins, he is faithful and just to forgive *us our* sins and to cleanse *us* from all unrighteousness. If *we* say *we* have not sinned, *we* make him a liar, and his word is not in *us*.

This is not a message being preached to lost people to bring them to the faith, nor is 1 John 1:9 addressed to the lost. To the contrary, it refers to John and the believers to whom he writes: "If *we* confess *our* sins"—not, if *you* unsaved Gnostic heretics confess *your* sins—"he is faithful and just to forgive *us our* sins and to cleanse *us* from all unrighteousness"—not, he is faithful and just to forgive *you your* sins and to cleanse *you* from all unrighteousness.[20]

As for the heretics and the unbelievers, they are consistently addressed as outsiders, as "they," as people who were not (or who were no longer) part of the community:

> Children, it is the last hour, and as you have heard that antichrist is coming, so now many antichrists have come. Therefore we know that it is the last hour. *They* went out from us, but *they* were not of us; for if *they* had been of us, *they* would have continued with us. But *they* went out, that it might become plain that *they* all are not of us. But you have been anointed by the Holy One, and you all have knowledge.
>
> —1 JOHN 2:18–20

> Little children, you are from God and have overcome *them*, for he who is in you is greater than he who is in the world. *They* are from the world; therefore *they* speak from the world, and the world listens to *them*. We are from God. Whoever knows God listens to us; whoever is not from God does not listen to us. By this we know the Spirit of truth and the spirit of error.
>
> —1 JOHN 4:4–6[21]

So, the context of 1 John explicitly rules out the idea that 1 John 1:9 was written to unbelievers who were being called to put their trust in Jesus and be saved. In fact, the exact opposite is true: *because* the heretics were claiming to be without sin, John was "countering his opponents' claim to be sinless," urging his readers to "confess their specific sinful deeds, that is, the evil they are actually doing."[22]

The Greek is even more explicitly against the hyper-grace interpretation, since the word *confess* in the Greek speaks of continuous, present action as opposed to a one-time act. (Any first-year Greek student would know this.) As one commentary explained:

> **1:9 "confess"** This is a compound Greek term from "to speak" and "the same." Believers continue to agree with God that they have violated His holiness (cf. Rom. 3:23). It is PRESENT TENSE, which implies ongoing action. Confession implies (1) a specific naming of sins (v. 9); (2) a public admitting of sins (cf. Matt. 10:32; James 5:16; and (3) a turning from specific sins (cf. Matt. 3:6; Mark 1:5; Acts 19:18; James 5:16). I John uses this term quite often (cf. 1:9; 4:2, 3, 15; II John 7). Jesus' death is the means of forgiveness, but sinful mankind must respond and continue to respond in faith to be saved (cf. John 1:12; 3:16).[23]

Or, as stated by 1 John commentator C. G. Kruse, "The author projects a situation in which people acknowledge their sins in an ongoing way. He portrays authentic Christian living as involving honest and ongoing acknowledgement of one's sins."[24] As Greek authority A. T. Robertson notes, the text literally says "if we keep on confessing."[25] That's why Lutheran Bible commentator R. C. H. Lenski translated 1 John 1:9 with this wording: "If we keep confessing our sins, faithful is he and righteous to remit to us the sins and to cleanse us from all unrighteousness."[26] And Greek scholar Kenneth Wuest actually argued that, in the language of John, "The sinner is to believe (John 3:16). The saint is to confess."[27]

Yes, this is part of our intimate relationship with God, not something born of condemnation or legalism or faultfinding, but of liberty and joy. And because we love our Father and don't want to grieve Him, because we are careful never to let anything stand between us, and because we are zealous to keep our consciences clear, when we are conscious of sin we acknowledge that before our Father. And He is not only faithful to forgive us our sins, but because Jesus has paid for them in full, therefore, it is also righteous for God to forgive our unrighteousness.

But this is not the forgiveness of salvation, nor do we need to "get saved" over and over again whenever we sin. This is the forgiveness of friendship, the forgiveness that takes place within the family, the forgiveness that is based on acceptance and love. Even a strong grace teacher like Pastor Colin Dye, one of the most respected leaders in the United Kingdom, at whose church I have had the pleasure of ministering in the past, acknowledged that there is a need for believers to receive ongoing forgiveness from the Lord, distinguishing between God's "*parental* forgiveness" and His "*judicial* forgiveness."

So Pastor Dye, who holds to the doctrine of once saved, always saved (which I do not; see the appendix) and who believes that all our future sins are forgiven the moment we are saved (as do hyper-grace teachers), writes:

> When God withholds his *parental* forgiveness, he does not put us back under condemnation. Our sins can never count against us again because God has totally forgiven and forgotten them. He cancelled our debt and credited us with the righteousness of Christ. We received this *judicial* forgiveness once and for all by faith in the blood of Jesus. God, the righteous judge, judged all our sins on the cross and removed condemnation from our lives forever![28]

Obviously, I differ with some of Pastor Dye's position here, but I absolutely agree with him that the issue before us is *not* one of being saved one day and lost the next, struggling to confess every last one of our sins before we fall asleep lest we die in our sleep and go to hell, always wondering if we might have "missed" one sin—what Colin Dye calls "the kind of morbid introspection some religious teachers demand."[29] No, this forgiveness is *relational*, not judicial, having to do with our fellowship with God and our *experience* of being cleansed and forgiven as opposed to our overall standing with God.[30] (The only thing that could affect our overall standing with God—meaning, our ultimate salvation—is if we repudiate Jesus by denying Him or living in ongoing, unrepentant rebellion.)

As Charles Spurgeon explained:

> It is quite certain that those whom Christ has washed in His precious blood need not make a confession of sin, as culprits or criminals, before God the Judge, for Christ has for ever taken away all their sins in a legal sense, so that they no longer stand where they can be condemned…but having become children, and offending as children, ought they not every day to go before their heavenly Father and confess their sin, and acknowledge their iniquity? Nature teaches that it is the duty of erring children to make a confession to their earthly father, and the grace of God in the heart teaches us that we, as Christians, owe the same duty to our heavenly Father.[31]

And this is what Jesus had in mind when He taught us to pray, even daily, "Forgive us our debts, as we also have forgiven our debtors," explaining, "For if you forgive others their trespasses, your heavenly Father will also forgive you, but if you do not forgive others their trespasses, neither will your Father forgive your trespasses" (Matt. 6:12, 14–15). He is not here talking about being saved one day if we forgive others and lost the next day if we don't forgive them. He is talking about being in harmony with the Father and in right relationship with Him.

In fact, this calling to forgive others was so important that Jesus repeated it in several other contexts, including Mark 11:24–25, where He reiterates this while teaching about praying in faith. (How can we pray in faith when we are holding something against another person and refusing to forgive them as God forgave us?)

Paul Ellis has a real problem with this, writing:

> Jesus said, "If you do not forgive men their sins, your Father will not forgive your sins" (Matthew 6:15). This is not good news. This is bad news that should make us shake in our boots for it links God's forgiveness to our own. It is not grace, it is law. It is quid pro quo and tit for tat. It is something you must give to get.[32]

And Dr. Ellis also claims that "before the cross Jesus preached conditional forgiveness; forgive to be forgiven,"[33] contrasting it with an allegedly different message after the cross. (We will discuss this claim further in chapter 6.) The fact is, these words were spoken by the One who epitomized grace and truth (see chapter 13 for more on this), and this is anything but law as opposed to grace. In fact, rather than simply teaching "forgive to be forgiven," Jesus devotes a whole parable to teach us that that we must forgive *because* we have been forgiven. (See Matthew 18:21–35.)

Yes, we must forgive others from the heart in light of the massive debt that we have been forgiven. (Even before the cross the Jewish people had an understanding of grace, recognizing how God forgave the many sins they had committed; see, for example, Nehemiah 9:17 and Psalms 32:1; 130:4. After the cross that understanding was now multiplied exponentially.)

In the parable the master says to the unforgiving servant, "You wicked servant! I forgave you all that debt because you pleaded with me. And should not you have had mercy on your fellow servant, as I had mercy on you?" As a result, Jesus says, "in anger his master delivered him to the jailers, until he should pay all his debt. So also my heavenly Father will do to every one of you, if you do not forgive your brother from your heart" (Matt. 18:32–35). Yes, our loving Father will discipline us if we refuse to forgive our brothers and sisters from the heart. Paul emphasizes this holy calling too, reminding us that we are to forgive each other: "As the Lord has forgiven you, so you also must forgive" (Col. 3:13).

Failure to forgive *does* have consequences—in our fellowship with God and with others—but this does not mean that God "unforgives" all our previous sins and puts us in the category of the lost again. God forbid! It means that as God's children, as saints, we still need to receive cleansing and mercy when we do sin against God and others or when we hold unforgiveness in our hearts.

For me, though, this doesn't necessarily mean daily reflection and introspection, although in intimate times with God at the end of the day, if I'm reminded of a sin I committed during the day, I'll immediately ask for forgiveness. For the most part, this is an element of my ongoing relationship with my Father. And when I'm conscious of doing wrong, or when I realize my actions or attitudes or words grieved Him, as a beloved son, a fully accepted member of the Father's family, I confess my sin and ask Him to cleanse me, without for a split second thinking to myself, "I hope I'm still saved!" (Honestly, I can't even relate to that kind of thinking, and my heart really goes out to you if you do think like that. There's obviously something very important about grace that you're still missing.)

This is beneficial in many ways, since it helps me not to trivialize sin or to deceive myself by allowing sin to grow incrementally in my heart. I bring my life into the light as a child of the light, and cleansing and forgiveness are applied afresh to my life, as one already forgiven and cleansed.

A Continual Cleansing

First John 1:7 is very relevant here. (Remember that 1 John 1:7 was allegedly the part of the letter written to unbelievers; again, this is completely untrue.) Starting in verse 6, John wrote, "If we say we have fellowship with him while we walk in darkness, we lie and do not practice the truth. But if we walk in the light, as he is in the light, we have fellowship with one another, and the blood of Jesus his Son cleanses us from all sin." The Greek word for "cleanses" (or, "purifies") is *katharizo*, and here it is in the present active indicative, speaking of continuous, ongoing activity. As one study guide explains, "The term 'sin' is SINGULAR with no ARTICLE. This implies every kind of sin. Notice this verse is not focusing on a one-time cleansing (salvation), but an ongoing cleansing (the Christian life). Both are part of the Christian experience (cf. John 13:10)."[34]

As explained in another commentary:

> By his use of the present tense for the verbs "to walk" and "to purify," the author represents both the walking and the cleansing as ongoing activities. One lesson that may be learned from this second consequence is that walking in the light does not mean that those who do so never sin, but that they do not seek to hide that fact from God. They "walk in the light" with him, and the

> result of their doing so is that the blood of his Son Jesus purifies them from their sins.[35]

Again, this is not rocket science. It is simple, basic Greek, reminding us that John is writing to believers here, not unbelievers. And he is telling us that as we walk in the light, the blood of Jesus is continually cleansing us from sin, from which we learn that "walking in the light" doesn't mean living without sin. It means living a life that is pleasing to the Lord, and so if we sin, we immediately turn away from that sin and turn back to Him, and we are continually being cleansed and purified by Jesus' blood.

This, of course, flies in the face of hyper-grace teaching that the moment you were saved, your future sins were pronounced forgiven and removed from God's sight along with your past and present sins. Obviously not. First John 1:7 says that as we walk with the Lord, there is continual cleansing of our sins, many of which we don't even know exist. Jesus addressed this concept in John 13 when He washed the disciples' feet.

To give the context, Jesus knew He was about to be betrayed and that He was about to return to God. Before He left this world, He wanted to show His disciples the full extent of His love (John 13:1–3). So what did He do? He "rose from supper. He laid aside his outer garments, and taking a towel, tied it around his waist. Then he poured water into a basin and began to wash the disciples' feet and to wipe them with the towel that was wrapped around him" (vv. 4–5).

This was too much for Simon Peter: "Lord," he exclaimed, "there's no way You're going to wash my feet!" But Jesus insisted: "If I do not wash you, you have no share with me." This left impetuous Peter with only one response: "Lord, not my feet only but also my hands and my head!" (vv. 6–9). Amen, Peter! You're my kind of guy, all or nothing at all, both feet in or both feet out. Peter was saying, "If getting my feet washed is essential to staying in right relationship with You, then wash my whole body. Give me the whole package, Lord!"

> Jesus said to him, "The one who has bathed does not need to wash, except for his feet, but is completely clean. And you are

> clean, but not every one of you." For he knew who was to betray him; that was why he said, "Not all of you are clean."
>
> —John 13:10–11

What did Jesus mean? Well, you need to remember the culture of the day. The houses back then didn't have running water or plumbing, and that meant homes had no private showers or baths. When you wanted to bathe, you would either go to the river or to a public bath house. There you would wash and get completely clean. But then you had to walk back home, and that meant trekking down grimy, dusty roads. No matter what you did, your feet would get dirty. So, when you arrived at someone's house, it was a customary act of kindness for them to have a basin of water ready and a servant waiting to wash your feet. But that didn't mean that you needed to take another bath. You only needed to get your feet washed.

How did Jesus apply this spiritually? Well, all of His disciples (except Judas, who was about to betray Him) were in good standing with Him. He had received them as His own, forgiving their sins, and in His words, they were already "clean." (See also John 15:3, "Already you are clean because of the word that I have spoken to you.") Their head, hands, and whole body were bathed. They only needed to have their feet washed.

"That's nice," you say, "but I still don't get it. What does this have to do with 1 John 1:7?"

Simply this: When we get saved, we get bathed from head to toe. God cleans us up big-time, scrubbing away the accumulated filth. And there is a lot of filth to wash away! For some of us, it amounted to decades of sin and pollution; in other words, *decades* without a bath. Can you imagine, spiritually speaking, how miserably we stunk when we first asked God for mercy?

I think immediately of the roadside beggars we see each year on our ministry trips to India. It is difficult to describe the utter squalor in which these men live. Dressed in torn clothes (or sometimes just soiled rags) that look as if they have been soaked in motor oil, their bodies are covered with dirt (and sometimes sores), and their long hair is stiff and totally matted. (God only knows what kind of little creatures live in that hair.) I once asked one of my Indian friends, "Why don't they shave their heads instead? Wouldn't they be more comfortable?" He explained, "No, they leave their hair like that to get more money begging." Really, it's hard to describe just how repulsive and tragic a sight it is.

Yet that's how we looked when we got saved! We were utterly repulsive, coated with grime, a mass of "bruises and sores and raw wounds...not pressed out or bound up or softened with oil" (Isa. 1:6).

And in one moment of time, when we put our faith in the Lord Jesus and asked Him to save us from our sins, He healed our sick spirits and made us white as snow. He made us pure and holy. He made us clean!

This is what the Word says: "You were washed, you were sanctified, you were justified in the name of the Lord Jesus Christ and by the Spirit of our God" (1 Cor. 6:11).[36] Yes, Jesus cleansed us, "by the washing with water with the word" (Eph. 5:26), and "saved us...by the washing of regeneration and renewal by the Holy Spirit" (Titus 3:5). Now, we can "draw near to God with a sincere heart in full assurance of faith, having our hearts sprinkled to cleanse us from a guilty conscience and having our bodies washed with pure water" (Heb. 10:22, NIV).

There's only one problem: we still live in this world. We still have to walk along dusty, dirty roads, and sometimes our feet get dirty, even though we have been washed and bathed. There is simply no way to avoid all the dirt all the time. It's like going into a room filled with cigarette smokers. Even though you don't smoke yourself, you come out smelling like smoke—and some of the fumes get into your lungs too. That's a picture of the polluting power of sin.

Sometimes we are enveloped by profanity on a job site, even though we ourselves never utter such words. Still, just hearing filth can make you feel unclean. Other times we find ourselves coming into contact with people whose dress and behavior are lewd and sensual, and we feel dragged down by their sinful ways, even though we have kept ourselves morally upright. We feel dirty. But that doesn't mean we need another bath! We just need to get our feet washed. "Father, cleanse me from this junk in Jesus' name!" Purification in the Bible can be for uncleanness as well as for sin.

Yet there are times when we *do* sin, and that means our feet get dirty—even though we are walking in the light and our lives are no longer dominated by disobedience and self-will. The fact is, every day all of us fall short to one extent or another. Perhaps we have a fleeting thought of envy or competition, or maybe we speak a judgmental word about a fellow believer or fail to focus on the Lord during prayer. Perhaps the problem one day is our lack of compassion for a church member in need, or maybe we cast a fleeting, lustful glance at someone or momentarily become swelled with pride because the Lord saw fit to use us.

One way or another, even as consecrated, dedicated, separated children of God, we still have some momentary blemishes and spots. But that doesn't mean that we need to get saved again every time we fall short. Instead we immediately turn to the Lord for cleansing, wiping the grime from our feet as soon as we recognize it, and receiving mercy and grace from His hand.[37]

David Ravenhill provided a vivid picture of what the Word teaches on this important subject and how our hyper-grace colleagues get this wrong.

> Imagine a car dealership that provides every car buyer with a free car wash for as long as they own the car. You purchase a car, and along with the required paperwork you are given a free car wash certificate. The dealer tells you he has fully paid for all the car washes you will ever need, saying he believes that a clean car is the greatest way of advertising and promoting his dealership.
>
> Several days later, you happen to drive down a muddy country road full of potholes and ruts. Later, you notice your car is covered with mud and decide to avail yourself of your free lifetime car wash. But before you have time to drive through the car wash, your *friends* inform you that you no longer have to go there. They tell you that your first car wash was all that was necessary. Any suggestion that you need another wash is not only wrong, but a lie.
>
> You try and reason with your friends and even show them your dirty car. They still refuse to acknowledge that the car needs washing, even after seeing the condition of the car. They inform you that what the dealer really meant was that once the dealership had purchased the car wash for you, that would keep the car

clean forever. They also argued that to suggest it needed washing again was an insult to the dealer and the dealership. "Don't you realize," your friends tell you, "when the dealer first paid for your car wash, that automatically washed it for life; all past, present and future dirt was washed away, and therefore it never needs to be washed again."

Such logic would, by anyone's reasoning, be considered imbecilic, ignorant or crazy, to say the least. Obviously, what the dealer intended was that anytime you needed your car washed, you could avail yourself of a car wash because he had already paid for it in advance.

Thinking back on your conversation with the dealer, you recall him telling you that he has a personal hatred for dirty cars and that is why he paid for a lifetime of free washes to anyone who asked. He went on to say that *if*—and not *when*—you happen to get your car dirty, the car wash would take care of it. He obviously never intended for you to drive around searching for dirty roads just so you could avail yourself of the car wash. That, he said, would be abusive to the car-wash program and an insult to his dealership.

In a similar way, the atoning work of Christ paid in full for *all* my sin. This, however, does not exclude my need for repentance, nor does it give me license to sin as I please. For my "friends" to tell me otherwise is totally false and misleading.

Sadly, this is the logic behind the new hyper-grace message. The essence behind this false teaching is that all sins past, present and future have already been atoned for and therefore there is no longer any need to repent. That, the proponents of this idea say, would be tantamount to telling God you don't believe He has paid for all your sin.

This type of fuzzy theology falls apart for this reason: If repentance is acknowledging a sin that has already been forgiven, thereby making repentance unnecessary, then why do we tell people to repent the first time in order to be saved? If repentance is wrong following salvation, then using the same "logic," repentance is wrong prior to salvation too.

The error here is that this type of teaching leads to *ultimate reconciliation* or *universalism*. Jesus paid for all sin; therefore, all

> are saved. [For more in this false theology, see chapter 14, "The New Gnostics."]
>
> The fact is that the *provision* for my cleansing was completed at the cross but the *process* of my cleansing is conditional upon my repentance, and not before.[38]

The bottom line is that everything we need has already been purchased and provided by the Son of God, and as we walk with Him in this world, we receive the needed forgiveness, cleansing, guidance, and provision, be it day by day or even moment by moment. And rather than making this into a theological debate, let's keep it relational. We have a loving God who is now our Father, and in every good relationship, there is good communication. And sometimes that involves confession. The wonderful news is that God will always respond with grace upon grace as we turn to Him.[39]

-6-

THE HOLY SPIRIT, CONVICTION OF SIN, AND REPENTANCE

One of the most common teachings of the hyper-grace movement is that the Holy Spirit does not convict believers of sin, since God has already forgiven and forgotten all our sins and He sees us as perfect in Jesus. Therefore He will never again bring our sins to our attention. There are even some modern grace teachers who claim that the Holy Spirit does not convict *unsaved sinners* of their sin. According to Pastor Steve McVey:

> It is pointless to hope or pray that the Holy Spirit will convict an unbeliever of the things they are doing wrong. He's not going to do that for one simple reason: Their sins are not the problem. Christ dealt with their sins on the cross. When He said, "It is finished," He was including the world, not just those who have already believed the gospel. You see, the specific sins—the detailed misbehavior—of a person who isn't trusting in Jesus Christ are just indicative of a deeper problem.[1]

The Holy Spirit doesn't convict unbelievers of their sins? That is certainly news to hundreds of millions of believers through the centuries who were made deeply aware of their own sinfulness by that very same Holy Spirit, leading to a glorious conversion. That is exactly what happened to me in 1971, even though I had no idea people were praying for me, and the conviction came upon me with real intensity.

Former slave trader John Newton, the author of "Amazing Grace," expressed this so well in another hymn, "In Evil I Took Long Delight":

> My conscience felt and owned its guilt,
> And plunged me in despair,

I saw my sins His blood had spilt,
And helped to nail Him there. [2]

The great grace preacher Charles Spurgeon also expressed this sentiment beautifully:

> Possibly, much of the flimsy piety of the present day arises from the ease with which men attain to peace and joy in these evangelistic days. We would not judge modern converts, but we certainly prefer that form of spiritual exercise which leads the soul by the way of Weeping-cross, and makes it see its blackness before assuring it that it is "clean every whit." Too many think lightly of sin, and therefore think lightly of the Saviour. He who has stood before his God, convicted and condemned, and with the rope about his neck, is the man to weep for joy when he is pardoned, to hate the evil which has been forgiven him, and to live to the honour of the Redeemer by whose blood he has been cleansed.[3]

Absolutely! Yes, it is often true that the depth of someone's conversion is directly related to the depth of conviction they experienced before coming to faith. The words of Scottish evangelist James A. Stewart, who died in 1975, still ring true:

> I refuse to entertain sinners on their way to hell.... I want to preach every time as though it were my last chance. I do not want souls to curse my name in the lake of fire and say, "Yes, I went to such-and-such a Gospel meeting, but that preacher Stewart only entertained and joked. He made Christianity a farce!"
>
> The old-fashioned method of evangelism was to make people weep, but the modern "Hollywood" way is to make people laugh. Everybody has to have a jolly good time.... We must have plenty of jokes or it would not be a good meeting. That is why there is such a woeful lack of conviction of sin in modern evangelism. The Holy Spirit cannot work in a frivolous atmosphere.
>
> Here is a solemn truth that very few of God's people seem to see: Everything depends on the atmosphere of the meeting.... For example, if you were saved in a jazzy sort of atmosphere, light and frivolous, with the song leader more like a clown and the preacher merely glorifying himself and using fleshly effort, you

> will also turn out to be a jazzy frivolous Christian with no depth in your spiritual life.[4]

And this makes perfect sense. When we get a real glimpse of the awesome holiness of God, we see the depth of our own sin, and we are transformed by His love. If you don't believe me, ask Isaiah (Isa. 6:5) or Peter (Luke 5:8–9) or Job (Job 42:1–6). This also refutes the notion of some hyper-grace teachers that, "You simply cannot focus on yourself and Jesus at the same time. You cannot attend to your shortcomings and behold his glorious perfections simultaneously. It's one or the other. It's you or him."[5]

To the contrary, often the only way we see ourselves for who we really are is by focusing on the Lord, and it is as we "behold his glorious perfections" that we are able to "attend to [our] shortcomings." And it begins with the moment of our salvation, which is often the result of searching, searing—and ultimately wonderful—conviction of sin. That's why one seasoned missionary to Indonesia who experienced the powerful outpouring of the Spirit there in the 1960s and 1970s wrote, "I think the greatest thing that I have heard and that I have seen is people being convicted of sin and of the need of a Savior."[6]

To quote Spurgeon again, "A spiritual experience which is thoroughly flavored with a deep and bitter sense of sin is of great value to him that hath it. It is terrible in the drinking, but it is most wholesome in the bowels, and in the whole of the after life."[7] He also wrote, "Stripping comes before clothing; digging out the foundation is the first thing in building and a thorough sense of sin is one of the earliest works of grace in the heart."[8]

What about Pastor McVey's argument that God already dealt with our sins at the cross, because of which He will no longer convict unbelievers of their sins? Or, in the words of Andre Rabe, "Repentance is not the event in which a person twists the arm of a reluctant God to forgive. God forgave even before you were born."[9] This is absolutely not what the Word teaches.[10]

First, there are many verses that indicate that those who do not believe in Jesus are still in their sins. (See, for example, Colossians 1:21; 2:13; Titus 3:3; and John 8:23–24.) And Scripture teaches explicitly that unbelievers will be judged for their sins. As Paul wrote, "For you may be sure of this, that everyone who is sexually immoral or impure, or who is covetous (that is, an idolater), has no inheritance in the kingdom of Christ and God. Let no one deceive you with empty words, for because of these things the wrath of God comes upon the sons of disobedience" (Eph. 5:5–6). This flies in the face of Pastor McVey's claim that "the Holy Spirit isn't going to convict unbelievers of their specific sins because that wouldn't meet the deepest need they have. Their biggest problem isn't their misbehavior. He's going to convict them of the one thing that ultimately matters—their unbelief in Christ. That's the core issue."[11]

Of course their sins matter deeply, and of course God will convict unbelievers of their sins. And the gospel message is one of repentance and forgiveness of sins, which is why Peter set the tone in Acts by calling his fellow Jews to account of their sin of rejecting the Messiah, after which they were deeply convicted:

> "Let all the house of Israel therefore know for certain that God has made him both Lord and Christ, this Jesus whom you crucified." Now when they heard this they were cut to the heart, and said to Peter and the rest of the apostles, "Brothers, what shall we do?" And Peter said to them, "Repent and be baptized every one of you in the name of Jesus Christ for the forgiveness of your sins, and you will receive the gift of the Holy Spirit."
>
> —Acts 2:36–38

You say, "But the sin they were convicted of was the sin of rejecting Jesus. You said so yourself." Correct! That is one of the sins the Spirit convicts us of, along with the sin of unbelief. But it is absolutely false to say, as McVey claims, "The Holy Spirit will convict an unbeliever of only one thing—his unbelief in Jesus Christ. He will show that person where he stands so that he can enter into the experience of knowing God through Jesus."[12] Peter preaches the forgiveness of *sins* (plural),[13] not simply the forgiveness of *the sin* (namely, of unbelief). That's why Ananias said to Saul (Paul) after his encounter with Jesus, "Rise and be baptized and wash away your sins [not "sin"], calling on his name" (Acts 22:16).

It is when the Holy Spirit convicts an unbeliever of his sins—again, as countless hundreds of millions of believers can attest—that the unbeliever recognizes his need for the Lord. As I wrote in *It's Time to Rock the Boat*, "Without conviction there is no conversion, and without conviction the Cross makes no sense."[14]

This is really so obvious that there's no need to debate this further.[15] The real question is this: Does the Holy Spirit convict *believers* of their sins? The almost totally unanimous answer from the hyper-grace camp is no. Joseph Prince states:

> The Holy Spirit never convicts (Christians) of your sins. He never comes to point out your faults.... It does not take a revelation from the Holy Spirit to see that you have failed. However, when you know that you've failed what you do need is for the Holy Spirit to convict you of your righteousness.[16]

Clark Whitten goes on to explain:

> The Holy Spirit's ministry to the world is to convince the world of sin "because they do not believe in me," Jesus says in John 16:9. The Holy Spirit has already convinced me of sin, and now I believe in Jesus! He is now convincing me of righteousness (see John 16:10). I am convinced that I am becoming "the righteousness of God in Him" (2 Cor. 5:21). The Holy Spirit convinced me of judgment and that truth helped me become a believer. Now He is convincing me that "the ruler of this world has been judged" (John 16:11)—not me![17]

We'll take up the definition of the Greek word for "convict" later in this chapter (Pastor Whitten here translates it to mean "convince"). But the deeper question is this: Does the Holy Spirit ever speak to us about our sins? Does He ever draw attention to things we have done wrong? Does He ever rebuke us or correct us? Of course He does. Why? Because He loves us so much! If He didn't love us, He would stand back and allow sin to damage and destroy us. But because of His boundless love and kindness, He makes us uncomfortable in our sins so that we will turn away from them and turn back to Him.

Hyper-grace teachers take issue with this, arguing that the Holy Spirit doesn't convict us of sin because God doesn't see our sins, as we discussed in chapter 4. But since He does see our sins, since sin is so destructive, and since our Father loves us so dearly, the Spirit of God deals with us to help us turn away from our sin.

Conviction vs. Condemnation

Unfortunately, some believers confuse conviction with condemnation, and the moment the Spirit speaks to them about something wrong in their lives, they feel hopeless and condemned, which only drives them further from the Lord. This is a lie from the enemy that must be exposed, and I stand with my colleagues in the hyper-grace camp when they seek to expose this destructive notion. Let the truth be shouted from the rooftops: *the Holy Spirit never speaks condemnation to a son or daughter of God.*

As I explained in my book *Go and Sin No More*, "If you are a born-again believer, a blood-washed child of God, you are not damned and doomed. God is not saying, 'To hell with you! Depart from Me, you wicked one.' Absolutely not! He is saying, 'You are Mine! I accept you fully through My Son.'"[18]

What then is the difference between conviction and condemnation? Conviction says to the believer, "You have sinned, so come to Me!" Condemnation says to the lost and damned sinner, "You are pronounced guilty. Away from Me!"

Conviction is good, not bad; it's something sent from heaven, not manufactured in hell. We should thank God when His conviction breaks our hearts, helping us to yield to the Spirit, since heeding His rebuke always brings life. In fact, the Spirit's work of conviction is part of His ministry to "guide [us] into all truth" (John 16:13). As the nineteenth-century theologian Charles Hodge wrote, "There is no form of conviction more intimate and irresistible than that which arises from the inward teaching of the Spirit."[19]

"But," you say, "from what I can see, according to the New Testament, the Holy Spirit only convicts the world of sin, not believers. That's what John 16:8 says, and I don't see anywhere else in the New Testament that the word *convict* is ever used with reference to the Spirit's ministry to the church."

Let's take a look at this and see exactly what God's Word says, searching things out in the original Greek. The Greek word translated "convict" in John 16:8 is *elencho*, which can mean "convince, convict; reprove, correct; rebuke, discipline." It occurs seventeen times in the Greek New Testament, and we'll look at every verse where *elencho* is found. In each citation I have highlighted the English word that corresponds to *elencho* so you can see for yourself exactly how it is used in the English Standard Version.

We'll start in the Gospels:

- "If your brother sins against you, go and *tell him his fault*, between you and him alone. If he listens to you, you have gained your brother" (Matt. 18:15).
- "But Herod the tetrarch, who had *been reproved* by [John] for Herodias, his brother's wife, and for all the evil things that Herod had done" (Luke 3:19).
- "For everyone who does wicked things hates the light and does not come to the light, lest his works should *be exposed*" (John 3:20).
- "Which one of you *convicts* me of sin? If I tell the truth, why do you not believe me?" (John 8:46).
- "And when he comes, he will *convict* the world concerning sin and righteousness and judgment" (John 16:8).

Are you getting a feel for how the word is used? And did you notice that it was used with reference to a brother reproving another brother who sinned against him?

Let's go to the Epistles now to see how *elencho* is used, first with reference to sinners in the world, then with reference to an elder who continues in sin:

- "But if all prophesy, and an unbeliever or outsider enters, he is *convicted* by all, he is called to account by all" (1 Cor. 14:24).

- "Take no part in the unfruitful works of darkness, but instead *expose* them.... But when anything is *exposed* by the light, it becomes visible" (Eph. 5:11, 13).
- "As for those who persist in sin, *rebuke* them in the presence of all, so that the rest may stand in fear" (1 Tim. 5:20).

Did you catch that? The same Greek word that is used with reference to *convicting* an unbeliever of his sin and *exposing* the darkness of the world is also used with reference to *rebuking* a sinning elder. But there's more. Paul calls on Timothy to be sure to *elencho*—convict, rebuke—his hearers when he preaches the Word (and the context makes clear he was speaking of his ministry to the church in Ephesus): "Preach the word; be ready in season and out of season; *reprove*, rebuke, and exhort, with complete patience and teaching" (2 Tim. 4:2).

If Timothy's congregation had read some of today's hyper-grace teaching, they would have protested: "But Timothy! You're not supposed to reprove us and convict us! We're already righteous, and God doesn't see our sins. Why then are you reproving us?" In fact, they would have told Paul himself he was wrong. "Paul, it's obvious you don't understand grace! You're giving Timothy some very poor advice!"

Well, he gave the same counsel to Titus. Speaking of the requirements of elders, Paul wrote, "He must hold firm to the trustworthy word as taught, so that he may be able to give instruction in sound doctrine and also to *rebuke* those who contradict it" (Titus 1:9). And speaking of some of the challenges involved in discipling the local population, Paul wrote, "This testimony is true. Therefore *rebuke* them sharply, that they may be sound in the faith" (v. 13).

Of course, it's possible that some of the people Titus was ministering to were not believers, but Paul made clear to Titus, just as he had to Timothy, that he was to convict and rebuke as a fundamental part of his ministry to the saved and lost alike: "Declare these things; exhort and *rebuke* with all authority. Let no one disregard you" (Titus 2:15). How ironic it is that the very style of ministry Paul insisted upon is the very style of ministry rejected today in the name of Paul!

The letter to the Hebrews takes things one step further. Speaking explicitly *to believers*, the author of Hebrews writes, "And have you forgotten the exhortation that addresses you as sons? 'My son, do not regard lightly the discipline of the Lord, nor be weary when *reproved* by him'" (Heb. 12:5). Do you see that? Divine reproof is a sign of the Father's love for His children! Indeed, "If you are left without discipline, in which all have participated, then you are illegitimate children and not sons" (v. 8).

Jacob (James) also has an explicit word for us as believers: "But if you show partiality, you are committing sin and are *convicted* by the law as transgressors" (James 2:9). Yes, *as believers* we are convicted. And note well: it is by *God's Law* that we are convicted—the very Law that hyper-grace teachers want to throw under the bus as dangerous and destructive, rather than recognizing its life-giving role of conviction. How many times I have been convicted of sin while reading the Torah—the Law—gaining a deeper revelation of God's holiness and perfection, causing me to run to Him and fall at His feet, wanting to be more like Him. (See chapter 12 for more on this.)

The verb *elencho* is used two more times in the New Testament, first in Judah (Jude) 15, speaking of the coming judgment on the ungodly: "to execute judgment on all and to *convict* all the ungodly of all their deeds of ungodliness that they have committed in such an ungodly way, and of all the harsh things that ungodly sinners have spoken against him." Hyper-grace teachers would have no problem with this verse at all, since it's speaking of the world, not the church.

But what do they do with the words of Jesus, identified explicitly with the voice of the Holy Spirit, in Revelation 3:19? There Jesus says, "'Those whom I love, I *reprove* and discipline, so be zealous and repent.... He who has an ear, let him hear what the Spirit says to the churches'" (Rev. 3:19, 22). The Holy Spirit is still convicting believers of sin!

Joseph Prince wrote, "The bottom line is that the Holy Spirit never convicts you of your sins. He NEVER comes to point out your faults. I challenge you to find a scripture in the Bible that the Holy Spirit comes to convict you of your sins."[20] It looks like that challenge has been met![21]

Godly Sorrow

In the midst of his beautiful and moving book *The Birthright: Out of the Servants' Quarters Into the Father's House*, teacher and evangelist John Sheasby makes what I believe is the same hyper-grace error, presenting a glorious truth in a way that ultimately negates what Scripture says. In the context of the Lord's offer to restore fellowship to the believers in Laodicea (Rev. 3:20), Sheasby writes:

> The pattern of Jesus' life on earth gives insight into God's method of transformation. He knows that you, like Zacchaeus [see Luke 19:1–10] will not be changed by performance but by his presence. The power of his love, the joy of his presence, and the peace coming from his acceptance are far more capable of changing the human heart than rebuke, censure, condemnation, and rejection.[22]

Of course, it is true that nothing changes us like an encounter with God's holy presence and a revelation of His love. But what Sheasby has completely overlooked is that Jesus, in the very same context of speaking to the church of Laodicea, said to them in Revelation 3:19, "Those *whom I love*, I reprove and discipline, so be zealous and repent." And so, rebuke and reproof are often a sign of God's love for us, an extension of His presence and goodness. Yet this sincere author quotes Revelation 3:20 ("I stand at the door and knock") while ignoring Revelation 3:19 (which speaks of Jesus disciplining and reproving us in His love and calling us to repent)!

That's why the Holy Spirit, speaking through Jacob (James), brought a strong word of rebuke to believers who were living in rebellion and sin:

> Submit yourselves therefore to God. Resist the devil, and he will flee from you. Draw near to God, and he will draw near to you. Cleanse your hands, you sinners, and purify your hearts, you double-minded. Be wretched and mourn and weep. Let your laughter be turned to mourning and your joy to gloom. Humble yourselves before the Lord, and he will exalt you.
>
> —Jacob (James) 4:7–10

Those verses, my friends, are in the New Testament, written to believers who had become enemies of God by their lifestyles (Jacob [James] 4:1–6), and they call for repentance and mourning over sin, promising God's mercy to those who humble themselves in His sight.

"But," someone says, "the Holy Spirit doesn't want me to feel bad. He only wants me to feel good!"

To be brutally honest, that is a very immature attitude. First, it reflects an incredibly superficial attitude to life itself. There are times to dance and there are times to mourn (Eccles. 3:1–8), as Jesus Himself said, "Blessed are those who mourn, for they shall be comforted.... Blessed are you who weep now, for you shall laugh" (Matt. 5:4; Luke 6:21).

Second, it reflects an incredibly superficial relationship with God. How should we, His beloved children, respond when we realize that we have grieved Him? How should we, His blood-bought family, respond when we understand that He is not pleased with us?

If a husband sinned against his wife and she said to him, "Honey, what you did really hurt me," would he respond, "But you're making me feel bad!" Obviously not—unless he was selfish and immature and had a very superficial relationship with his spouse. Otherwise he would say, "I am so sorry that I hurt you, and I want to make things right." And he would be pained that he had pained his wife. Isn't that what relationships are about? And isn't that the way God relates to us throughout the Word, expecting us to respond in turn?

Consider this concrete example from 2 Corinthians 7, where Paul is commending the Corinthians for their heartfelt response to his earlier rebuke. He explains first how painful it was for him to cause them pain, but he rejoiced because the pain led them to godly repentance:

> For even if I made you grieve with my letter, I do not regret it—though I did regret it, for I see that that letter grieved you, though only for a while. As it is, I rejoice, not because you were grieved, but because you were grieved into repenting. For you felt a godly grief, so that you suffered no loss through us. For godly grief produces a repentance that leads to salvation without regret, whereas worldly grief produces death.
>
> —2 Corinthians 7:8–10

Let's not skip over this (and I urge all hyper-grace adherents to chew on these words from Paul). There is such a thing as godly grief (or godly sorrow), and according to Paul, it is a wonderful thing, because it leads to true repentance. And I repeat: he is dealing with believers here, not unbelievers.

Then he describes what this godly grief and true repentance looked like, and it was far more than just "agreeing with God," as many hyper-grace teachers like to say. It was heartfelt, it was intense, and it was thorough: "For see what earnestness this godly grief has produced in you, but also what eagerness to clear yourselves, what indignation, what fear, what longing, what zeal, what punishment! At every point you have proved yourselves innocent in the matter" (v. 11).

It is striking that Andre Rabe, in a mini-book devoted exclusively to the subject of *metanoia* (which he wrongly defines as "clarity" rather than "repentance") could write: "You could not and cannot die to sin through your own efforts and discipline. Neither is it your regret or the sincerity of your confession that will accomplish this separation from sin. It is not the depth of your sorrow, but the clarity of your insight that will set you free from destructive habits and thoughts."[23]

Obviously, no one here is talking about dying to sin through our "own efforts and discipline," but it is crystal clear in the Word—in particular here in 2 Corinthians 7—that there is often deep sorrow and regret when the Spirit convicts us of our sins, and that Spirit-birthed sorrow and regret is part of a transformational repentance process.

We neglect the convicting ministry of the Holy Spirit today to our own great harm, and there are some modern grace teachers who recognize this too, such as Pastor Rob Rufus, who wrote:

> Godly sorrow comes when we realize we are doing something wrong, sinning and disobeying God. As Paul says in 2 Corinthians 7:10: "Godly sorrow brings repentance that leads to salvation and leaves no regret, but worldly sorrow brings death." Godly sorrow comes when
>
> - we have lost our zeal
> - we are just going through religious routines
> - we are half-hearted
> - we are compromising on the sidelines

- we are hiding bitterness in our hearts
- we have immorality hidden somewhere in secret places

> When that is our state, the Holy Spirit comes to help us. He loves us so much he will come and convict us of sin. He will not come to condemn, threaten or intimidate us. He will come and break our hearts with the loveliness of God. We will sense by revelation the goodness of our God and it will lead us to repentance when we see how great, good and merciful God is. Our hearts will be broken with grief when we see the sin we are doing and realize that we have hurt God. Everything in our being will be motivated positively to change and get rid of wrong in our lives. Godly sorrow brings change for the better, but worldly sorrow brings psychological guilt that is demotivating, destructive and paralyzing.[24]

Thank you, Pastor Rufus! And when we are convicted of our sin by the Spirit, or when our own conscience convicts us, we turn away from that sin and turn back to God, helped and empowered by that same Spirit. That is called repentance, which is also something precious and beautiful. Unfortunately, it too has been misunderstood by hyper-grace teachers.

Steve McVey writes:

> What is repentance? Many people confuse it with remorse, which is to feel badly about something you've done. They think, "You haven't really repented unless you are groveling and wallowing in your guilt and shame. That's how you will allow God to release good into your life."
>
> Although that view is common, it's not what the Bible means by repentance.[25]

Well, it's one thing to talk about "groveling and wallowing in your guilt and shame"; it's another thing to talk about "feel[ing] badly about something you've done," which is certainly what is meant by repentance in 2 Corinthians 7, as well as often throughout the Scriptures. And it is certainly what happened to the prodigal son in Luke 15 when he came to his senses and repented:

> But when he came to himself, he said, "How many of my father's hired servants have more than enough bread, but I perish here with hunger! I will arise and go to my father, and I will say to him, 'Father, I have sinned against heaven and before you. I am no longer worthy to be called your son. Treat me as one of your hired servants.'"
>
> —LUKE 15:17–19[26]

Hyper-grace teachers sometimes point to this very passage, rightly emphasizing how the father embraced his son without condemnation, running out to meet him, fully accepting him back, and throwing a party on his behalf. And they'll sometimes accuse those outside the hyper-grace camp of being like the older brother who was indignant over the celebration. Yet it is this passage that paints such a vivid picture of repentance: the prodigal son recognizes the folly of his ways, he is stung by his guilt, and he is eager to confess his sins and get right with his father.

In stark contrast with this account—and with the witness of many other scriptures—Pastor Whitten writes, "I believe that New Testament repentance is not the Holy Spirit convicting of sin, me feeling sorry, confessing the sin, asking for forgiveness, and committing to stop doing it. That typical scenario is a grotesque misrepresentation of the gift of repentance. It is heathenish!"[27]

Heathenish? What? Unfortunately, virtually every hyper-grace teacher I have read to date gives the same basic definition of *repent* and *repentance* in the New Testament, telling us:

> The New Testament was written in Greek, and the word *repentance* is the Greek word *metanoia*. It comes from two words. The first (*meta*) means "after," and the second (*noieō*) means "to think as the result of observing." So the word *repent* in the New Testament is a compound word that means "to think differently after taking a closer look at a matter." Simply put, it means to change your mind. It's an about-face in the way you think. It's an afterthought, and it's different from what we thought before we looked closer. So repentance, then, isn't about groveling before God and being racked with guilt and shame. It's about changing our minds.[28]

And:

> By the way, for all of you who feel that there should be more preaching on repentance, do you know what the word "repent" means in the first place? The word "repent" is the Greek word *metanoeo*, which according to *Thayer's Greek Lexicon*, simply means "to change one's mind." But because we have been influenced by our denominational background as well as our own religious upbringing, many of us have the impression that repentance is something that involves mourning and sorrow.[29]

And:

> In the old covenant repentance essentially meant "stop sinning" because the blessing and cursing was based on obedience to the Law. In the new covenant it is tied to the terms of the covenant too but the primary sins we are being called to repent of is unbelief. The Greek for "repent" simply means "change your mind." Change your mind about God and sin so you can believe with your heart.... So we are not repenting of behavior in order to get forgiveness but changing our minds about the finished work of Christ, opening our heart and believing the good news.[30]

Is repentance merely "changing my mind" and coming into agreement with God? Is that what the Greek noun and verb mean? Absolutely not. Every major New Testament Greek dictionary is against this (including Thayer's, which was actually *misquoted* above); the testimony of many scriptures is against this; the Aramaic (and/or Hebrew) language that Jesus and the apostles preached in is against this; and common sense is against this.

To start with a commonsense example, let's say that I'm driving in the car with you, heading north when we're supposed to be heading south. You point out to me that we're going in the wrong direction, but I insist that I know the way and we're heading toward our destination. After a while you give me undeniable evidence that we're going north instead of south, and I say to you, "You're absolutely right! I'm totally wrong! We are heading in the wrong direction!" And then I continue to drive the wrong way.

Is that a picture of "repentance"? Obviously not. Why? Because a change of mind without an accompanying change of action—direction!—is absolutely worthless. As the Greek scholar and Irish church leader Richard Trench once observed, repentance is "that mighty change in mind, heart, and life, wrought by the Spirit of God."[31] It is far more than "an about-face in the way you think."

To be sure, some hyper-grace teachers emphasize the dramatic change of direction that true repentance brings, as Pastor Whitten rightly notes: "True repentance gets at the root of our sin instead of dealing with the behavioral symptoms. Legalism only deals with the surface, behavioral problems; and therefore, there are few lasting victories."[32] He also makes this great observation: "True repentance can break the power sin has over us by allowing the Spirit of God to reveal truth to us and renewing our minds in the specific area of deception that is producing sin. He guides or coaches us in becoming like Christ in the way we think. If we become like Christ in the way we think, we become like Christ in the way we act!"[33] And Chuck Crisco correctly states that, "Right believing will always produce right behavior."[34]

But with the constant downplaying of the Spirit's work of conviction, with the continual denial that repentance ever involves remorse and sorrow, and with the consistent emphasis that "repent" simply means "change your mind," hyper-grace teachers actually hinder many believers from truly repenting and experiencing God's glorious liberty. In fact, they sometimes reject true repentance and life-saving conviction in the name of "grace."

Now, to say this once more: I absolutely agree that it is an encounter with the presence of God, the life of God, and the truth of God that radically changes us, and we can grovel and feel miserable and confess our sins for years without experiencing change. The Holy Spirit helps us to repent, and it is often God's patience and kindness—His goodness—that leads us to repentance (Rom. 2:4).[35]

So I agree with my hyper-grace colleagues here. Where I disagree is with the nature and definition of repentance, which often includes sorrow and grief, often comes as the result of the Spirit's conviction and rebuke, and means far more than changing our minds and agreeing with God that we are righteous.

That's why all the major Greek lexicons and theological dictionaries define the Greek words related to "repentance" (again, the noun is *metanoia* and the verb is *metanoeō*) with something more than "a change of mind." To be sure, in some contexts, the Greek *can* have this meaning,[36] but it is abundantly clear that in the vast majority of cases, it doesn't mean that.

A Change of Mind

Now, you might say, "I'm into the Spirit, not the letter, and I don't really care what these dictionaries have to say," but that would be a very unwise attitude. First, have you noticed that the modern grace teachers often tell us what the Greek allegedly says? Why is it OK for them to do it, but it's not OK for someone who differs with them to do it? Second, do you believe words have meanings? Do you believe God communicated with purpose and accuracy? Then you should do your best to understand what those divine words mean—I'm referring to the words of Scripture—and since God preserved His Word for us in Hebrew and Greek (with a few portions in Aramaic), we do well to understand those languages. Third, God has put teachers and scholars in the body to help us, not to hurt us, and if you read your Bible in English or any language other than the original Hebrew and Greek, you owe that to Bible scholars who labored many long years to get that translation into your hands.

I personally love word studies. In fact, my doctoral dissertation was based on the Hebrew word for "healing" (from the root *rapha'*), compared to its usage in the other ancient Semitic languages. Yes, my PhD thesis focused on one word! Since then I've had the joy of writing quite a few in-depth articles on different words in the Hebrew Bible, and each time I was massively enriched. What amazing treasures there are in the Word!

When it comes to the *metanoia*, repentance, and *metanoeō*, to repent, the major dictionaries all agree on its primary meaning in the New Testament. So, *A Greek-English Lexicon of the New Testament and Other Early Christian Literature*, recognized as the number one dictionary of New Testament Greek, defines the noun *metanoia* as having the basic meaning of "a change of mind," then explains that throughout the New Testament writings it means "repentance, turning about, conversion." As for *metanoeō*, the dictionary states that one meaning is "change one's mind," but it finds no examples of this in the New Testament.[37] The second definition is "feel remorse, repent, be converted," with many examples in the New Testament. (By the way, if you've never worked with one of these dictionaries—I mean held one in your hands and gone through its pages—you would be stunned to see how much research is involved in a single entry. From a careful scholarly viewpoint, it is staggering.)

The *Analytical Lexicon of the Greek New Testament*, after stating that the technical meaning of the word is "perceive afterward, with the implication of being too late to avoid consequences," explains that *metanoia* has two main uses in the New Testament: "(1) predominately of a religious and ethical change in the way one thinks about acts repent, change one's mind, be converted (MT 3.2); (2) as feeling remorse regret, feel sorry (LU 17.3, 4)."[38]

The *Greek-English Lexicon of the New Testament: Based on Semantic Domains* explains that in the New Testament *metanoia* means "to change one's way of life as the result of a complete change of thought and attitude with regard to sin and righteousness." It goes on to say, "Though in English a focal component of repent is the sorrow or contrition that a person experiences because of sin, the emphasis in μετανοέω [*metanoeō*] and μετάνοια [*metanoia*] seems to be more specifically the total change, both in thought and behavior, with respect to how one should both think and act."[39]

Thayer's Greek English Lexicon of the New Testament (which was cited in an incomplete, misleading way by a hyper-grace leader, as noted above) actually says this about *metanoeō*:

> the verb *metanoeō* means, "*to change one's mind, i.e., to repent* (to feel sorry that one has done this or that, Jonah 3:9), of having offended someone, Luke 17:3f;...used especially of those who, conscious of their sins and with manifest tokens of sorrow, are intent on obtaining God's pardon;...*to change one's mind for the better, heartily to amend with abhorrence of one's past sins:...* Luke 3:8...i.e., conduct worthy of a heart changed and abhorring sin).[40]

For the noun *metanoia*, Thayer writes:

> ... *a change of mind*: as it appears in one who repents of a purpose he has formed or of something he has done, Heb. 12:17 ... especially the change of mind of those who have begun to abhor their errors and misdeeds, and have determined to enter upon a better course of life, so that it embraces both a recognition of sin and sorrow for it and hearty amendment, the tokens and effects of which are good deeds ... used merely of the improved spiritual state resulting from deep sorrow for sin, 2 Cor. 7:9f.[41]

The massive *Theological Dictionary of the New Testament* explains the words this way:

> ... *metanoeō* and *metanoia* are the forms in which the NT gives new expression to the ancient concept of religious and moral conversion.... [The repentance preaching of Jesus] demands radical conversion, a transformation of nature, a definitive turning from evil, a resolute turning to God in total obedience (Mark 1:15; Matt. 4:17; 18:3).[42]

A. T. Robertson, one of the greatest Greek scholars of his day, stated that the New Testament preaching of repentance said, "Change your mind and life. Turn right about and do it now."[43] The widely acclaimed, multivolume *New International Dictionary of New Testament Theology* states, "The predominantly intellectual understanding of *metanoia* as change of mind plays very little part in the NT. Rather the decision by the whole man to turn around is stressed. It is clear that we are concerned neither with a purely outward turning nor with a merely intellectual change of ideas."[44] And another fine multivolume work, *The Exegetical Dictionary of the New Testament*, defines *metanoeō* as "turn around, change one's mind, repent," while defining *metanoia* as "change of direction, conversion, repentance."[45]

This same dictionary explains that, beginning in the Gospels, "*Repentance* is first of all a turning away from sin (Mark 1:4f.).... *Repentance* furthermore refers to a radical acknowledgment of God, who stands over against Israel in his wrath, as well as a radical confession of a sinful fallenness that is so total that recourse to the former means of salvation appears hopeless."[46]

This is hardly just a change of mind or, in the words of one modern grace teacher, a matter of "rethink[ing] my position about impossibilities in light of the truth that God can do all things," which means that when Jesus preached repentance (see, for example, Matthew 4:17), He simply required a "great adjustment of thinking."[47] It was obviously a lot more than that. As I wrote in 1989, "Repentance means spiritual revolution. Strongholds of sin are demolished. Lifetime bondages are overcome. Hardened hearts break open. Satan's grip is undone. Repentance sets the prisoners free!"[48]

I also stated above that the original spoken language of Jesus, John the Baptizer, and the apostles was Aramaic and possibly Hebrew. So when they preached to their fellow Jews in their native language, they would not have been speaking Greek. This is important to remember, since they would absolutely not have been saying, "Change your mind." Rather, as I noted in *It's Time to Rock the Boat*, "The fundamental Aramaic and Hebrew word for *repent* means 'turn around, turn back, do an about-face.' (The other Hebrew word used for *repent* means 'feel sorrow, grief, and regret; have second thoughts, change your mind.')."[49]

As noted by the *Exegetical Dictionary of the New Testament*, "Decisive for the NT understanding of the word [repent] is OT *šûb* ([pronounced *shoov*] 'turning around,' in the sense of a turning away from present things and returning to the point of departure)."[50] Yes, the repentance preaching of the apostles, following on the heels of the Old Testament prophets, clearly meant, "Turn around! Turn back to God! Turn away from your sins and turn to Him! Make an about-face! God's mercy is here to forgive you and change you!" This is confirmed by the fact that "the New Testament makes it perfectly clear that the *proof* of repentance is seen in one's actions (see Luke 3:7–14 and Acts 26:20)."[51]

Just think of how silly it would be if *repent* only meant "change your mind." The words of Jesus would then become preposterous:

> Woe to you, Korazin! Woe to you, Bethsaida! If the miracles that were performed in you had been performed in Tyre and Sidon,

> they would have repented [changed their mind?] long ago *in sackcloth and ashes.*
>
> —MATTHEW 11:21, NIV

No! They would have "*repented* long ago in sackcloth and ashes." John's baptism too would have become nonsense:

> ...a baptism of repentance *[changing of mind?]* for the *forgiveness of sins.*
>
> —LUKE 3:3

No! It was a baptism of *repentance* for forgiveness of sins.

If repentance is only a change of mind with no conviction involved, then why did Paul tell the Corinthians, "*Godly sorrow* brings repentance that leads to salvation and leaves no regret" (2 Cor. 7:10, NIV)?

Is it too much to think that the sinner should feel sorry that he has sinned against God Almighty? Was this primarily an Old Testament phenomenon? (I've heard that taught too!) Is it unreasonable to believe that when the transgressor realizes it was his own sin that nailed the Savior to the cross, he might be cut to the heart?[52]

Of course, we do not tell the unsaved, "Feel bad, become good, reform your ways, and then believe." Absolutely not! If the Holy Spirit is dealing with them, we tell them, "Right now, in your heart, cry out to God to save you from your sins by the blood of Jesus. Right now, with your mouth, ask Him to deliver you from the snare of the devil and to make you His own. Ask Him to deliver you from your sinful self-will and help you to turn to God. Jesus will set you free and make you whole! Put your faith in Him."

Here are some other verses that make it perfectly clear that *repent* doesn't simply mean "change your mind" or "rethink my position about impossibilities in light of the truth that God can do all things." Consider these examples from Revelation:

> The rest of mankind, who were not killed by these plagues, did not *repent of the works* of their hands nor give up worshiping demons and idols of gold and silver and bronze and stone and wood, which cannot see or hear or walk, nor did they *repent of*

> *their murders or their sorceries or their sexual immorality or their thefts.*
>
> —Revelation 9:20–21

> They were scorched by the fierce heat, and they cursed the name of God who had power over these plagues. They did not *repent* and give him glory. The fifth angel poured out his bowl on the throne of the beast, and its kingdom was plunged into darkness. People gnawed their tongues in anguish and cursed the God of heaven for their pain and sores. They did not *repent of their deeds.*
>
> —Revelation 16:9–11

These verses, among many others in the New Testament, also refute the idea that "repentance in the old covenant meant turning from sin but repentance in the new means turning to God."[53] To the contrary, throughout the Word, repentance means turning away from sin and turning to God—it's what happens when you do an about-face. But in the New Testament there is a supernatural grace to repent because God's kingdom has broken into this world, Jesus has died for our sins and risen from the dead, and the Holy Spirit has been given in a unique way.

All of which means this: God loves us more than we can possibly imagine, and because sin is so destructive, when we become insensitive to the Lord and get caught up in disobedience, His Spirit makes us aware of our sin and makes us uncomfortable in it—praise God for that!—calling us to turn away from that sin and turn back to Him.

That is God's grace at work. That is the love of the Father. That is the path to life. Embrace it, and it will help you live life in Him to the full.

-7-

SANCTIFIED OR NOT?

IT IS MY goal throughout this book to keep things as simple and clear as possible so that readers without much background in theology or without any knowledge of the biblical languages can follow along. At the same time, everything I present to you is based on decades of careful study of the Scriptures in Hebrew, Aramaic, and Greek, and in some chapters we'll need to dive more deeply into the Word together. Are you ready to take the plunge? This is one of those chapters where we need to go a little deeper.

Let's look, then, at one of the most important—and controversial—issues that we need to tackle. The question is this: Are we *already* totally sanctified, are we in the *process* of being totally sanctified, or is total sanctification still *future*? (Since "sanctification" and "holiness" are virtually synonymous, another way we could ask the question is: Are we already totally holy, are we in the process of being made totally holy, or is total holiness still future?)

I believe the Scriptures clearly teach three things about sanctification: 1) The moment we were born again, we were set apart as holy to the Lord. 2) From that moment until our dying day, we are called by God to grow in holiness, with His help and empowerment. 3) When we are resurrected, we will be made perfectly holy forever. In theological terms, we *have been* sanctified, we *are being* sanctified, and *we will be* totally sanctified. Put another way, sanctification is progressive.

Modern grace teachers reject this in the strongest of terms. As John Crowder stated, "The moment you decide to *do something* to be holy, you have trusted in yourself, instead of Christ, for salvation."[1] Or in the words of Pastor Clark Whitten, "You are like Him, my friend, and are in a *permanent and unchangeable state of being of holiness.*"[2] As we noted in the previous chapter, according to the modern grace message the concept of progressive sanctification, meaning the idea that we are called to grow in holiness and that we must pursue holiness, is a "spiritually murderous lie" (to quote Clark Whitten again).[3]

For those of you who might not feel comfortable with all these theological concepts, let me simplify things as much as possible, laying out where I agree with the modern grace teachers and where I disagree with them, based on the Word.

I agree with them that the moment we were born again, we were justified (meaning, pronounced "righteous" and "not guilty" in God's sight), and this was by faith and not by good works. I also agree with them that the moment we were saved, we were set apart to God as holy ("sanctified"), also by faith and not by our good works. That's why we are addressed as "saints" ("holy ones") in the New Testament, even when our conduct is not particularly saintly.

But modern grace teachers claim that the moment we were saved, we were made perfectly, totally, and forever holy in God's sight, regardless of what we do or how we live. So we were not only completely justified by faith, once and for all, but we were also completely sanctified by faith, once and for all. As Pastor Ryan Rufus says, "Sanctification isn't a process! We do not become more and more holy—no—we become holy once and for all! We are sanctified once and for all and the life we live is the overflow of what has happened! That miracle of overflow goes through our mind and through our body!"[4]

In the words of Pastor Joseph Prince, "Colossians 2 tells us we are already made perfect in Christ. We don't work towards perfection. Christ has made us perfect from the Cross. The minute you believe you are made perfect in Christ. You work from your perfection not to it."[5] And, "God has taken us out from a prison called 'sin' and has now transferred to a prison called 'righteousness'. Is there anything you can do to take yourself from the prison of 'sin' to the prison called 'righteousness'? If the answer is 'no', what makes you think anything you did can now put you back into the prison call 'sin'?"[6] More emphatically still, "The moment you accepted Jesus, God gave you an eternal 'A+' for your right standing with Him."[7] And John Crowder explains, "We are not climbing an unseen ladder. We have already arrived."[8]

Indeed, while Crowder speaks against a poor theology that makes excuses for bad behavior, he claims that we are now "perfect" and that, "Whenever someone is saved, the battle against sin is decisively over."[9]

What then do these teachers do with the verses that call us to "pursue holiness" or to "be holy" or to "be perfect" or that speak of us as presently "being sanctified"? They either ignore them or reinterpret them, sometimes in grossly wrong ways.

But that's not the only issue. If the modern grace teachers are right, that means the finest grace teachers who ever lived got this wrong. In other words, not only the Reformers (men like Martin Luther and John Calvin) misunderstood this point, but also grace preachers like John Bunyan, author of *Pilgrim's Progress* and the autobiographical *Grace Abounding to the Chiefest of Sinners*, and Charles Spurgeon, author of *All of Grace* and arguably the greatest grace preacher of them all, misunderstood this point as well.[10] All these leaders believed in progressive sanctification in one form or another, meaning that once we are saved and set apart to God as holy, we grow in holiness for the rest of our lives.

Now, I want to state again that I have no problem with Luther, Calvin, Bunyan, or Spurgeon being wrong in some of their doctrines. In fact, they had differences among them, none of them were infallible, and I certainly have some different perspectives than they do. It's just important that we understand the implications of what the modern grace teachers are saying: virtually every major grace teacher in the past got this very crucial—even foundational—point wrong, while only the modern grace teachers have it right.[11]

How can we sort this out? Actually, it's not that complicated. The modern grace teachers focus all their attention on the scriptures that speak of our past sanctification while overlooking (or misinterpreting) the scriptures that speak of our ongoing, progressive sanctification, as well as our final sanctification. All we need to do is take in the whole counsel of God here and things will become very clear.

But first let me affirm a very important point that the modern grace teachers make, and it is one I have made for many years as well:[12] As born-again followers of Jesus, we are called "saints" in the New Testament ("saints" literally means "holy ones") rather than "sinners," and that is how we should identify ourselves. In other words, rather than saying, "I'm just a sinner saved by grace," each of us who know the Lord should say, "I was a sinner but now I'm a saint, forgiven by grace and empowered by grace!"

This is what Paul expressed in 1 Corinthians 1:2: "To the church of God that is in Corinth, to those *sanctified* in Christ Jesus, called to be *saints*" (the words "sanctified" and "saints" come from the same Greek root). The passage is rendered this way in the New Living Translation (with the sentence order reversed), "to you who have been called by God to be his own holy people. He made you holy by means of Christ Jesus."

As I pointed out in *Go and Sin No More*:

> According to the Scriptures, "sinners" are the enemies of God whereas His people are called "saints." In other words, it is one thing to sin and repent, even as a believer; it is another thing to *be* a sinner. It is one thing to do something bad and then correct it; it is another thing to *be* bad. It is one thing to think an adulterous thought and turn from it immediately; it is another thing to *be* an adulterer. I *was* a heavy drug user, I *was* a rebellious snob, I *was* a filthy sinner. Now I'm a saint—imperfect, but nonetheless radically transformed and wonderfully changed. Sin is no longer the rule of my life, it's the exception to the rule. My habit now is to live for God, whereas before I knew Him, my habit was to sin.[13]

That's why some churches still have the habit of referring to one another as "saints," as in the Sunday morning greeting, "How are you doing, saints?" or as in the classic spiritual, "When the Saints Go Marching In." How different it would be if the pastor stood up on Sunday morning and said, "How are you doing, sinners?" That's not who we are anymore in the Lord, and we do well to follow the pattern of the New Testament where we are *called* saints (as in Ephesians 1:1) and *called to be* saints (as in Romans 1:7)—or "holy ones,"[14] meaning, "This is who you are and this is how you should live." It is only when we live in blatant, willful sin that we are addressed as "sinners." (See Jacob [James] 4:1–10, especially verse 8).

So I agree wholeheartedly with my modern grace brothers when they emphasize who we are in Jesus, when they encourage us to live according to our new nature, and when they remind us that we have died to sin and cannot live in it any longer. That is the transforming power of the gospel. That is the transforming power of grace. The problem arises when these sincere teachers build their theology on one set of verses while ignoring, rejecting, or wrongly reinterpreting many other verses, thereby drawing theological conclusions that are contrary to the Word. (I'll come back to that point later in the chapter.)

Already, Not Yet

They also seem unaware of (or reject) the New Testament idea of "already, not yet."[15] As my colleague at FIRE School of Ministry Dr. Bob Gladstone explained:

> Failure to grasp the biblical tension of "already/not yet" is a failure to grasp biblical grace, and Jesus Himself. The kingdom is now; the kingdom is not yet. I am saved; I am being saved. The hour has come; the hour is yet future. I am sanctified; I am being sanctified. I am a new creation; I await resurrection. I am now a child of God; I am exhorted—sometimes warned—to endure to the end. So grace is both the virtue that saved me as a free gift and that governs me throughout the process of ongoing sanctification. But it never erases my free will or the call to be a faithful steward.[16]

So, we are already redeemed (Eph. 1:7) and we already have the Spirit, but at present the Spirit "is a deposit guaranteeing our inheritance *until* the redemption of those who are God's possession" (v. 14, NIV). We are already seated in heavenly places with Jesus (Eph. 2:6), but at present we are living in earthly bodies, because of which we groan (2 Cor. 5:2), "so that what is mortal may be swallowed up by life" (v. 4). We are already adopted as sons (Rom. 8:15), but for now, we "groan inwardly as we wait eagerly for adoption as sons, the redemption of our bodies" (v. 23).

We have already died to sin and cannot live in it in any longer (Rom. 6:1–7), yet we must consider ourselves dead to sin and not let it rule in our lives (vv. 11–19). We have already put off the old self and put on the new self (Eph. 4:22–24). Yet we are instructed to "put to death" and "put off" that which pertains to our earthly nature and "put on" that which pertains to our new self (Col. 3:1–14). This is what is meant by "already and not yet."

And this is what I meant when I wrote previously that "we *have been* sanctified, we *are being* sanctified, and *we will be* totally sanctified." As explained by one theologian, our sanctification is *positional* (past), *progressive* (present), and *perfect* (future):

> Sanctification or Holiness of life has a threefold aspect: 1) Positional, which is past, through the work of Christ in our redemption, and confers upon the Christian a perfect position, as a child of God (Heb. 10:10); 2) Progressive, which is the present work of the Holy Spirit in the life of the believer, bringing one's character development into conformity with his position in Christ, and this is experiential throughout one's lifetime (II Tim. 3:16, 17; Col. 1:28; II Peter 3:18); 3) Perfection, which is future and will be completed when the Christian arrives in heaven, and then his character behaviors will be as perfect as his position is in Christ (I Thess. 3:12,13; Phil. 1:6; I John 3:2,3).[17]

Hyper-grace teachers reject this, claiming that, "Even the reformers were not reformed enough. You will see how the cross united us to Christ, not just positionally, but effectively. It doesn't just cover our sins, but eradicates sinfulness itself from us."[18]

I believe this is one of the fundamental errors of interpretation within the modern grace movement, which is why its leaders do such a poor job explaining verses like Jacob (James) 1:13–14: "Let no one say when he is tempted, 'I am being tempted by God,' for God cannot be tempted with evil, and he himself tempts no one. *But each person is tempted when he is lured and enticed by his own desire.*" The obvious question is, "If sinfulness has been totally eradicated from me in this world, why do I still have evil desires inside of me?

Then there is Jacob (James) 4:1: "What causes quarrels and what causes fights among you? Is it not this, that your passions are at war within you?" According to John Crowder, Jacob (James) isn't speaking about the war that is waged inside our own souls; rather, he is speaking of the divisions and fights within the church.[19] But where, pray tell, do the divisions and fights within the church come from, if not from us, the believers?

The reality is that we are overcomers in Jesus (1 John 5:4), and yet in this world we still fall short of the mark of perfection (note Jacob [James] 3:2, "we all stumble in many ways"). We are new creations (2 Cor. 5:17), yet we must be transformed by the renewal of our minds (Rom. 12:2).

As Raymond E. Brown, a leading scholar on the writings on John, explained with reference to 1 John:

> We are God's children already, and there is freedom from sin attached to that state. Jesus had issued the challenge, "If you really are Abraham's children, you would do works worthy of Abraham" (John 8:39). The epistolary author [meaning the author of 1 John] has his own variation on that theme, "You really are God's children, and so you must do works worthy of God, and not sin which is the work of the devil." But in this last hour he recognizes that we are not yet all that we shall be, and so there is growth in God's children. The divine seed abides and continues to transform the child of God into the image of God's Son which is the image of God Himself, until at the final revelation we are like God Himself. The more that this divine seed transforms the Christian, the more impossible it is for the Christian to sin.[20]

Hyper-grace teachers seem not to grasp these realities, basing most (or all) of their theology on our *positional standing* in Jesus, which leads to many serious errors in interpreting Scripture. But because they so powerfully stress what Jesus has *already done for us* and *who we already are in Him*, many lives are radically changed by their message. The problem is that when truth is mixed with error, there will always be casualties, and those casualties are mounting by the day, especially as the hyper-grace message becomes more and more extreme.

Being Made Holy

Let's look, then, at some of the verses that speak of us being made holy (sanctified) when we were born again, instantly and without self-improvement. In 1 Corinthians 6:11, after a list of sinful lifestyles, Paul writes, "And such were some of you. But you were washed, *you were sanctified*, you were justified in the name of the Lord Jesus Christ and by the Spirit of our God."

Notice that Paul puts three verbs together—washed, sanctified, and justified—all in the past tense.[21] And while it is absolutely true that these Corinthians believers had been transformed ("some of you" used to be unrighteous and wicked) in this context, giving up their unrighteous ways is not what made them "sanctified." Rather, it was because they were sanctified that they gave up their unrighteous ways.

Other verses that point to this same truth include 1 Corinthians 1:30, where Paul states, "And because of him you are in Christ Jesus, who became to us wisdom from God, righteousness and sanctification and redemption." Yes, in a very real sense, Jesus is our righteousness, our sanctification, and our redemption, which is absolutely glorious.[22]

Hebrews 10:10 is also very strong, explaining that "we have been sanctified through the offering of the body of Jesus Christ once for all." Or, as rendered in *The Mirror Bible*, which reflects the modern grace theology for better or worse, "By his resolution he sees us immediately sanctified through one sacrifice, the slain body of Jesus Christ." Andre Rabe, while not quoting this verse but pointing to the cross, states, "In this one man, in this one event, all sin of all men and in all time would be dealt with, with such finality that God would never think of sin again!"[23]

Obviously, it is ridiculous to claim that since the cross God has "never [thought] of sin again" (although some have tried to argue that from 2 Corinthians 5:18–20).[24] But based on Hebrews 10:10, you can see how modern grace teachers get the idea that our sanctification is total and complete, already finished in the past, with nothing for us to add to it. (We'll return to this verse later in the chapter.)

To repeat, I agree with the modern grace teachers when they state that we have already been sanctified, but that is only part of the story. The Word states plainly that we are also *being* sanctified (a process in which we participate actively) and one day we will be *ultimately* sanctified. In other words, what these modern grace teachers understand to be the end of the story is actually the beginning of the story.[25] In short, because we have been set apart as holy by the Lord and designated as holy by the Lord (called "saints"!), and because Jesus has become our sanctification and our righteousness and our redemption, we are now called to live this out progressively in every area of our lives—to be holy in all our conduct and to pursue holiness. And we do this in Him, empowered by His grace.

Let's look at New Testament texts that state this quite plainly. I'll intersperse my comments in the midst of the verses, which I have put in bold italics. In 1 Thessalonians 4:3 Paul writes, ***"For this is the will of God, your sanctification: that you abstain from sexual immorality."*** Notice that this is something they are called to live out. God wants their sanctification—their holiness—and so Paul gives them specific instructions in terms of what this means: it is God's will that you be holy and that you stay away from sexual sin.

As explained by Thessalonians scholar C. A. Wannamaker, "Paul understood God to be the holy God of the OT who was set apart from every form of sin and impurity and who demanded similar holiness from the people of Israel through separation (Lv. 11:44f.; 19:2; 21:8). God had not changed, so the same requirement was laid on the new people of God, the Christians." He also explains that "separation from sinful existence, that is sanctification, was a fundamental part of Paul's understanding of Christian existence (cf. Rom. 6:19, 22). According to Rom. 6:22 the goal of sanctification is nothing less than eternal life. This explains why Paul can say it is the will of God for the Thessalonians."[26]

Paul is speaking here of a lifestyle that requires action and obedience. And so sanctification here is progressive, and the Thessalonian believers were commanded to participate in that process. As noted by F. F. Bruce, perhaps the top New Testament scholar of the last generation and one of the greatest authorities on Paul in particular, the Greek word used for sanctification is *hagiasmos*, which means "the process of making holy."[27]

Paul continues: ***"That each one of you know how to control his own body in holiness and honor, not in the passion of lust like the Gentiles who do not know God"*** (1 Thess. 4:4–5). This is the exact opposite of what John Crowder said, quoted at the beginning of this chapter: "The moment you decide to do something to be holy, you have trusted in yourself, instead of Christ, for salvation."[28] Not so! As those who trust Christ and who have been consecrated to the Lord, we are called to do certain things in order to live out that consecration—to be holy. (We'll see this again in 1 Peter 1, which we will explore later in this chapter.)

Paul goes on to say: ***"That no one transgress and wrong his brother in this matter, because the Lord is an avenger in all these things, as we told you beforehand and solemnly warned you"*** (1 Thess. 4:6). Paul is warning these believers about the consequences of spurning this call to holy living. Yet if you try to quote verses like this to modern grace adherents, they will tell you that you are being legalistic and fear-based! Paul concludes this segment in 1 Thessalonians 4 with, ***"For God has not called us for impurity, but in holiness. Therefore whoever disregards this, disregards not man but God, who gives his Holy Spirit to you"*** (vv. 7–8). Because God has given us His Holy Spirit and called us in holiness, we must live holy lives.

Note also Paul's prayer for the Thessalonians in 1 Thessalonians 5:23: ***"Now may the God of peace himself sanctify you completely, and may your whole spirit and soul and body be kept blameless at the coming of our Lord Jesus Christ."*** Why would Paul pray for the complete sanctification of these believers if they were already completely sanctified? The simple answer is that they were not. Sanctification is progressive.[29]

Since Romans is probably the favorite book of the modern grace preachers, we should look carefully at Paul's words about sanctification there. (For the record, Romans is one of my favorite books too!) Paul wrote this in Romans 6:19: ***"I am speaking in human terms, because of your natural limitations. For just as you once presented your members as slaves to impurity and to lawlessness leading to more lawlessness, so now present your members as slaves to righteousness leading to sanctification."*** Did you get that? We are to present the members of our physical body "as slaves to righteousness *leading to sanctification*" (or, as some versions render, "leading to holiness"). Sanctification is a process!

Paul continues: ***"For when you were slaves of sin, you were free in regard to righteousness"*** (Rom. 6:20). Once again he talks about the way we used to live when we were sinners, not saints. ***"But what fruit***

were you getting at that time from the things of which you are now ashamed? For the end of those things is death. But now that you have been set free from sin and have become slaves of God, the fruit you get leads to sanctification and its end, eternal life" (Rom. 6:21–22). Remarkable! We used to be slaves to sin, but we are now slaves of God. As a result we live differently—that's the "fruit" of which Paul speaks—which "*leads to sanctification* and its end, eternal life," the verse speaking here of the eternal life we will enjoy with the Lord forever.

Obviously, if we were already completely sanctified, Paul would not exhort us to live a certain way that *leads to sanctification.* As New Testament scholar Leon Morris explains:

> They have given up slavery to evil; they must accept slavery to righteousness (see on v. 18) with all that that means. This is "with a view to sanctification"...that is, to becoming holy as befits the slave of God. The lives of the Roman Christians are to reflect the reality of their full commitment to the service of God.[30]

And to quote A. T. Robertson again:

> **Unto sanctification...**
>
> This the goal, the blessed consummation that demands and deserves the new slavery without occasional lapses or sprees (verse 15)....Paul includes sanctification in his conception of the God-kind (1:17) of righteousness (both justification, 1:18–5:21 and sanctification, chapters 6 to 8). *It is a life process of consecration, not an instantaneous act.* Paul shows that we ought to be sanctified (6:1–7:6) and illustrates the obligation by death (6:1–14), by slavery (6:15–23), and by marriage (7:1–6).[31]

Yes, Paul speaks of "a life process of consecration, not an instantaneous act."

How do we reconcile these truths with Hebrews 10:10, where we learned that "we have been sanctified through the offering of the body of Jesus Christ once for all"? To begin with, the words "once for all" apply first to the sacrifice of Jesus the Messiah and then to our sanctification, and based on that "once for all" act, there has been a "once for all" sanctification on our behalf. As New Testament scholar F. F.

Bruce explains, "The sanctification which his people receive in consequence [of the once for all sacrifice of Jesus] is their inward cleansing of sin and their being made fit for the presence of God, so that henceforth they can offer him acceptable worship."[32]

Well then, doesn't that make the modern grace teachers right if Hebrews 10:10 says that we have been sanctified once and for all by the sacrifice of Jesus? Not at all. You see, Hebrews 10:14—just four verses after verse 10—states that "by a single offering he has perfected for all time those *who are being sanctified*." So even though the verb in Hebrews 10:10 refers to "a completed state," the verb in Hebrews 10:14 refers to "a process here."[33] (If you give me a minute to finish this present point, we'll get to the words "perfected for all time" in Hebrews 10:14.) And Hebrews 10:26–29 warns about severe judgment that will come on believers who *were sanctified* by the blood of Jesus but who turned away from the cross. (We'll return to those verses in a moment as well.)

To recap things briefly, at the beginning of this chapter I explained that we *have been sanctified* by the death of Jesus and the work of the Spirit, and we *are being sanctified* by the application of what Jesus has done, with the help of the Spirit. Hebrews 10:10 and 10:14 say this very thing: "*We have been sanctified* through the offering of the body of Jesus Christ once for all.... For by a single offering he has perfected for all time those who *are being sanctified*."[34] As noted by Hebrews scholar William L. Lane, the Greek verb quite definitely means "those who are in the process of sanctification."[35]

Now, I know that all this technical language can be confusing, but the Greek verbal system is very precise, and when the same author uses such specific and exacting terminology in the space of just a few verses (Hebrews 10:10 and 10:14), it's important that we understand exactly what he is saying. To paraphrase, "Through the once for all sacrifice of Jesus, you have been set apart as holy, and now, by that same sacrifice, having been made fit for complete and perfect access into God's presence, you are being made holy in your daily lives."

This is reinforced in Hebrews 12:14, which says, "Strive for peace with everyone, and for the holiness without which no one will see the Lord." Or, as rendered in the New American Standard Bible, "Pursue peace with all men, and the sanctification without which no one will see the Lord." (Compare also the New International Version: "Make every effort to live in peace with all men and to be holy; without holiness no one will see the Lord.") So we are called to pursue sanctification (or holiness), something that makes no sense if, in fact, we have already been made totally holy and there is nothing we can do to be holy.

Yes, if Pastor Whitten is right and as a believer you "are in a permanent and unchangeable state of being of holiness,"[36] why does God call us to *be* holy, why does Scripture speak of us as being in the *process* of being made holy, and why does the Word call us to *pursue* holiness? This underlying hyper-grace theology seems also to be the reason that *The Mirror Bible* translates Hebrews 12:14 with, "Pursue peace with all men; true friendship can only be enjoyed in an environment of total forgiveness and innocence. This makes God visible in your life." That is quite a change!

Perfected for All Time

How then do we explain the first part of Hebrews 10:14, which states that "by a single offering he has *perfected for all time* those who are being sanctified"? Obviously the author of Hebrews is not contradicting himself within the same verse, telling us that we are already totally perfect and at the same time that we are in the process of being made holy. So it's clear that "perfected" must have another beginning, and it's easy to discover what that meaning is by looking at the verb "make perfect" (*teleō* in the Greek) in Hebrews.

But first, let's look at Paul's words in Philippians 3:12, where he writes, "Not that I have already obtained this [speaking of his ultimate spiritual goals] or *am already perfect*." Well, if Paul was not already perfect, it's obvious that we ourselves are not "already perfect."

Turning to Hebrews, we see that the verb "be, become perfect, perfected" occurs frequently. When referring to Jesus being made "perfect," the verses mean "made perfect for His role." (See Hebrews 2:10; 5:9; 7:28.) So by suffering as He did, Jesus became our perfect leader and high priest.

As far as the law and the sacrificial system were concerned, they could not make people (or things) "perfect," meaning, giving the worshippers "immediate and permanent access to God."[37] (See Hebrews 7:19; 9:9; 10:1.) As for Hebrews 11:40, the meaning there is that believers before the cross could not experience the fullness of redemption without us, while Hebrews 12:23 speaks of the heavenly scene at the throne of God, where the spirits of believers have reached their full goal—hence, been made perfect.

With this in mind, remembering in particular what we learned in verses about the Law, let's look again at Hebrews 10:14: "For by a single offering he has perfected for all time those who are being sanctified." What does this mean? The text is saying that rather than the worshipper having to bring offerings again and again, year after year, without being fully and completely right with God, Jesus brought one single offering, making us righteous in God's sight once and for all and giving us complete and unhindered access to God's presence. And it is on that basis that we participate in the process of sanctification.

Here is how some commentators on Hebrews explain Hebrews 10:14:

> On the cross Christ has already made a single offering so that in generation after generation he is continually making holy all who respond in faith. To become **perfect** did not promise sinless perfection, but it promised believers the full realization of God's saving purpose.[38]

> "He has perfected" is in emphatic contrast with the inability of the old sacrifices to deal with sin (10:1, 11).... Christ's own are a "perfected" or "cleansed" people. This "perfecting" is of such a quality that it will never need renewal or supplementation, any more than Christian session might need repetition. Nothing more need be done for God's people to be delivered from sin and brought into God's presence.[39]

To sum it up, Jesus the Messiah, in His one, single, glorious sacrifice, did everything necessary to present us to God, washing our sins away and paying our debt in full, making us children of the Father the moment we were saved. Yes, from the first second we were born again, before we were even conscious of the many ways we needed to change, we had access to the holiest place in the universe, the very throne of

God—and that was through the power of the cross of Christ. What a Savior! To cite the Complete Jewish Bible, "For by a single offering he has brought to the goal for all time those who are being set apart for God and made holy" (Heb. 10:14).

But there is more to the story: if we reject this once-for-all sacrifice, if we decide that we can continue in willful, unrepentant sin because we have been forgiven and set apart to God, or if, as a first-century Jewish believer in Jesus might have been tempted to do, we forsake the sacrifice of Jesus and seek out other means of atonement, there is a stern and fearful warning for us:

> For if we go on sinning deliberately after receiving the knowledge of the truth, there no longer remains a sacrifice for sins, but a fearful expectation of judgment, and a fury of fire that will consume the adversaries. Anyone who has set aside the law of Moses dies without mercy on the evidence of two or three witnesses. How much worse punishment, do you think, will be deserved by the one who has trampled underfoot the Son of God, and has profaned the blood of the covenant by which he was sanctified, and has outraged the Spirit of grace?
>
> —Hebrews 10:26–29

Please take a moment to look at these verses carefully. This is a warning to believers! And notice how it ends: "For we know him who said, 'Vengeance is mine; I will repay.' And again, 'The Lord will judge his people.' It is a fearful thing to fall into the hands of the living God" (Heb. 10:30–31).

The author of Hebrews is speaking here of those who have received the knowledge of the truth and *have been sanctified* by the Messiah's blood. But by deliberately continuing to sin—not a momentary lapse or an ongoing struggle with temptation, but rather a determined, willful, turning away from the Lord—we spurn the Son of God, we profane the blood of the covenant, and we outrage the Spirit of grace. (Yes, *the Spirit of grace* can be outraged.) And the author of Hebrews writes this after declaring in verse 10 of this chapter that *we have been sanctified* once and for all by Jesus's once-for-all sacrifice and stating in verse 14 that *we have been perfected* for all time.

Now, it's easy to see how hyper-grace teachers have misunderstood these verses by taking them out of the larger context of Hebrews—and even out of the specific context of Hebrews 10—but there can be no mistaking what Hebrews is saying: the finished work of the cross never needs to be repeated and nothing can be added to it, and by that finished work we have been presented to God as holy with full and complete access to His holy presence. (This will be discussed further in chapter 15.) Our consciences have been cleansed from guilt, God has forgiven and forgotten our sins, and He now calls us to walk out that holiness and to pursue holiness, warning us not to disparage a holy God and the holy blood that was shed. As some scholars have expressed it, "Sanctification has taken place, but it still remains a task" (Braun); and, "The appropriation of the enduring effects of Christ's act is an ongoing present reality" (Attridge).[40]

Hebrews also states clearly that if we scorn God's grace and turn away from the cross and go back into sin, we forfeit everything He has done for us. That's why the book is filled with so many warnings, including this one:

> Strive for peace with everyone, and for the holiness without which no one will see the Lord. *See to it that no one fails to obtain the grace of God*; that no "root of bitterness" springs up and causes trouble, and by it many become defiled; *that no one is sexually immoral or unholy like Esau*, who sold his birthright for a single meal. For you know that afterward, when he desired to inherit the blessing, he was rejected, for he found no chance to repent, though he sought it with tears.
>
> —Hebrews 12:14–17

This may not jibe with the modern definition of grace and sanctification, but it is clearly what the New Testament teaches. As the Lutheran scholar R. C. H. Lenski explained:

> It is after the whole exposition about Christ's sacrifice that the writer can now say of this sin: "no longer is there left a sacrifice for sins," i.e., any sacrifice for sins that would have any effect on sinners of this kind. Since they permanently repudiate the one, final, supreme sacrifice of Christ, what is there left that might

> be brought to bear on these sinners? The thought is not that we must necessarily say that Christ did not expiate also their sin, but that repudiation of him and his sacrifice leaves them nothing.[41]

This obviously contradicts what Clark Whitten stated so emphatically: "Grace with conditions that depend on humanity's performance to stay in it is no grace at all. Grace, so called, that is uncertain, conditional, or fearful is flat out *no grace at all. Period! Exclamation mark!*"[42] Put simply, Jesus paid it all. If we repudiate Him and what He did, we lose it all.

And let's not forget that before the readers of Hebrews would even get to the statements we've looked at in Hebrews 10, they would have already encountered these exhortations to persevere in Hebrews 2:1–3; 3:6–14; and 4:1, 11, followed by a strong warning at the end of Hebrews 12, culminating with, "Therefore let us be grateful for receiving a kingdom that cannot be shaken, and thus let us offer to God acceptable worship, with reverence and awe, for our God is a consuming fire" (Heb. 12:28–29, quoting from Deut. 4:24).

That's why Peter exhorted his readers to live holy lives in light of the great salvation they had experienced and in light of the holiness of the God they were now called to serve, love, and emulate. As believers, we are called to walk worthy of the Lord! (See chapter 8.) "Therefore," Peter writes, "preparing your minds for action, and being sober-minded, set your hope fully on the grace that will be brought to you at the revelation of Jesus Christ" (1 Pet. 1:13).

Yes, there is a *future grace* that we still await, a grace that will complete our sanctification. As John expressed in his epistle, "Beloved, we are God's children now, and what we will be has not yet appeared; but we know that when he appears we shall be like him, because we shall see him as he is. And everyone who thus hopes in him purifies himself as he is pure" (1 John 3:2–3).

Peter continues, "As obedient children, do not be conformed to the passions of your former ignorance, but as he who called you is holy, you also be holy in all your conduct"—yes, our conduct matters to the Lord—"since it is written, 'You shall be holy, for I am holy'" (1 Pet. 1:14–16). And notice how Peter quotes Leviticus 19 here without having to apologize for the quote—as in, "I know this is from the Law and the Law really doesn't apply to us anymore"—just as the writer of Hebrews quoted Deuteronomy 4:24 in Hebrews 12:29 without having to apologize.

"And," Peter writes, "if you call on him as Father who judges impartially according to each one's deeds, conduct yourselves with fear throughout the time of your exile, knowing that you were ransomed from the futile ways inherited from your forefathers, not with perishable things such as silver or gold, but with the precious blood of Christ, like that of a lamb without blemish or spot" (1 Pet. 1:17–19).

And how did Peter begin his letter?

> From Peter, an apostle of Jesus Christ, to those temporarily residing abroad (in Pontus, Galatia, Cappadocia, the province of Asia, and Bithynia) who are chosen according to the foreknowledge of God the Father by being set apart [i.e., sanctified] by the Spirit for obedience and for sprinkling with Jesus Christ's blood. May grace and peace be yours in full measure!
>
> —1 PETER 1:1–2, NET

He is writing to believers who *have been set apart to God as holy* by the Spirit "for obedience and for sprinkling with Jesus Christ's blood." (Note that "obedience" and the blood of Jesus go hand in hand.)

And so, after we are saved by the sanctifying work of the Spirit, we are then called to live sanctified lives with the help of the Holy Spirit, and on that final day, by God's grace, we will "stand, rejoicing, without blemish before his glorious presence" (Judah [Jude] 24, NET). This is exactly what Paul wrote to the Colossians:

> And you, who once were alienated and hostile in mind, doing evil deeds, he has now reconciled in his body of flesh by his death, in order to present you holy and blameless and above reproach before him, if indeed you continue in the faith, stable and steadfast, not shifting from the hope of the gospel that you heard, which has been proclaimed in all creation under heaven, and of which I, Paul, became a minister.
>
> —COLOSSIANS 1:21–23

Has this fallen into place for you now? Was it worth digging into these scriptures to get a clearer understanding? And do my opening comments now make more sense? "In theological terms, we *have been* sanctified, we *are being* sanctified, and *we will be* totally sanctified. Put another way, sanctification is progressive." It has nothing to do with earning our salvation or holding to salvation by works. It has to do with living out our calling to be "saints" (holy ones), with walking out the realities of what Jesus has already done for us and in us.

Turning back to Peter, we see that his letter is filled with exhortations to holy conduct: he calls us to love one another deeply (1 Pet. 1:22); to "put away all malice and all deceit and hypocrisy and envy and all slander" (1 Pet. 2:1); "to abstain from the passions of the flesh, which wage war against your soul" (v. 11)—and to do as a chosen people and royal priesthood, as the people of God (vv. 9–10), keeping our conduct honorable before the world (v. 12); to be submissive to authority and to follow the example of Jesus in not retaliating (vv. 13–23); for wives and husbands to conduct themselves in purity (1 Pet. 3:1–7); to "have unity of mind, sympathy, brotherly love, a tender heart, and a humble mind" (v. 8); to do good to others and to bless those who curse us (vv. 9–17); and to "live for the rest of the time in the flesh no longer for human passions but for the will of God. For the time that is past suffices for doing what the Gentiles want to do, living in sensuality, passions, drunkenness, orgies, drinking parties, and lawless idolatry" (1 Pet. 4:2–3).

He urges us to "be self-controlled and sober-minded" (v. 7). He reminds us again of our calling to love one another earnestly (v. 8), to show hospitality without grumbling (v. 9), to use our gifts for the good of others (vv. 10–11), and to suffer joyfully for the gospel (vv. 12–16), even stating that "it is time for judgment to begin at the household of God; and if it begins with us, what will be the outcome for those who do not obey the gospel of God?" (v. 17). Then he urges his fellow elders to be true shepherds and godly examples (1 Pet. 5:1–4), exhorting the younger men to humble themselves (vv. 5–6) and urging all to be sober and vigilant against the onslaughts of the devil (vv. 8–9), reminding his readers that "after you have suffered a little while, the God of all grace, who has called you to his eternal glory in Christ, will himself restore, confirm, strengthen, and establish you" (v. 10). For Peter, this is what it means to "be holy in all your conduct" (1 Pet. 1:15).

To be sure, with a letter like this (which is actually very much like Paul's letters), Peter would be branded a legalist in many "grace" camps today, which makes this last verse all the more remarkable, as Peter sums up his book: "By Silvanus, a faithful brother as I regard him, I have written briefly to you, exhorting and declaring that *this is the true grace of God*. Stand firm in it" (1 Pet. 5:12).[43]

How incredible! Yes, *this*—this calling to live holy lives, empowered by the Spirit, because of the extraordinary gift of salvation through Jesus—"*this* is the true grace of God. Stand firm in it!" Will you?

> For the grace of God has appeared, bringing salvation for all people, training us to renounce ungodliness and worldly passions, and to live self-controlled, upright, and godly lives in the present age, waiting for our blessed hope, the appearing of the glory of our great God and Savior Jesus Christ, who gave himself for us to redeem us from all lawlessness and to purify for himself a people for his own possession who are zealous for good works.
>
> —Titus 2:11–14

-8-

FIND OUT WHAT PLEASES THE LORD

ALONG WITH TEACHING that we are completely and totally sanctified the moment we are saved (see chapter 7), modern grace teachers also claim that God always sees us as perfect in His sight (and therefore doesn't see our sins, a concept we addressed in chapter 4). And because we are always seen as perfectly righteous before God, there is nothing we can (or should) do to try to please God. We are already totally pleasing in His sight!

As Clark Whitten writes, "When God looks at me, He doesn't see me through the blood of Christ, He sees me—cleansed! Likewise, He sees us as holy and righteous. He sees us, and He loves what He sees!"[1] Or in the words of Ryan Rufus:

> There will be some mistakes and failures but God isn't looking at them. He sees us perfect and righteous in Christ all the time. Now He is helping us to overcome our struggles so that we can go on to maturity in Christ and live in our destiny. He is proud of us![2]

Yes, no matter how we live and no matter what we do, God "is proud of us!" Indeed, Pastor Ryan Rufus says, "You need to hear your Heavenly Father's praises. He is thrilled with you. He is beside Himself with love for you and takes enormous pleasure in you. There is no failure or fall that could ever separate you from His love!"[3]

Our Father is always proud of us, always thrilled with us, always praising us, and always taking enormous pleasure in us? Always? (We'll address the question of whether anything can separate us from God's love in the Appendix.)

To quote Pastor Rufus once more:

> To reign in life is to know that you are right with God. It is to know that God is not mad at you but mad about you. It is to know that He is happy with you, approving of you, and pleased with you. It is to know that His love is toward you constantly and His favor continually upon you. To reign in life is to live totally free from crippling guilt and condemnation with an awareness that your right standing before God can never change![4]

As for the idea that there is nothing we can try to do to please God (since He relates to us as if we were His Son, Jesus, who is perfect in every way), Pastor Whitten writes, "If you are 'working' to please Him, you are in for a lifetime of unfinished business, and it will leave you perpetually exhausted!"[5] According to Paul Ellis, "There is nothing wrong with wanting to better yourself, but you have to understand that in Christ, you are already as good and pleasing to God as you ever will be."[6] More bluntly, John Crowder states, "It is high time the church gets delivered from *God pleasing*."[7]

Andrew Farley explains that before he understood grace, "having raised my antennae toward the Christian world around me, I intercepted the subtle message that there are requirements to remain in God's favor,"[8] and he makes clear through the rest of his book *The Naked Gospel* that there are, in fact, no requirements to remain in God's favor.

Steve McVey is even more direct: "We may talk about disappointing God, but the truth of the Scripture is this: *It is impossible for you to disappoint God.* Not only is the idea we can disappoint God a lie—it's impossible."[9] Joseph Prince affirms this as well: "Because you did **nothing** to deserve His presence in your life, there is **nothing** you can do that will cause His presence to leave you."[10]

Is there any truth to what these men are saying? On the one hand it is absolutely true that God sees us as His precious and beloved children, redeemed by the blood of His Son and part of His very own family, accepted because of what Jesus did rather than because of our performance, and all this is the result of His grace. On the other hand, it is absolutely false to claim that when God looks at us, He always "loves what He sees" or that He is always "happy with [us], approving of [us], and pleased with [us]" or that is impossible for us to disappoint God or that there is nothing we can do to drive away His presence.

Now I want to be sensitive here as I address this point, since some of you reading this book used to suffer terribly from a perpetually guilty conscience, always feeling inadequate, never believing that you had done enough to please God, feeling as though you were always falling short. Perhaps you are a very sensitive person, or perhaps you are prone to introspection, and when you measure yourself against the two great commandments, namely, to love God with all your heart, soul, and strength, and to love your neighbor as yourself, you say, "There's no way I can ever live up to that! God must be disgusted with me."

That's why the message of grace was so liberating for you. You realized that you were accepted because of what Jesus did and that even on your worst day you were dearly loved by the Father. And the idea that God always saw you as perfect and holy was so liberating to you that you found yourself more in love with the Lord than ever before and more devoted to holiness.

As Andrew Wommack expressed:

> He moves in our life because of mercy and grace, not justice. Once you understand that, God's love will abound in your heart more than ever before. Once you understand the Gospel, love comes. And once you understand God's love, your faith will work because faith works by love. (Gal. 5:6.) This understanding doesn't set you free *to* sin, but free *from* sin.[11]

I have no doubt that this has been the experience of many who have embraced the modern grace message, and it has truly been life-giving for them. So if I have just described your own spiritual history and temperament, I want to be very careful as we separate truth from error, helping you to rest secure in the Lord and be assured of His goodness and favor while at the same time helping you to take hold of our biblical calling to "find out what pleases the Lord" (Eph. 5:10, NIV).

Let's begin by drinking deep of the incredible words written by Paul to the believers in Ephesus.[12] I remember reading and memorizing them as a new believer, and I was overwhelmed by the beauty and depth of each verse. There is so much in every phrase that it would take whole books just to explore what Paul expressed, so we'll focus on Ephesians 1:3–14 in the New English Translation.

> Blessed is the God and Father of our Lord Jesus Christ, who has blessed us with every spiritual blessing in the heavenly realms in Christ. For he chose us in Christ before the foundation of the world that we may be holy and unblemished in his sight in love.
>
> —Ephesians 1:3–4, NET

The God and Father of Jesus is our God and Father (see John 20:17), and in the heavenly realms, where Jesus is seated, the Father has already bestowed on us "every spiritual blessing…in Christ." Yes, before we were born or even the world was created, God determined that He would have a people in His Son—we are not chosen in ourselves but "in Christ"—with a divine purpose and destiny, namely, "that we may be holy and unblemished in his sight in love."

As the Puritan leader Joseph Caryl wrote, "Perfect holiness is the aim of the saints on earth, and it is the reward of the saints in heaven."[13] That's why Oswald Chambers could say, "God has one destined end for mankind, namely, holiness! His one aim is the production of saints. God is not an eternal blessing-machine for men; He did not come to save men out of pity: He came to save men because He had created them to be holy."[14]

> He did this by predestining us to adoption as his sons through Jesus Christ, according to the pleasure of his will—to the praise of the glory of his grace that he has freely bestowed on us in his dearly loved Son.
>
> —Ephesians 1:5–6, NET

The way that God would bring about this glorious transformation was by adopting us as sons through Jesus, and so, "because you are sons, God has sent the Spirit of his Son into our hearts, crying, 'Abba! Father!' So you are no longer a slave, but a son, and if a son, then an heir through God" (Gal. 4:6–7; see also Heb. 2:11; Rom. 8:15). The same spirit of sonship that was in Jesus is now in us, and that's why we too can cry out, "Abba! Father!"

God performed this extraordinary act freely, transforming sinful rebels who by nature were objects of wrath and by action were servants of Satan's kingdom, and making us into His holy and beloved children. It is all to the praise of His grace!

> In him we have redemption through his blood, the forgiveness of our trespasses, according to the riches of his grace that he lavished on us in all wisdom and insight. He did this when he revealed to us the secret of his will, according to his good pleasure that he set forth in Christ, toward the administration of the fullness of the times, to head up all things in Christ—the things in heaven and the things on earth.
>
> —EPHESIANS 1:7–10, NET

This is just staggering. Jesus' blood was so powerful that in God's sight it offered complete redemption and forgiveness for us, providing the complete and total payment of every one of our sins, all in accordance with God's amazing, abundant, extravagant grace—grace that God lavished on us. (When is the last time you had something "lavished" on you? The Greek word here means "to be or exist in abundance, with the implication of being considerably more than what would be expected."[15]) And somehow, what God is doing in us is part of His amazing plan to establish Jesus the Messiah as the preeminent one in heaven and earth.

> In Christ we too have been claimed as God's own possession, since we were predestined according to the one purpose of him who accomplishes all things according to the counsel of his will so that we, who were the first to set our hope on Christ, would be to the praise of his glory.
>
> —EPHESIANS 1:11–12, NET

Notice the repeated phrase "in Christ," a phrase that occurs *seventy-six times* in Paul's letters—and otherwise, just three times in the rest of the New Testament (1 Pet. 3:16; 5:10, 14). And that is in addition to the many times Paul speaks of our being "in Him"—meaning, in Jesus.[16] Everything we have, everything we are, is "in Him"—and through Him and by Him and because of Him—and it is all to the praise of God's glory.

> And when you heard the word of truth (the gospel of your salvation)—when you believed in Christ—you were marked with the seal of the promised Holy Spirit, who is the down payment of our inheritance, until the redemption of God's own possession, to the praise of his glory.
>
> —EPHESIANS 1:13–14, NET

When was God's grace lavished on us? Was it after we proved our loyalty to the Lord? Was it after years of faithful service? Was it after we had given up a sufficient amount of sin? No. It was when we put our faith in Jesus to save us and give us new life. It was at that time that our names were written in heaven (Luke 10:20), that we were rescued from the dominion of darkness (Col. 1:13), that we were made alive and redeemed and forgiven (Eph. 2:1–9), that we became children of God (John 1:12–13), and that we "were marked with the seal of the promised Holy Spirit."

As Ephesians scholar William Klein explains, "Paul intends the seal as a mark of ownership or possession.... In that case, the presence of the Spirit in the believers' lives marks them out as God's property (also confirmed in 2 Co[r.] 1:22)." He also notes that the Spirit here "constitutes God's 'earnest money,' a kind of deposit from him by which he assures that he will give them their full inheritance.... The Spirit is the down payment; the remaining riches will follow. A Spirit-filled life is a foretaste of what heaven will be like (cf. 5:18-21)."[17]

And we've only touched on the riches of what Paul was saying in these twelve verses. Do you realize just how incredibly extravagant and overflowing God's love for us is in Jesus? Let's feast together on one more passage from Ephesians:

> Once you were dead because of your disobedience and your many sins. You used to live in sin, just like the rest of the world, obeying the devil—the commander of the powers in the unseen world. He is the spirit at work in the hearts of those who refuse to obey God. All of us used to live that way, following the passionate desires and inclinations of our sinful nature. By our very nature we were subject to God's anger, just like everyone else.
>
> But God is so rich in mercy, and he loved us so much, that even though we were dead because of our sins, he gave us life

> when he raised Christ from the dead. (It is only by God's grace that you have been saved!) For he raised us from the dead along with Christ and seated us with him in the heavenly realms because we are united with Christ Jesus. So God can point to us in all future ages as examples of the incredible wealth of his grace and kindness toward us, as shown in all he has done for us who are united with Christ Jesus.
>
> God saved you by his grace when you believed. And you can't take credit for this; it is a gift from God. Salvation is not a reward for the good things we have done, so none of us can boast about it. For we are God's masterpiece. He has created us anew in Christ Jesus, so we can do the good things he planned for us long ago.
>
> —Ephesians 2:1–10, NLT

Yes, God "raised us from the dead along with Christ and seated us with him in the heavenly realms because we are united with Christ Jesus." It is an act so amazing that "in all future ages" God can "point to us...as examples of the incredible wealth of his grace and kindness." These are "things into which angels long to look" (1 Pet. 1:12). How glorious and incomprehensible God's grace must appear to them, and yet all of it is true, every word of it, and we really are spiritually seated with the Son of God—and therefore with God Himself—in the heavenly realms.

We Must Walk Worthy of Our Calling

How then should we live here on this earth? How should we conduct ourselves? Those are questions that Paul addresses in Ephesians 4–6, and we need to pay attention to the second half of his letter as much as the first half. You see, our citizenship is in heaven (Phil. 3:20), and we have a heavenly standing in Jesus, but we are also in this world, and there are things that God requires of us while we are here—as beloved, redeemed, children; as insiders, not as outsiders.

Peter describes our life on earth as the time of our exile (1 Pet. 1:17), and he writes, "Beloved, I urge you as sojourners and exiles to abstain from the passions of the flesh, which wage war against your soul" (1 Pet. 2:11). He also writes:

> And if you call on him as Father who judges impartially according to each one's deeds, conduct yourselves with fear throughout the time of your exile, knowing that you were ransomed from the futile ways inherited from your forefathers, not with perishable things such as silver or gold, but with the precious blood of Christ, like that of a lamb without blemish or spot.
>
> —1 PETER 1:17–19

What he is saying is that fleshly, worldly things are not for us. They are at war with our heavenly calling and our new nature in the Messiah, and because God has paid such a great price for our salvation, we need to live our lives here with reverential fear.

In the same way, because of our lofty calling and our heavenly position in Jesus, Paul urges us "to walk in a manner worthy of the calling to which you have been called" (Eph. 4:1). This was a repeated theme in his letters: "Only let your manner of life be worthy of the gospel of Christ.... From the day we heard [about your faith], we have not ceased to pray for you, asking that you may be filled with the knowledge of his will in all spiritual wisdom and understanding, so as to walk in a manner worthy of the Lord, fully pleasing to him, bearing fruit in every good work and increasing in the knowledge of God.... We exhorted each one of you and encouraged you and charged you to walk in a manner worthy of God, who calls you into his own kingdom and glory" (Phil. 1:27; Col. 1:9–10; 1 Thess. 2:12).

This means that we can walk in a manner that is *unworthy* of our high calling, and if Paul could exhort the Thessalonians as to how they "ought to walk and to please God" (1 Thess. 4:1)—as they had already been doing, in keeping with his instructions—then it is possible to walk in a way that does *not* please God. And if Paul could urge the Ephesians not to "grieve the Holy Spirit of God" by their conduct, words, and attitudes (Eph. 4:30), then it is possible to live and act in such a way that we *do* grieve the Holy Spirit.

But this is what we need to keep in mind: Paul and Peter are telling us these things *because* of our union with Jesus. They are exhorting us to please God in thought, word, and deed *because* we are His sons and daughters, *because* we are redeemed and forgiven, *because* we are new creations, *because* we are spiritually seated in heavenly places, *because* we are the objects of His grace, not His wrath.

That's why the author of Hebrews explains that when God disciplines us, He is treating us as children:

> And have you forgotten the exhortation that addresses you as sons? "My son, do not regard lightly the discipline of the Lord, nor be weary when reproved by him. For the Lord disciplines the one he loves, and chastises every son whom he receives" [citing Prov. 3:11–12]. It is for discipline that you have to endure. God is treating you as sons. For what son is there whom his father does not discipline? If you are left without discipline, in which all have participated, then you are illegitimate children and not sons.
>
> —Hebrews 12:5–8

In their books and sermons and on their blogs, many hyper-grace teachers have virtually eliminated the Father's loving discipline—which implies disobedience in our lives or something lacking on our end; otherwise, He would not discipline us—because of their overstated depiction of how God sees us. Put another way, while these teachers have done a great job of painting an incredible picture of what it means for us to be "in Christ" as the objects of God's lavish grace, they don't present the rest of the picture, namely, that we must walk this calling out here on earth and sometimes we fall short of God's ideal and displease Him.

But that is no reason for us to hang our heads in despair and feel condemned. Not at all! Everything we read in Ephesians 1 and 2 is true, and that is who we are in Jesus. God is simply saying to us, "In light of what I have done for you, and in light of your exalted standing as children of the heavenly Father and blood-bought, blood-washed saints—holy ones!—I want you to be very careful with how you live."

This is the basis of Paul's exhortation to the Corinthians:

> What agreement has the temple of God with idols? For we are the temple of the living God; as God said, "I will make my dwelling among them and walk among them, and I will be their God, and they shall be my people. Therefore go out from their midst, and be separate from them, says the Lord, and touch no unclean

> thing; then I will welcome you, and I will be a father to you, and you shall be sons and daughters to me, says the LORD Almighty." Since we have these promises, beloved, let us cleanse ourselves from every defilement of body and spirit, bringing holiness to completion in the fear of God.
>
> —2 CORINTHIANS 6:16–7:1

We know for a fact that there were things that took place at Corinth that displeased the Lord—He certainly didn't love everything He saw there, He certainly wasn't thrilled with everything His people were doing there, and He certainly wasn't just singing their praises—but that didn't mean they weren't His precious, beloved children. It meant that because they had these promises, they needed to separate themselves from "every defilement of body and spirit, bringing holiness to completion in the fear of God."[18]

Why can't we accept these twofold spiritual realities at the same time? We are dearly loved by the Father *and* we are called to please Him. We are seated in heavenly places with Jesus *and* we need to live lives that reflect that on earth. God considers us to be redeemed saints *and* He sees our faults and blemishes. As Jesus Himself expressed with unmistakable clarity, "Those whom I love, I reprove and discipline, so be zealous and repent" (Rev. 3:19).

Divine reproof, divine discipline, and the divine call to repent—which means to turn away from sin and turn to God (see chapter 6)—are all a sign of His love. Why can't we embrace that?

Is God *Always* Pleased With Us?

At the beginning of this chapter, I quoted the words of Ryan Rufus, who said, "You need to hear your Heavenly Father's praises. He is thrilled with you. He is beside Himself with love for you and takes enormous pleasure in you."

Yet, according to the Word, our heavenly Father is *not* always praising us and does *not* always take enormous pleasure in us, but as long as we are His children, we need not cower in fear and hopelessness. When He corrects us or rebukes us or disciplines us, it is because

He loves us and is committed to us. That is good news, and that is simply part of having a relationship with the Lord.

The fact is that He is *not* the accuser of the brethren. He is *not* the condemner of the weak. He is *not* the author of despair. He is for us, not against us, and that's why He speaks correction into our lives. Can you feel the Father's love—even when it is stern—in all of this? Can you find a place of security in which you can freely confess your sins to God and freely receive fresh cleansing and freely respond to the conviction of the Spirit? (We discussed this in chapters 5 and 6.) And can you take hold of the fact that *He* is the center of attention rather than us? (In other words, we live for His glory and we belong to Him rather than Him being our celestial bellboy.)[19]

Let's consider some of Paul's words to the Corinthians, whom he addresses as "those sanctified in Christ Jesus, called to be saints" (1 Cor. 1:2; see chapter 7 for more on this verse). He has glowing words of praise for them and expresses great confidence about their future, and in speaking this over them, he is certainly expressing God's heart:

> I give thanks to my God always for you because of the grace of God that was given you in Christ Jesus, that in every way you were enriched in him in all speech and all knowledge—even as the testimony about Christ was confirmed among you—so that you are not lacking in any spiritual gift, as you wait for the revealing of our Lord Jesus Christ, who will sustain you to the end, guiltless in the day of our Lord Jesus Christ.
>
> —1 Corinthians 1:4–8

Yet Paul also had sharp words of rebuke for the Corinthian believers, and in this too he was reflecting God's heart. Put another way, God was hardly pleased with some of what He saw in His beloved people, and He was certainly not always singing their praises.

Paul wrote, "In the following directives I have no praise for you, for your meetings do more harm than good" (1 Cor. 11:17, NIV). And in terms of abuses at the Lord's Supper, he asked, "Don't you have homes to eat and drink in? Or do you despise the church of God and humiliate those who have nothing? What shall I say to you? Shall I praise you for this? Certainly not!" (v. 22, NIV). Can we really believe that Paul, *the* source of the grace message for the modern grace preachers, was so out of tune with God here? That God was praising the Corinthians and Paul was not?

Because of the sacredness of the Lord's Supper, which commemorates the body and blood of Jesus, Paul issued this strong warning:

> Whoever, therefore, eats the bread or drinks the cup of the Lord in an unworthy manner will be guilty concerning the body and blood of the Lord. Let a person examine himself, then, and so eat of the bread and drink of the cup. For anyone who eats and drinks without discerning the body eats and drinks judgment on himself. That is why many of you are weak and ill, and some have died. But if we judged ourselves truly, we would not be judged. But when we are judged by the Lord, we are disciplined so that we may not be condemned along with the world.
>
> —1 CORINTHIANS 11:27–32

Did God "love what He saw" when the Corinthians were getting sick or even dying because they partook of the Lord's Supper in an unworthy manner? Was He "thrilled" with them at that time?

When Paul heard about the incestuous sin that was taking place in their midst, he wrote, "It is actually reported that there is sexual immorality among you, and of a kind that is not tolerated even among pagans, for a man has his father's wife. And you are arrogant! Ought you not rather to mourn? Let him who has done this be removed from among you" (1 Cor. 5:1–2). He even ordered that the offending, unrepentant brother be delivered "to Satan for the destruction of the flesh, so that his spirit may be saved in the day of the Lord" (v. 5).

Perhaps the Corinthians should have said to Paul, "Why are you so upset with us? You are such a petty legalist! Don't you know that our Father is always thrilled with us and always singing our praises? Don't you understand that there's nothing we could ever do to disappoint Him? You really need to get a revelation of grace!"

The difference couldn't be clearer. Joseph Prince wrote, "Stop examining yourself and searching your heart for sin. Remember that when someone takes his sin offering to the priest, the priest does not examine him. He examines the sin offering."[20] In contrast, Paul wrote in 1 Corinthians, "A man ought to examine himself before he eats of the bread and drinks of the cup" (1 Cor. 11:28, NIV). Again, in 2 Corinthians he wrote, "Examine yourselves" (2 Cor. 13:5).[21]

And what about Jesus, the Son of God, the very image of God, the exact representation of His character (Col. 1; Heb. 1), the One who said that whoever saw Him saw the Father (John 14:9)? It looks like He too did not agree with the modern grace teachers.

If God always sees us as perfectly holy and righteous in His sight and is never looking at our faults,[22] why did Jesus rebuke five out of the seven congregations in Asia Minor, saying repeatedly "I know your works," after which He enumerated the good things they had done and the sins they were committing? Can you imagine how shocked these believers would have been to hear these words from the Lord if they had been fed a steady diet of the hyper-grace message?

"Lord, why are You rebuking us? Why are You reminding us of our sins? Why are You threatening us with judgment? And why do You sound disappointed with us? We were taught that You don't see our faults, that You're always thrilled with us, and that there's nothing we could ever do to disappoint You! Jesus, don't You understand grace?"

To the believers in Ephesus Jesus said, "I have this against you, that you have abandoned the love you had at first" (Rev. 2:4); to the believers in Pergamum He said, "I have a few things against you," before listing His grievances with them (v. 14); to the believers in Thyatira He said, "I have this against you, that you tolerate that woman Jezebel, who calls herself a prophetess and is teaching and seducing my servants to practice sexual immorality and to eat food sacrificed to idols" (v. 20).

According to the modern grace preachers, Jesus says, "I see each of you as beautiful, holy, and righteous, and I love what I see!" The Son of God Himself takes strong exception to this. That's why He said to the believers in Sardis, "I know your works. You have the reputation of being alive, but you are dead. Wake up, and strengthen what remains and is about to die, for *I have not found your works complete in the sight of my God*" (Rev. 3:1–2).

Does not that one verse utterly destroy the hyper-grace claims? Jesus *does* look at our works, and sometimes He finds them incomplete, calling us to repent because of His great love for us.

As for always seeing us as perfect, nothing could be further from the truth for the believers in Laodicea, to whom He said, "I know your works: you are neither cold nor hot. Would that you were either cold or hot! So, because you are lukewarm, and neither hot nor cold, I will spit you out of my mouth. For you say, I am rich, I have prospered, and I need nothing, not realizing that *you are wretched, pitiable, poor, blind, and naked*" (vv. 15–17).[23]

But here's what we need to remember: God still loves us deeply even when He *does* see our flaws and failures, and rather than cast us off and condemn us, He calls us back to Himself. That's the whole purpose of the Holy Spirit's conviction (see chapter 6) and the reason for the Lord's loving rebuke. (See again Revelation 3:19: "Those whom I love, I reprove and discipline, so be zealous and repent.")

Think about it for a moment. As a parent, do you have to see your child as perfect and without fault to love him or her? (All the more can this be asked of grandparents!) Do you say to them when they have a bad day, "You're not my child and I am not your parent!"? Then why do we need to erect an unbiblical theology that states that God doesn't see our faults and blemishes in order for us to feel loved and secure? We are accepted because of Jesus, and that's the ground of our security. Now it is our holy privilege to walk worthy of that high calling, drawing near to God in confidence, "with our hearts sprinkled clean from an evil conscience and our bodies washed with pure water" (Heb. 10:22).

And let's remember that to each of these congregations addressed in Revelation 2–3, Jesus gave wonderful words of encouragement, including precious promises to overcomers (Rev. 2:7, 11, 17, 26–28; 3:5, 12), culminating with verse 21 in chapter 3: "To him who overcomes, I will give the right to sit with me on my throne, just as I overcame and sat down with my Father on his throne" (NIV). And those who overcame certainly brought joy to the Father's heart. Without a doubt, they were the ones who pleased Him!

John Crowder wrote, "It is high time the church gets delivered from God pleasing."[24] In stark contrast, Paul wrote:

- "Find out what *pleases the Lord*" (Eph. 5:10, NIV).
- "So we make it our goal to *please him*" (2 Cor. 5:9, NIV).
- "And we pray this in order that you may live a life worthy of the Lord and *may please him in every way*: bearing fruit in every good work, growing in the knowledge of God" (Col. 1:10, NIV).
- "Finally, brothers, we instructed you *how to live in order to please God*, as in fact you are living. Now we ask you and urge you in the Lord Jesus to do this more and more" (1 Thess. 4:1, NIV).
- "We are not trying *to please men but God*, who tests our hearts" (1 Thess. 2:4, NIV).

And so, when we look at the second half of Ephesians (chapters 4–6), Paul gives us specific instructions on how we are to live to please God, including these exhortations, just in chapter 4:

- "Walk in a manner worthy of the calling to which you have been called, with all humility and gentleness, with patience, bearing with one another in love, eager to maintain the unity of the Spirit in the bond of peace" (vv. 1–3).
- "Speaking the truth in love, we are to grow up in every way into him who is the head, into Christ" (v. 15).
- "You must no longer walk as the Gentiles do, in the futility of their minds" (v. 17).
- "Having put away falsehood, let each one of you speak the truth with his neighbor, for we are members one of another. Be angry and do not sin; do not let the sun go down on your anger, and give no opportunity to the devil. Let the thief no longer steal, but rather let him labor, doing honest work with his own hands, so that he may have something to share with anyone in need. Let no corrupting talk come out of your mouths, but

> only such as is good for building up, as fits the occasion, that it may give grace to those who hear. And do not grieve the Holy Spirit of God, by whom you were sealed for the day of redemption. Let all bitterness and wrath and anger and clamor and slander be put away from you, along with all malice. Be kind to one another, tender-hearted, forgiving one another, as God in Christ forgave you" (vv. 25–32).

Nowadays, when you call believers to live like this, you're immediately charged with being into "sin management" and "behavior modification,"[25] whereas Paul's heart—and mine—is to say, "Jesus has wonderfully redeemed us and transformed us by His grace and mercy, and we now belong to Him. Let's live lives that are worthy of His great name. Let's become like Him in thought, word, and deed! Let's stop living in the old way of life, and let's live in the newness of life in the Spirit!"

That is Paul's whole emphasis, as he continues in Ephesians 5 with specific instructions based on our calling to imitate God:

> Therefore be imitators of God, as beloved children. And walk in love, as Christ loved us and gave himself up for us, a fragrant offering and sacrifice to God. But sexual immorality and all impurity or covetousness must not even be named among you, as is proper among saints. Let there be no filthiness nor foolish talk nor crude joking, which are out of place, but instead let there be thanksgiving. For you may be sure of this, that everyone who is sexually immoral or impure, or who is covetous (that is, an idolater), has no inheritance in the kingdom of Christ and God. Let no one deceive you with empty words, for because of these things the wrath of God comes upon the sons of disobedience. Therefore do not become partners with them; for at one time you were darkness, but now you are light in the Lord. Walk as children of light (for the fruit of light is found in all that is good and right and true), and try to discern what is pleasing to the Lord.
>
> —Ephesians 5:1–10

And so, with all respect to the good intentions of the hyper-grace teachers, I'll stay with Jesus and Paul and the rest of the scriptures here, confident that I have been accepted in Jesus, the beloved Son (Eph. 1:1–6), that the One who began a good work in me will bring it to completion (Phil. 1:6), that the Father has lavished His grace on me and called me His own (Eph. 2:4–7), and that no one can bring a condemning accusation against me, since Christ Jesus, who died—more than that, who was raised to life—is at the right hand of God and is also interceding for us (Rom. 8:34).

Because of this we make it our business to please Him, bringing Him joy, not grief... pride, not pain... always remembering the depth of His kindness toward us. For, "as a father shows compassion to his children, so the LORD shows compassion to those who fear him. For he knows our frame; he remembers that we are dust" (Ps. 103:13–14). And perhaps the most amazing thing of all is this: when you get to know Him intimately, He is really not hard to please.

Doesn't your heart just burst with a holy desire to bring Him joy and to walk worthy of your high calling as a child of the Father, seated with Jesus in heavenly places? With Paul, I desire to say at the end of my life, "I have fought the good fight, I have finished the race, I have kept the faith" (2 Tim. 4:7). And I can't wait to hear Him say on that day, "Well done, my good and faithful servant.... Let's celebrate together!" (Matt. 25:21, NLT).

I am driven and carried and captured by love. Are you?

-9-

IS SPIRITUALITY EFFORTLESS?

John Crowder asks the question, "Does happy, *effortless* Christianity sound scandalous to you? Does a daily walk of joyful, sinless existence seem like an impossibility?"[1] Putting aside the question of "sinless existence" for the moment, what about the concept of "*effortless* Christianity"? Does it "sound scandalous to you"?

According to Crowder, "There is a reason that the gospel was first called 'good news.' It is a gloriously happy message of *effortless* union with God. It comes as an utter shock and outrage to the depressive human willpower that is common to religion." He goes on to say, "Your union with God in Christ is instant and *effortless*. It happened the first moment you believed. It is from this vantage point of being 'in Christ' that all other doctrines of the church must be built." Indeed, "real conversion *effortlessly* leads you to a happy holy life."[2]

Crowder explains that a man who doesn't put his faith to work is worse than an unbeliever, rightly emphasizing that a true believer cannot help but to manifest his faith through his works. But what does that look like according to Crowder? He says, "Prayers that are *effortless*, trusting ones—reliant upon God by faith—are the ones infused with God's energy."[3]

British preacher John Henry Jowett (1864–1923) had a very different perspective:

> The ministers of Calvary must supplicate in bloody sweat, and their intercession must often touch the point of agony. If we pray in cold blood we are no longer the ministers of the Cross. True intercession is a sacrifice, a bleeding sacrifice, a perpetuation of Calvary, a "filling up" of the sufferings of Christ....
>
> My brethren, this is the ministry which the Master owns, the

> agonized yearnings which perfect the sufferings of His own intercession. Are we in the succession? Do our prayers bleed? Have we felt the painful fellowship of the pierced hand? I am so often ashamed of my prayers. They so frequently cost me nothing; they shed no blood. I am ashamed at the grace and condescension of my Lord that he confers any fruitfulness upon my superficial pains....
>
> As soon as we cease to bleed we cease to bless.[4]

Can both Crowder and Jowett be right? Is one of them preaching the truth and another preaching error? Or is there some truth to both positions?

In his book *The Birthright*, John Sheasby suggests that God's children need not persist in prayer. Using an illustration from the story of the persistent friend in Luke 11:5–8, where the friend is outside and the children are in bed with their father, Sheasby writes:

> The picture is of the warmth, closeness, and intimacy that is ours within the father's house. If the man reluctantly answers the request of his friend on the outside, how much more eagerly will he answer the request of his children on the inside? The friend standing at the door has to knock; the children lying next to him in bed have only to whisper. The one has to persist; the other has only to tug on his nightshirt. Here is the point: we are not the friend on the outside; we are the children on the inside. Lying next to him. Snuggled warmly by his side. He is that near to us. And we are that dear to him.[5]

But the fact that we are God's children "on the inside" is not the point here, since Jesus gave this parable in answer to His disciples' request to teach them to pray (v. 1). And, more importantly, the application of the parable that Jesus offered is the exact opposite of the claim that God's children need not knock. Yes, it was Jesus who concluded the parable by saying, "And I tell you, ask, and it will be given to you; seek, and you will find; *knock, and it will be opened to you.* For everyone who asks receives, and the one who seeks finds, *and to the one who knocks it will be opened*" (vv. 9–10). The whole point of the parable was to encourage importunity (boldness!) in prayer (v. 8).

Jesus tells us to knock. A modern grace teacher tells us we need not knock. Who do we follow?

John Crowder says that in the days to come, our work for the Lord in the harvest fields will be "completely effortless." Can all believers really expect this? Is this scriptural and realistic? Or is Crowder on to something powerful but is presenting it in overstated terms?

Let's consider the writings of Joseph Prince, who also stresses "effortless spirituality." A few years ago people starting asking me about his teachings. "He's a heretic," some said, "and he preaches a false gospel. Something isn't right about that guy." Others said, "My life has been radically changed listening to his messages!"

Because I don't watch much TV and hardly ever see Christian TV, and because I don't travel in certain Christian circles, I wasn't familiar with his ministry at that time. But soon enough I began hearing some of Joseph Prince's messages, prompting me to get his book *Unmerited Favor* (and then *Destined to Reign*). I started to read his writings with real interest and an open heart before God, even praying as I read, "Father, show me what this brother is preaching that I need to hear. Reveal any area in my life where I am not walking in the light of Your unmerited favor. Give me a fresh revelation of Your grace!"

As I stated in chapter 2, I don't believe that I am the perfect standard by which everyone will be judged. I don't believe that I am walking in the fullness of truth and revelation on every subject, as if I have something to teach others but nothing to learn myself. God forbid! And, to repeat myself again, when it comes to the subject of grace, I never want to denigrate, downplay, or deny God's amazing kindness, mercy, and love, even for a split second. I am sustained by grace, empowered by grace, and dependent on grace every day of my life.

So I came to Joseph Prince's book with an open mind rather than a critical attitude, and I found much in his book that was excellent. (I would say the same thing about his earlier book *Destined to Reign*.) He writes like a man who knows the Lord and has experienced God's goodness, like a man who takes delight in God's Word and who knows what it is to worship and love Jesus.

My heart resonated with much of what he wrote, especially lines like these (although I can't relate to his latte illustration, since I've never had a cup of coffee in my life!):

> Reading His Word has become a great personal time of intimacy between Jesus and me. I get completely lost and absorbed in His presence until I lose track of time. I can't tell you the number of times when I had looked up at my clock after digging into His Word and realized that it was already five in the morning! You know what it's like when you are enjoying a steaming cup of latte in a café with friends that you love, and you are having so much fun, laughing and sharing, that time just seems to disappear? Well, you can enjoy Jesus' presence in the same way![6]

Amen! And I totally agree with Pastor Prince when he says, "Some people think that grace will compromise God's holiness. Absolutely not! The standards that grace sets are much higher than the standards of the law of Moses."[7] But he also adds, "When you are under grace, you will effortlessly fulfill and even superexceed the expectations of the law of Moses!"[8] Is this true?

Will we "effortlessly...superexceed the expectations of the law of Moses" when we are "under grace"? Is that what God's Word teaches? Is there such a thing as "effortless spirituality"? If so, I would love to have more of it!

Prince writes, "When you are overflowing with God's love, you will fulfill the law effortlessly without even trying."[9] To a great extent, that is true, but sometimes we backslide from that love, as the church at Ephesus did, in which case Jesus says to us, "Remember therefore from where you have fallen; repent, and do the works you did at first. If not, I will come to you and remove your lampstand from its place, unless you repent" (Rev. 2:5). Those are urgent words of warning from the Lord. And those are words that call for an intentional, effort-filled response, don't they?[10]

Fourteen times in his book *Unmerited Favor* Pastor Prince makes reference to "effortless" spirituality, and the word *effort* occurs a total of sixty-eight times in one form or another. In *Destined to Reign* the word *effortless* even makes its way into the subtitle: *The Secret to Effortless Success, Wholeness and Victorious Living.* Where is the truth, and where is the error in what he has written?

Self-Effort or Running With Perseverance?

Evangelist and musician Benjamin Dunn also uses "effortless" in the subtitle of his book *The Happy Gospel: Effortless Union With a Happy God* (we will devote a separate chapter to the subject of a "happy God"), while faith teacher Andrew Wommack uses "effortless" in the title of his book *Effortless Change: The Word Is the Seed That Can Change Your Life.*[11] What are we to make of this so-called "effortless spirituality"?

According to Joseph Prince:

> We can never bring about good success that comes from God by depending on our self-efforts. No matter how we strive and struggle, we cannot work for our own righteousness or attain our own forgiveness. Any success that we may achieve is only partial success.... People who trust in their own efforts have no ability to see and receive blessings from the Lord. They only believe in the "good" that can come from their own efforts.[12]

I concur! And who would argue with this? He writes, "You know, all our struggling, willpower, discipline and self-effort cannot do what the presence of the Lord can do in an instant."[13] Absolutely! I would rather have one thirty-minute, true encounter with the living God than ten thousand hours implementing my latest brainstorms. But along with many solid, powerful statements, Prince also makes potentially misleading statements like this: "My friend, there is no middle road. You cannot mix your own efforts with God's grace."[14]

So we just take our foot off the pedal and let God take over? Why then does God call us to labor and strive, empowered and helped by His grace? Why then does He call us to "work out [our] own salvation with fear and trembling" for the very reason that "it is God who works in [us], both to will and to work for his good pleasure" (Phil. 2:12–13)?

Pastor Prince writes, "When you receive completely what Jesus has done for you, your 'doing' will flow effortlessly."[15] Then why does the Lord exhort us repeatedly to run and fight and persevere? That is hardly "effortless"!

Prince explains, "Several years ago, I shared with my church that there are essentially two ways in which you can go about your life. The first is to depend entirely on your self-efforts, and the other is to depend completely on the unmerited favor and blessings of God."[16]

But why make such a sharp dichotomy? Why not depend on God's unmerited favor and blessings and then run your race with perseverance in obedience to Him?

I fully understand the point that Pastor Prince is trying to make, but I have seen the effect that these unbalanced teachings have on too many believers. They have shifted into neutral, they reject all loving exhortation, and the moment you quote the Word to them, they accuse you of trying to put them under the Law. How much better it would be to do our best to teach "the whole counsel of God" (Acts 20:27) rather than preaching and practicing a "gospel" that makes no demands.

Without a doubt, *many* believers have been transformed listening to Joseph Prince and others teach about grace, and it is because much of what they are saying is biblical. I affirm that part of the message wholeheartedly, and I wish I could recommend their material without reserve. The problem, I believe, is that he and other hyper-grace leaders sometimes teach about grace in exaggerated form or, worse still, mixed with serious errors, and that's why there are all too many casualties and divisions among the listeners and readers.

Prince writes, "To ask the Lord for wisdom is to say, 'I can't, Lord, but You can. I give up on my own efforts and depend entirely upon Your unmerited favor and wisdom.' As you receive His wisdom, riches and honor, as well as long life, will follow after you. Run to Him right now!"[17] But doesn't it require effort to "run to Him right now," and aren't there often obstacles to overcome as we run?

Again Prince states, "While success to the world comes by one's self-effort, willpower and striving by one's own strength, God's way to supernatural, effortless success is for you to *depend totally on His unmerited favor.*"[18] Does that mean that we do nothing and just wait for God to do the work?

Unfortunately, because Pastor Prince often does not qualify his words (or sufficiently explain them), his teaching all too often produces an unfocused, undisciplined, unholy spirituality, even if that is the last thing he intends. As a result, many who embrace the message of "effortless spirituality" reject the call to press in to the Lord in prayer or carry His burden or say no to the flesh. After all, with hyper-grace teachers stating that the only work we have to do is believe, it's no surprise that many hearers become spiritually lazy, and the very fact that you call them to make an effort turns you into a legalistic Pharisee in their eyes. What then do we make of the words of Jacob (James)? He wrote, "Show me your faith apart from your works, and I will show you my faith by my works" (Jacob [James] 2:18).

Benjamin Dunn's teachings are more extreme than Joseph Prince's, although he too has many wonderful things to say about the beauty of fellowshipping with Jesus and the transforming power of His presence. He writes as one who understands the words of the old hymn writer Fanny Crosby: "O the pure delight of a single hour / That before Thy throne I spend/ When I kneel in prayer, and with Thee, my God / I commune as friend with friend!"[19]

It is really a shame, with all the insights that Dunn shares, that he is so extreme in his attack on making efforts to please the Lord. He goes so far as to say, "Those who demand to please the Lord through effort and Law, heartbreakingly miss out on the benefits of being married to grace. Being Christians, they should enjoy being wedded to grace, but instead they are *committing adultery with the Law*."[20]

According to Acts 21:18–26, the Jewish believers in Yeshua with whom Paul sided were "all zealous for the law" (v. 20). Were they committing adultery with the Law? That is what Dunn implies, not to mention his strong statement about "those who demand to please the Lord through effort," as if making an effort to please God was sinful. (We discussed this in chapter 8.)

Dunn does state that, "The effortlessness of the Gospel should not be misunderstood to be apathy. On the contrary, when such bliss and love come to possess our hearts, we cannot stop the divine flow of holy works."[21] This is a wonderful truth, for sure. Unfortunately, his repeated resistance to the idea that God requires us to make an effort, coupled with the way he sometimes defines "effortlessness," easily leads to apathy, and I have seen this attitude in all too many who embrace this message.

He asks:

> *So where do our efforts belong in all of this? What is our place as followers of Jesus?*
>
> Our place in Christianity is simply to be His—to be in Christ. Just surrender to what He has done. Surrender to mystical union!
>
> There are some amazing things that take place when you recognize your union with Christ. You begin to notice that love comes when you least expect it, and flows to the most unlikely of suspects.
>
> Instead of throwing insults, you find yourself throwing hugs.
>
> A holy life becomes a simple outflow of love.
>
> Things, for which we once worked so hard, now come to us so effortlessly.
>
> We must *realize* that we are one with Christ, and that we take part in His *attributes* only because we have partaken *of Him*.[22]

He writes, "The only efforts necessary for this union with God were Christ's. Just simply respond with childlike wonder and amazement at the work of Christ. Just shout, '*Yes, I believe it!*'"[23]

Is this a biblical concept? Does the Lord simply call us to do nothing more than "surrender to mystical union" with Him and shout, "Yes, I believe it!"?

As we'll see in a moment, the entire testimony of the New Testament is against this message, and it is really is a shame that Dunn makes several overstated and even untrue claims in his book, since he says so much that is excellent.

Some of Andrew Wommack's statements on this topic are similarly problematic. He writes: "Effortless change—it sounds impossible. Yet, that's what the Word reveals about how the kingdom of God works." He continues, "In this book, I want to share with you some truths from the Word of God that can totally transform the way you understand and approach change. If you receive these truths into your heart and apply them to your life, you'll be able to see change take place in your life effortlessly."[24]

But it requires effort to receive biblical truths into our heart and apply them into our lives, doesn't it? Wommack states that, "If you're struggling with depression, you're not meditating on the Word of God day and night."[25] But it requires determination and discipline to meditate on God's Word day and night. (By the way, to someone trapped in depression, advice like this might not be as helpful as it appears.)

Along with Andrew Wommack, I have experienced the reality that "when I changed on the inside, immediately everything in my life began to change on the outside."[26] But changing on the inside often requires serious spiritual effort.

Wommack claims that, "If you will just cooperate and let the Word of God germinate, you will change effortlessly."[27] But this is like saying, "If you will be disciplined in your diet and will exercise regularly, you will lose weight effortlessly." Right!

What then are we to make of the message of "effortless" spirituality? Without a doubt, there are important truths that these brothers are bringing, and those truths can be liberating and life-changing. But the message is being presented in such an unbalanced and exaggerated way that, in the end, it often does more harm than good, hurting believers more than helping them.

The message of effortless spirituality basically says this: "Don't strive. Don't try to work at being spiritual. Jesus already paid the price. All you have to do is accept it. There's nothing you can add to what He's done. Don't be a legalist. Don't mix faith with works or grace with law. God wants you to rest and enjoy the ride. The old you is dead. The new you is seated in heavenly places, and you don't need to *do* anything other than let the Lord do His work through you."

Again, there are parts of this message that are wonderfully true. The problem is that the parts that are not true—really, the parts that are missing—can prove fatal.

To be sure, it is gloriously true that Jesus paid for all our sins, and there's nothing we can add to His once-for-all sacrifice (Heb. 9:13–28; 10:1–14). That's enough to keep us rejoicing for the next trillion years. And it is true that God calls us to rest in Him (Matt. 11:28–30; Heb. 4:9–10), to receive His peace (John 14:27), to put our trust in His keeping power (John 10:27–29; 1 Cor. 1:8; Phil. 1:6), and to recognize that we are justified by faith and not by works (Rom. 3:20–31; 4:1–16; Gal. 3:1–14; Eph. 2:8–9; 2 Tim. 1:8–10; Titus 3:4–7). What glorious truths are contained in these wonderful verses! They are the foundation for my own walk with the Lord.

It is also true that as we abide in Jesus the Vine, we will automatically bear fruit (John 15:1–7). And it is true that God works miracles among us by faith and not by works (Gal. 3:5) and that, however hard we labor for the Lord, it is God's grace working in and through us (1 Cor. 15:10).

Speaking for myself, I can honestly say that following Jesus is much more of a joy than a struggle, and when I really abide in Him, being spiritual comes "naturally" and with ease. At the same time, to really honor the Lord and do the right thing and consistently abide in Him requires determination and discipline, and there is often an intense battle involved in walking in full obedience to Jesus and saying no to the flesh and the world. As Smith Wigglesworth, the "apostle of faith," famously said, "Great faith is the product of great fights. Great testimonies are the outcome of great tests. Great triumphs can only come out of great trials."[28]

Wigglesworth also said:

> There is no man who can be clothed with the Spirit and catch the fire and zeal of the Master every day and many times a day, without ceasing in every way to be connected with the "arm of flesh" which would draw him aside from the power of God. Many men have lost the glory because they have been taken up with the natural. If we are going to accomplish in the Spirit the things that God has purposed for us, we must never turn again to the flesh. If we are Spirit-filled, God has brought us into relationship with Himself, and now He is all in all to us.[29]

This hardly sounds "effortless"! Could it be that some of those who embrace effortless spirituality are simply coasting and not resisting? Could it be that rather than crucifying the flesh they are catering to carnality, floating rather than fighting? (I'm not speaking of *all* here; I'm speaking of some—and by "some," I mean a considerable minority, if not a growing majority.)

The undeniable truth is that the New Testament is filled with exhortations to us, God's people, urging us to make every effort to please the Lord, to run and finish our race, to fulfill our calling in Him. Will we accept the testimony of God's life-giving Word? Can we let the Scriptures speak for themselves?

Rest and Run

Allow me to share a number of New Testament scriptures with you, and as I do, please examine your reaction to these verses as you read them. If you feel the need to explain them away, or if they threaten your theology, or if you find yourself getting defensive, then something is seriously wrong.

Let's see what Jesus has to say about the matter. In fact, let's ask Him directly.

"Jesus, do You believe in effortless spirituality? I read in Ben Dunn's book about "the ease and effortlessness of the Gospel." Is this an accurate concept?"

> Strive to enter through the narrow door. For many, I tell you, will seek to enter and will not be able.
>
> —LUKE 13:24

> No one who puts his hand to the plow and looks back is fit for the kingdom of God.
>
> —LUKE 9:62

> If anyone would come after me, let him deny himself and take up his cross daily and follow me.... Whoever does not bear his own cross and come after me cannot be my disciple.... Any one of you who does not renounce all that he has cannot be my disciple.
>
> —LUKE 9:23; 14:27, 33

> In the world you will have tribulation. But take heart; I have overcome the world.
>
> —JOHN 16:33

"Lord, what about the issue of sin? Is our victory over sin effortless?"

> If your hand causes you to sin, cut it off. It is better for you to enter life crippled than with two hands to go to hell, to the unquenchable fire. And if your foot causes you to sin, cut it off. It is better for you to enter life lame than with two feet to be thrown into hell. And if your eye causes you to sin, tear it out. It is better for you to enter the kingdom of God with one eye than with two eyes to be thrown into hell, "where their worm does not die and the fire is not quenched." For everyone will be salted with fire.
>
> —MARK 9:43–49

"But Jesus, wasn't Your spiritual walk effortless?"

> I came to cast fire on the earth, and would that it were already kindled! I have a baptism to be baptized with, and how great is my distress until it is accomplished!
>
> —LUKE 12:49–50

> And being in an agony [I] prayed more earnestly; and [my] sweat became like great drops of blood falling down to the ground.
>
> —LUKE 22:44

Now, let's see what Paul has to say about the matter.

"Paul, do you believe in effortless spirituality?"

> Do you not know that in a race all the runners run, but only one gets the prize? Run in such a way as to get the prize. Everyone who competes in the games goes into strict training. They do it to get a crown that will not last; but we do it to get a crown that will last forever.
>
> —1 CORINTHIANS 9:24–25, NIV

> Endure hardship with us like a good soldier of Christ Jesus.
>
> —2 TIMOTHY 2:3, NIV

> We must go through many hardships to enter the kingdom of God.
>
> —ACTS 14:22, NIV

"Paul, what about the issue of sin? Is our victory over sin effortless?"

> Let not sin therefore reign in your mortal body, to make you obey its passions. Do not present your members to sin as instruments for unrighteousness, but present yourselves to God as those who have been brought from death to life, and your members to God as instruments for righteousness.
>
> —Romans 6:12–13

> The hour has come for you to wake from sleep. For salvation is nearer to us now than when we first believed. The night is far gone; the day is at hand. So then let us cast off the works of darkness and put on the armor of light. Let us walk properly as in the daytime, not in orgies and drunkenness, not in sexual immorality and sensuality, not in quarreling and jealousy. But put on the Lord Jesus Christ, and make no provision for the flesh, to gratify its desires.
>
> —Romans 13:11–14

"But does that really require a conscious effort?"

> Flee from sexual immorality. . . . Flee from idolatry. . . . Flee youthful passions and pursue righteousness, faith, love, and peace, along with those who call on the Lord from a pure heart.
>
> —1 Corinthians 6:18; 10:14; 2 Timothy 2:22

> But as for you, O man of God, flee these things [meaning the love of money and a covetousness heart]. Pursue righteousness, godliness, faith, love, steadfastness, gentleness. Fight the good fight of the faith. Take hold of the eternal life to which you were called and about which you made the good confession in the presence of many witnesses.
>
> —1 Timothy 6:11–12[30]

"So are we engaged in some kind of spiritual struggle?"

> Finally, be strong in the Lord and in his mighty power. Put on the full armor of God so that you can take your stand against the devil's schemes. For our struggle is not against flesh and

blood, but against the rulers, against the authorities, against the powers of this dark world and against the spiritual forces of evil in the heavenly realms. Therefore put on the full armor of God, so that when the day of evil comes, you may be able to stand your ground, and after you have done everything, to stand.

—EPHESIANS 6:10–13, NIV

"But Paul, wasn't your own spiritual walk effortless?"

So I do not run aimlessly; I do not box as one beating the air. But I discipline my body and keep it under control, lest after preaching to others I myself should be disqualified.

—1 CORINTHIANS 9:26–27

I want to know Christ and the power of his resurrection and the fellowship of sharing in his sufferings, becoming like him in his death, and so, somehow, to attain to the resurrection from the dead. Not that I have already obtained all this, or have already been made perfect, but I press on to take hold of that for which Christ Jesus took hold of me. Brothers, I do not consider myself yet to have taken hold of it. But one thing I do: Forgetting what is behind and straining toward what is ahead, I press on toward the goal to win the prize for which God has called me heavenward in Christ Jesus.

—PHILIPPIANS 3:10–14, NIV

To the present hour we hunger and thirst, we are poorly dressed and buffeted and homeless, and we labor, working with our own hands. When reviled, we bless; when persecuted, we endure; when slandered, we entreat. We have become, and are still, like the scum of the world, the refuse of all things.

—1 CORINTHIANS 4:11–13

[Jesus] we proclaim, warning everyone and teaching everyone with all wisdom, that we may present everyone mature in Christ. For this I toil, struggling with all his energy that he powerfully works within me.

—COLOSSIANS 1:28–29

> I have fought the good fight, I have finished the race, I have kept the faith.
>
> —2 Timothy 4:7; see also Acts 20:24

"Could you share a few more details about what your own walk with the Lord looked like, including your ministry experience?"

> We are afflicted in every way, but not crushed; perplexed, but not driven to despair; persecuted, but not forsaken; struck down, but not destroyed; always carrying in the body the death of Jesus, so that the life of Jesus may also be manifested in our bodies.
>
> —2 Corinthians 4:8–10

> As servants of God we commend ourselves in every way: by great endurance, in afflictions, hardships, calamities, beatings, imprisonments, riots, labors, sleepless nights, hunger; by purity, knowledge, patience, kindness, the Holy Spirit, genuine love; by truthful speech, and the power of God; with the weapons of righteousness for the right hand and for the left; through honor and dishonor, through slander and praise. We are treated as impostors, and yet are true; as unknown, and yet well known; as dying, and behold, we live; as punished, and yet not killed; as sorrowful, yet always rejoicing; as poor, yet making many rich; as having nothing, yet possessing everything.
>
> —2 Corinthians 6:4–10

> For even when we came into Macedonia, our bodies had no rest, but we were afflicted at every turn—fighting without and fear within.
>
> —2 Corinthians 7:5

> And as for us, why do we endanger ourselves every hour? I die every day—I mean that, brothers—just as surely as I glory over you in Christ Jesus our Lord. If I fought wild beasts in Ephesus for merely human reasons, what have I gained?
>
> —1 Corinthians 15:30–32, NIV

Somehow I don't equate descriptions like these (and there are plenty more from Paul) with the word *effortless*. But there's still Peter. Let's ask him what he has to say.

"Peter, surely you believe in effortless spirituality, right?"

> [In light of God's promises and power on our behalf], *make every effort* to supplement your faith with virtue, and virtue with knowledge, and knowledge with self-control, and self-control with steadfastness, and steadfastness with godliness, and godliness with brotherly affection, and brotherly affection with love. For if these qualities are yours and are increasing, they keep you from being ineffective or unfruitful in the knowledge of our Lord Jesus Christ. For whoever lacks these qualities is so nearsighted that he is blind, having forgotten that he was cleansed from his former sins. Therefore, brothers, *be all the more diligent to confirm your calling and election,* for if you practice these qualities you will never fall. For in this way there will be richly provided for you an entrance into the eternal kingdom of our Lord and Savior Jesus Christ.
>
> —2 PETER 1:5–11

> In keeping with his promise we are looking forward to a new heaven and a new earth, the home of righteousness. So then, dear friends, since you are looking forward to this, *make every effort* to be found spotless, blameless and at peace with him.
>
> —2 PETER 3:13–14, NIV

"But Peter, we have effortless victory over sin, don't we?"

> Dear friends, I urge you, as aliens and strangers in the world, to abstain from sinful desires, which war against your soul.
>
> —1 PETER 2:11, NIV

> Since therefore Christ suffered in the flesh, arm yourselves with the same way of thinking, for whoever has suffered in the flesh has ceased from sin, so as to live for the rest of the time in the flesh no longer for human passions but for the will of God. For the time that is past suffices for doing what the Gentiles want to

> do, living in sensuality, passions, drunkenness, orgies, drinking parties, and lawless idolatry.
>
> —1 PETER 4:1–3

> Be sober-minded; be watchful. Your adversary the devil prowls around like a roaring lion, seeking someone to devour. Resist him, firm in your faith, knowing that the same kinds of suffering are being experienced by your brotherhood throughout the world.
>
> —1 PETER 5:8–9

"Are you saying that in some sense we are called to suffer for the Lord?"

> In this [glorious salvation] you greatly rejoice, though now for a little while you may have had to *suffer* grief in all kinds of trials.... For it is commendable if a man bears up under the pain of unjust *suffering* because he is conscious of God.... But if you *suffer* for doing good and you endure it, this is commendable before God. To this you were called, because Christ *suffered* for you, leaving you an example, that you should follow in his steps.... But even if you should *suffer* for what is right, you are blessed.... It is better, if it is God's will, to *suffer* for doing good than for doing evil.... Dear friends, do not be surprised at the painful trial you are *suffering*, as though something strange were happening to you. But rejoice that you participate in the *sufferings* of Christ, so that you may be overjoyed when his glory is revealed.... So then, those who *suffer* according to God's will should commit themselves to their faithful Creator and continue to do good.... And the God of all grace, who called you to his eternal glory in Christ, after you have *suffered* a little while, will himself restore you and make you strong, firm and steadfast.
>
> —1 PETER 1:6; 2:19–21; 3:14, 17; 4:12–13, 19; 5:10, NIV

It seems that Jesus, Paul, and Peter have made themselves perfectly clear. What about the author of Hebrews, whoever he was? Let's ask him if he believed in "effortless spirituality."

"So, author of Hebrews, what do you have to say?"

> Therefore we must pay much closer attention to what we have heard, lest we drift away from it.
>
> —Hebrews 2:1

> Take care, brothers, lest there be in any of you an evil, unbelieving heart, leading you to fall away from the living God. But exhort one another every day, as long as it is called "today," that none of you may be hardened by the deceitfulness of sin. For we have come to share in Christ, if indeed we hold our original confidence firm to the end.
>
> —Hebrews 3:12–14

> Therefore, while the promise of entering his rest still stands, let us fear lest any of you should seem to have failed to reach it.... Let us therefore strive to enter that rest, so that no one may fall by the same sort of disobedience.
>
> —Hebrews 4:1, 11

> Therefore do not throw away your confidence, which has a great reward. For you have need of endurance, so that when you have done the will of God you may receive what is promised.
>
> —Hebrews 10:35–36

"Are you saying, then, that our walk with the Lord is like a race that we need to run with determination, just as Paul taught?"

> Therefore, since we are surrounded by so great a cloud of witnesses, let us also lay aside every weight, and sin which clings so closely, and let us run with endurance the race that is set before us, looking to Jesus, the founder and perfecter of our faith, who for the joy that was set before him endured the cross, despising the shame, and is seated at the right hand of the throne of God. Consider him who endured from sinners such hostility against himself, so that you may not grow weary or fainthearted. In your struggle against sin you have not yet resisted to the point of shedding your blood.
>
> —Hebrews 12:1–4[31]

This Christian walk requires effort! So I ask you: In light of the consistent, clear, and abundant testimony of God's Word, how can anyone believe in effortless spirituality? The Word of God utterly demolishes this false and exaggerated concept, and the same God who offers us rest in His Son also calls us to run.

And let's not forget Jacob (James), who wrote, "But the one who looks into the perfect law, the law of liberty, and perseveres, being no hearer who forgets but a doer who acts, he will be blessed in his doing" (Jacob [James] 1:25). Perseverance, along with "doing" rather than just "hearing," requires effort, and so "faith by itself, if it is does not have works, is dead" (Jacob [James] 2:17, NIV).

And let's not forget the witness of Judah (Jude), who said, "Beloved, although I was very eager to write to you about our common salvation, I found it necessary to write appealing to you to contend for the faith that was once for all delivered to the saints" (Judah [Jude] 3). So, there is a battle that must be fought just for the purity of the gospel.

There is also a battle that must be waged against sin: "Have mercy on those who doubt; save others by snatching them out of the fire; to others show mercy with fear, hating even the garment stained by the flesh" (Judah [Jude] 22–23). And note that Judah (Jude) wrote those words immediately before invoking the One "who is able to keep [us] from falling and to present [us] before his glorious presence without fault and with great joy" (Judah [Jude] 24, NIV). He will do His part, but we must do ours, which is why Judah (Jude) exhorts his readers to build themselves up in the faith and to keep themselves in God's love (vv. 20–21).

That's why Paul wrote that God "has reconciled [us] by Christ's physical body through death to present [us] holy in his sight, without blemish and free from accusation—*if [we] continue in [our] faith*, established and firm, not moved from the hope held out in the gospel" (Col. 1:22–23, NIV). God's grace goes hand in hand with our obedience.

Bishop J. C. Ryle encountered a similar, exaggerated teaching in the nineteenth century—that of effortless sanctification—and examined this doctrine by the clear teaching of the Word. He asked, "Is it wise to teach believers that they ought not to think so much of fighting and struggling against sin, but ought rather to 'yield themselves to God' and be passive in the hands of Christ? Is this according to the proportion of God's Word? I doubt it."[32]

He wrote:

> It would not be difficult to point out at least twenty-five or thirty distinct passages in the Epistles where believers are plainly taught to use active personal exertion, and are addressed as responsible for doing energetically what Christ would have them do, and are not told to "yield themselves" up as passive agents and sit still, but to arise and work. A holy violence, a conflict, a warfare, a fight, a soldier's life, a wrestling, are spoken of as characteristic of the true Christian.[33]

Expressed in theological terms, "In justification our own works have no place at all, and simple faith in Christ is the one thing needful. In sanctification our own works are of vast importance and God bids us fight, and watch, and pray, and strive, and take pains, and labour."[34]

He taught accurately that "this Christian warfare is a great reality, and a subject of vast importance," explaining that:

> We must fight. There are no promises in the Lord Jesus Christ's Epistles to the Seven Churches, except to those who "overcome." Where there is grace there will be conflict. The believer is a soldier. There is no holiness without a warfare. Saved souls will always be found to have fought a fight. It is a fight of absolute necessity. Let us not think that in this war we can remain neutral and sit still.... We have no choice or option. We must either fight or be lost. It is a fight of universal necessity.... The foe we have to do with keeps no holidays, never slumbers, and never sleeps. So long as we have breath in our bodies we must keep on our armour, and remember we are on an enemy's ground. "Even on the brink of Jordan," said a dying saint, "I find Satan nibbling at my heels." We must fight till we die.[35]

Paul encouraged the believers in Corinth that their "labor in the Lord" was not in vain (1 Cor. 15:58, NIV)—and labor is the exact opposite of effortlessness! So finding a place of rest and security in the Lord, and empowered by God's grace, let us work; let us run; let us fight; let us overcome in Jesus's name. The effort will be worth the reward. Rest and run!

-10-

IS GOD ALWAYS IN A GOOD MOOD?

SOME OF MY respected ministry colleagues—men and women whom I deeply honor, people who have been used by the Lord to minister grace, healing, mercy, and deliverance to countless thousands of people—love to emphasize that "God is in a good mood," and I certainly understand their intent. They have seen so many believers beaten down by wrong images of the Lord, living under constant condemnation and fear, not wanting to get on God's "bad side," looking at Him as a bigger (and "badder"?) version of their flawed earthly fathers and authority figures. To such people, these colleagues of mine proclaim that "God is always in a good mood!"

One graduate of a ministry school in California had this to say about the powerful effect this message had on her:

> God has been doing a lot of refining in me this season. He is taking out everything that isn't Him and filling me with more of Him. I have experienced so much freedom! Sharing my heart used to be something that I didn't do often, or I didn't want to confront someone because I was afraid of hurting their feelings. It feels good to have a voice now. I am now a brave communicator haha. I have also realized that I have so much more freedom in worship than I used to. When you are in the presence of God nothing else matters. I now know that God is always in a good mood. I've always known that in my head, but now I truly know it in my heart. There are so many things to process through here, but I am learning the beauty of process. So to sum it up Papa is SO GOOD, and I am loving this dance with Him.[1]

Another believer offered these scriptural reflections on God being in a "good mood."

> God is not one to control us like puppets or to unleash evil on man. There is no evil or darkness in God (1 Jn 1:5). God is good (Psalm 25:8, Psalm 34:8). He is also in a good mood (Psalm 2:4, 37:13). He laughs at the devil's schemes. He guffaws at the nations plans. He will cause all things to work together for good (Romans 8:28). The craziness of this world doesn't faze Him. It shouldn't faze us.
>
> His throne room sits in the foundation of all the universe. The atmosphere there should set the spiritual thermostat of the church here. What do you think? In other words, God's attitude should be our attitude. Anything else is stupid, fearful, fleshly, and based in lies. What is the atmosphere of God's throne room like?[2]

These are really great insights, and they are filled with divine truth. But do they tell the whole story? Is God's attitude always one of joy?

With all honor to my friends who preach this, and with respect to my theologically minded readers who will be quick to point out that it's wrong to talk about God being in a "mood" of any kind (as if God is "moody"!),[3] let's simply ask the question: according to the Scriptures, is God always in a good mood?

Well, it depends on what you mean by "good mood." If you mean that He is always good, always kind, always righteous, always compassionate, always full of truth and light and love, then yes, you can say that God is always in a good mood. If you mean that He is never depressed, hopeless, erratic, or short-tempered, that there is nothing morbid in God or about God, then yes, you can say that God is always in a good mood.

If you mean that He never gets angry or wrathful or that He is never grieved or in pain, then no, He is not always in a good mood. In fact, it's impossible to read the Bible without seeing at once that God is not always in a "good mood." Shall we survey the Scriptures together?

According to grace teacher Chuck Crisco:

> The good news...is that he is happy in his relationship with you because of what Christ has done. He has established you in a state that brings him immense joy because he has established you "in Christ." Even when his children make mistakes, are

> immature and fail, Father God wants you to believe he is not manic depressive in his heart toward you. He is not angry one minute, indifferent the next and then glad when you finally get it right. No, there is an abiding joyful attitude toward us. God is in a good mood.[4]

There is much truth in what Chuck Crisco writes, but again, does it tell the whole story? Is God always "in a good mood"?

Benjamin Dunn's book *The Happy Gospel* is subtitled *Effortless Union With a Happy God*, and he finds support for this view of the Lord as a "happy God" in 1 Timothy 1:11, where Paul makes reference to "'the glad-message of the happy God' as Rotherham translates it."[5] Most other translations render this with "the blessed God," but it is true that the Greek word used for "blessed" is *makarios*, which often means "truly happy" (as in the Beatitudes in Matthew 5:3–12). So, is God always "happy"?

Psalm 16 teaches us that in God's presence is fullness of joy (Ps. 16:11), while Nehemiah 8:10 reminds us that "the joy of the LORD is [our] strength," which would imply that we receive that joy from Him. Hebrews 12:22 tells us that, through the new covenant, we "have come to thousands upon thousands of angels in joyful assembly" (NIV), while Zephaniah 3:17 paints this incredible picture of our God when His people are restored: "The LORD your God is in your midst, a mighty one who will save; he will rejoice over you with gladness; he will quiet you by his love; he will exult over you with loud singing." That is our God and King—a rejoicing, singing God![6]

According to Luke 15:7 and 10, there is joy in God's presence over one sinner who repents, and surely, day and night, sinners are repenting and being saved, which means there must be a lot of joy before His throne. And so, on the earthly side of things, when the gospel brought liberty and salvation to the people of Samaria, "there was much joy in that city" (Acts 8:8).

As for Jesus Himself, Hebrews 1:9, quoting Psalm 45:7, tells us that He was anointed with the oil of joy beyond His companions, while Luke 10:21 speaks of Him being full of joy by the Holy Spirit. And Jesus gave instructions to His disciples so "that my joy may be in you, and that your joy may be full" (John 15:11). Joy itself is a fruit of the Spirit (Gal. 5:22).

As one believer explained:

> The atmosphere of his throne room is filled with joy. When we come into his presence we will be filled with joy (Jude 24). The ground, temple, angels (Job 38:7), everything that makes up heaven oozes with joy. It's thicker than poi; fatter than the pork steaming forth from fresh lau lau (Hawaiian dish). It behooves us then to walk in a place of joy and peace, not fear, anger, stress, worry, or hatred. We are citizens of heaven (Ephesians 2:19) and should reflect its characteristics. We should be the most joyful people on the face of this earth. We represent heaven.[7]

But that is only part of the story, and there is a reason Ecclesiastes tells us that there is "a time to weep, and a time to laugh; a time to mourn, and a time to dance" (Eccles. 3:4). That's why the Gospels speak of Jesus being angry, being grieved, being burdened, and weeping. And He is the express image and exact reflection of the Father! In fact, throughout the Bible God is depicted as being both angry and joyful, both displeased and pleased, both overflowing with wrath and overflowing with love. And that's why Paul exhorted the Gentile believers in Rome to "note…the kindness and the severity [or, sternness or harshness] of God: severity toward those who have fallen [meaning Jewish unbelievers], but God's kindness to you, provided you continue in his kindness. Otherwise you too will be cut off" (Rom. 11:22).

Modern grace teachers want us to focus almost exclusively on God's kindness, as if there was no possibility that His severity could ever apply to us. Paul taught otherwise, explaining to the Roman believers that yes, Jewish branches of the olive tree "were broken off because of their unbelief, but you stand fast through faith. So do not become proud, but fear" (Rom. 11:20). This is a stern warning from the apostle, one of many in his writings.

Back to Where It All Began

Let's go all the way back to the beginning of human history. Was God in a good mood when Adam and Eve sinned in the garden? Was

He in a good mood when He drove them out of the garden? Was He in a good mood when He confronted Cain after Cain had killed his brother Abel? Was He in a good mood—was He "happy"—when He had to destroy every living creature on the earth in Noah's day, aside from Noah and his family? The Bible tells us, "The LORD saw that the wickedness of man was great in the earth, and that every intention of the thoughts of his heart was only evil continually. And *the Lord regretted that he had made man on the earth, and it grieved him to his heart*" (Gen. 6:5–6).

God experiencing regret? God's heart being grieved? Would you call this "God being in a good mood"? "So the Lord said, 'I will blot out man whom I have created from the face of the land, man and animals and creeping things and birds of the heavens, for I am sorry that I have made them'" (v. 7).

Do you think the Lord said these words in a jovial, happy-go-lucky way? Do you think He smiled and laughed as He destroyed every human being on the planet—the people He lovingly fashioned and made for His glory and purposes—along with the entire animal creation?

> And all flesh died that moved on the earth, birds, livestock, beasts, all swarming creatures that swarm on the earth, and all mankind. Everything on the dry land in whose nostrils was the breath of life died. He blotted out every living thing that was on the face of the ground, man and animals and creeping things and birds of the heavens. They were blotted out from the earth. Only Noah was left, and those who were with him in the ark.
>
> —GENESIS 7:21–23

Was there a party in heaven when this was taking place? In *God Is in a Good Mood*, author Chuck Crisco asks the question, "What if God is in party mode all the time?"[8] (In the second edition of the book, now titled *Extraordinary Gospel: Experiencing the Goodness of God*, this is changed to, "What if God is in celebration mode all the time?"). Party mode? Celebration mode? While He wiped out His precious creation with a flood?

Centuries later, after the Israelites sinned with the golden calf,

Moses spent forty days and nights lying prostrate before the Lord, eating no bread and drinking no water because of his people's evil deeds. "For I was afraid," Moses said, "*of the anger and hot displeasure* that the LORD bore against you, so that he was ready to destroy you" (Deut. 9:19). Does this sound like God was "happy"? Yes, He heard Moses's prayer and did not wipe out the nation, but to think that He was in a good mood at a tragic time like this would be to paint a false picture of God.

And this was the constant pattern in the Old Testament where God reached out to His people time and time again, calling them to repentance and offering them life and mercy if they would only turn back to Him, but they consistently refused. This caused Him great pain, as He expressed numerous times, especially in the prophetic books,[9] even describing Himself as a devoted husband whose wife was committing adultery with everyone who passed by.[10] Was He happy when His beloved bride was, spiritually speaking, fornicating with other lovers, worshipping gods of wood and stone, destroying herself in the process?

Was He happy when the people of Judah were burning their babies alive to the god Molech? (See Jeremiah 7:28–34; 19:1–15.) Would you call these the words of a "happy God"? "Therefore thus says the Lord GOD: Behold, my anger and my wrath will be poured out on this place, upon man and beast, upon the trees of the field and the fruit of the ground; it will burn and not be quenched" (Jer. 7:20).

Or do you think this is a picture of God being in "party" (or "celebration") mode?

> The LORD, the God of their fathers, sent persistently to them by his messengers, because he had compassion on his people and on his dwelling place. But they kept mocking the messengers of God, despising his words and scoffing at his prophets, until the wrath of the LORD rose against his people, until there was no remedy. Therefore he brought up against them the king of the Chaldeans, who killed their young men with the sword in the house of their sanctuary and had no compassion on young man or virgin, old man or aged. He gave them all into his hand.
>
> —2 CHRONICLES 36:15–17

I could easily quote scores of similar verses from the Old Testament, including many that speak of God's broken heart, of His grief and pain, of His fierce wrath and burning anger. But for now, let's jump over to the New Testament, remembering that when we see Jesus, we see the Father.

Was Jesus in a good mood when He sighed over the unbelief of His fellow Jews? "The Pharisees came and began to argue with him, seeking from him a sign from heaven to test him. And he sighed deeply in his spirit and said, 'Why does this generation seek a sign? Truly, I say to you, no sign will be given to this generation'" (Mark 8:11–12).

Was He in a good mood when He rebuked the hypocritical religious leaders, pronouncing seven woes on them, using stinging words like these: "Woe to you, scribes and Pharisees, hypocrites! For you shut the kingdom of heaven in people's faces. For you neither enter yourselves nor allow those who would enter to go in" (Matt. 23:13). Would you say Jesus was "happy" when He made these shattering pronouncements?

Was He in a good mood when He wept over Jerusalem and said:

> Would that you, even you, had known on this day the things that make for peace! But now they are hidden from your eyes. For the days will come upon you, when your enemies will set up a barricade around you and surround you and hem you in on every side and tear you down to the ground, you and your children within you. And they will not leave one stone upon another in you, because you did not know the time of your visitation.
>
> —Luke 19:42–44

Did He say these words with a big grin on His face, winking at His disciples as they smiled back at Him? Was He in a party mode at this time?

Was He in a good mood in the Garden of Gethsemane when He took Peter, Jacob (James), and John with Him, and "began to be deeply distressed and troubled"? Was He in a good mood when He said to them, "My soul is overwhelmed with sorrow to the point of death"? (Mark 14:33–34, NIV). Is this how we describe being "happy" or in a "celebration mode"? Were the disciples slapping one another on the back and laughing with joy as they heard Him speak these words of agony?

A God of Mercy and of Wrath

It really is superficial to make the blanket, unqualified statement that God is always in a good mood. The very fact that we are created in His image and can experience both holy joy and holy grief, both holy love and holy indignation, should tell us that it is misleading and, at times, downright wrong to say, "God is always in a good mood." Why should He be?

It is one thing to say, "All the time, God is good. God is good, all the time." That is 100 percent true. It's another thing entirely to say that, "God is always in a good mood." Not so!

Is He in a good mood when His children are hurting? Is He in a good mood when they believe wrong things about Him, causing them to run away from Him rather than to Him? Is He in a good mood when He hears the cries of suffering babies and children around the world?

Isaiah 63:9 tells us that in all Israel's affliction, He was afflicted, while Hebrews reminds us that "we do not have a high priest who is unable to sympathize with our weaknesses, but one who in every respect has been tempted as we are, yet without sin" (Heb. 4:15). Surely our God is moved with His people's pain, and that is *because* He is so good and compassionate and caring and kind.

Was Jesus in a good mood when He spoke through John to some of the congregations in Asia Minor in Revelation 2–3? To the believers in Thyatira He said:

> I have this against you, that you tolerate that woman Jezebel, who calls herself a prophetess and is teaching and seducing my servants to practice sexual immorality and to eat food sacrificed to idols. I gave her time to repent, but she refuses to repent of her sexual immorality. Behold, I will throw her onto a sickbed, and those who commit adultery with her I will throw into great tribulation, unless they repent of her works, and I will strike her children dead. And all the churches will know that I am he who

> searches mind and heart, and I will give to each of you according to your works.
>
> —REVELATION 2:20–23

Do you think He said this with a mischievous twinkle in His eye or sang the words to a cute little tune? Was Jesus beside Himself with joy as He threatened to "strike her children dead"? And did John record these words and say, "Let's party, God! You rock!" Chuck Crisco wrote that, "We see that Jesus Christ is always in a good mood toward us,"[11] but even that more nuanced statement is not entirely true.

And what about the people in the world who reject Him? Is He always in a good mood toward them? In Revelation 6 John describes a staggering vision of judgment as the sixth seal is opened:

> When he opened the sixth seal, I looked, and behold, there was a great earthquake, and the sun became black as sackcloth, the full moon became like blood, and the stars of the sky fell to the earth as the fig tree sheds its winter fruit when shaken by a gale. The sky vanished like a scroll that is being rolled up, and every mountain and island was removed from its place.
>
> —REVELATION 6:12–14

In response, John records:

> Then the kings of the earth and the great ones and the generals and the rich and the powerful, and everyone, slave and free, hid themselves in the caves and among the rocks of the mountains, calling to the mountains and rocks, "Fall on us and hide us from the face of him who is seated on the throne, and from the wrath of the Lamb, for the great day of their wrath has come, and who can stand?"
>
> —REVELATION 6:15–17

Would all these people, great and small alike, cowering in terror at "the face of him who is seated on the throne, and…the wrath of the Lamb" agree that God is always in a good mood? Would they describe God and the Lamb as being "jocular" or "happy" on the "the great day of their wrath"? And is it a coincidence that Paul speaks of God's *wrath* seventeen times in his letters?[12]

While some contemporary teachers want to emphasize that "God is always in a good mood," Paul wanted to emphasize that our loving, compassionate Father, the God of all grace and comfort and mercy, was also a God of wrath:

> The wrath of God is being revealed from heaven against all the godlessness and wickedness of men who suppress the truth by their wickedness.... For those who are self-seeking and who reject the truth and follow evil, there will be wrath and anger. There will be trouble and distress for every human being who does evil: first for the Jew, then for the Gentile.... Let no one deceive you with empty words, for because of such things God's wrath comes on those who are disobedient.... Because of these [sins], the wrath of God is coming.
>
> —Romans 1:18; 2:8–9;
> Ephesians 5:6;
> Colossians 3:6, niv

We say, "Be carefree! God is always in a good mood!" Paul said, "Be careful! The wrath of God is coming."

According to Revelation 19:15, Jesus is described as the one who "treads the winepress of the fury of the wrath of God Almighty" (niv). Other translations say, "It is he who treads the winepress from which flows the wine of the furious rage of ADONAI, God of heaven's armies" (cjb); "He will release the fierce wrath of God, the Almighty, like juice flowing from a winepress" (nlt); "and He treads the wine press of the fierce wrath of God, the Almighty" (nas); "and he treadeth the winepress of the fierceness and wrath of Almighty God" (kjv).

Does this sound like a fun event to you? Do you think Jesus will be laughing as He does this? And what of the fact that *it is Jesus* who will tread this winepress of divine wrath? Does that fit into your picture of Him? Paul also describes a most dreadful day:

> ...when the Lord Jesus [will be] revealed from heaven with his mighty angels in flaming fire, inflicting vengeance on those who do not know God and on those who do not obey the gospel of our Lord Jesus. They will suffer the punishment of eternal destruction, away from the presence of the Lord and from the glory of

> his might, when he comes on that day to be glorified in his saints, and to be marveled at among all who have believed, because our testimony to you was believed.
>
> —2 THESSALONIANS 1:7–10

Is this part of our preaching and teaching? Is this part of the picture of the Lord we want to see?

Revising Scripture

What, then, do the modern grace teachers do with these verses on wrath? Some of them simply say, "Yes, we believe that God's wrath is coming, but it is not for believers, since we have not been appointed to wrath." (See 1 Thessalonians 5:9; 1:10.)

I agree with this to a point: God's wrath is never for His new covenant children. (His discipline and loving judgment, yes; His wrath, no.) But my question to my hyper-grace friends is this: If you believe God's wrath is coming, why do you hardly ever (if ever) speak about it? And why don't you warn the world about it?

Taking this a step further, why did Paul and the other authors of the New Testament speak about it often, whereas modern grace teachers give the impression that it has no place in their message at all? And why, for that matter, did the New Testament speak to us, God's people, His children, so often about His wrath? Why is this important for us to understand too? What does it tell us about the character of God and the nature of holiness and the ugliness of sin?

Other modern grace teachers actually *make God's wrath disappear*—I'm not exaggerating—simply translating it out of their Bibles. A perfect example of this is found in Mick Mooney's expanded paraphrase of Paul's prison letters (Ephesians, Colossians, Philippians, and Philemon). Some of his work is excellent and really inspiring, but some of it is simply wrong—very wrong. In some places he imposes his theology on the Word of God rather than building his theology from the Word.

For example, some hyper-grace teachers have a problem with the idea that we can grieve the Spirit, but Ephesians 4:30 says, "And do not grieve the Holy Spirit of God, by whom you were sealed for the day of redemption." In Mooney's paraphrase, this becomes:

> The Holy Spirit is now living in you, so remind yourself of his wonderful presence in your life, and, in accordance with his leading, empty yourself of any remaining bitterness, rage and anger. Allow the full work of the Spirit to heal and refresh your inner being so that you may be kind and compassionate to one another.[13]

Grieving the Spirit is totally gone! What about passages speaking to believers about God's wrath? Paul wrote this in Ephesians 5:5–6: "For you may be sure of this, that everyone who is sexually immoral or impure, or who is covetous (that is, an idolater), has no inheritance in the kingdom of Christ and God. Let no one deceive you with empty words, for because of these things the wrath of God comes upon the sons of disobedience."

This is how it reads in the Mooney paraphrase:

> God's kingdom is one of love, and those who indulge in the immoral and impure things of this world have not yet crossed over into God's kingdom. Don't let anyone deceive you with empty words, for your salvation is not empty of power, but powerful enough to free you from all the things that deceive and trap those still walking along darkened paths.[14]

God's wrath is totally gone! In another passage where Paul warns about God's coming wrath, Mooney this time puts the wrath on Jesus at the cross. In Colossians 3:5–6, Paul wrote, "Put to death therefore what is earthly in you: sexual immorality, impurity, passion, evil desire, and covetousness, which is idolatry. On account of these the wrath of God is coming." Mick Mooney changed this to:

> Don't seek the things that belong to your old, earthly nature. Things that arouse lust and greed and entice you to pursue evil desires. For we know that Christ carried the punishment for all these unloving acts and passions. Remember that Jesus loved not only us, but the entire world so much that he took the wrath

> of God's punishment for all these unloving and self gratifying actions so that we could be free from them.[15]

How remarkable and how revealing. This "grace paraphrase" actually rewrites Scripture, eliminating God's coming wrath entirely and instead putting it on Jesus in the past.[16] It is serious business to tamper with the Word.

What makes this all the more unfortunate is that Mick Mooney has so many wonderful things to say in his paraphrase and in some of his other writings, such as *Look! The Finished Work of Jesus*.[17] But, along with the other hyper-grace teachers, I believe he mixes glorious truth with serious error, and his "grace paraphrase" serves as a glaring case in point.

In the same way, the *Mirror Bible* translation of Francois du Toit consistently removes references to God's wrath, despite the translator's obvious gifts and insights. Romans 1:18 reads: "For the wrath of God is revealed from heaven against all ungodliness and unrighteousness of men, who by their unrighteousness suppress the truth." In *The Mirror Bible* it becomes: "The righteousness of God that is endorsed in the heavens is in such contrast to the counterfeit earthly reference that blindfolds people in their own unrighteousness." What?

Let's look again at Ephesians 5:5–6, where Paul wrote: "For you may be sure of this, that everyone who is sexually immoral or impure, or who is covetous (that is, an idolater), has no inheritance in the kingdom of Christ and God. Let no one deceive you with empty words, for because of these things the wrath of God comes upon the sons of disobedience."

In the *Mirror Bible* this now becomes:

> The Christ-life gives distinct definition to the kingdom of God. You cannot live a double-standard life. Abusing people through adultery, lust, and greed is like worshipping a distorted image of yourself, which is what idolatry is all about. Avoid any association with those who employ hollow words to entice you; unbelief only produces a breed of people that distorts the pattern of their design as image bearers of God; this certainly does not please God.[18]

In similar fashion, Colossians 3:6, "On account of these the wrath of God is coming," becomes, "These distorted expressions are in total contradiction to God's design and desire for your life." Yes, "wrath" has completely disappeared once again!

Note also Hebrews 10:31, "It is a fearful thing to fall into the hands of the living God," which becomes, "What a foolish thing it would be to deliberately shun the hands that bled for your salvation." That is not the picture Hebrews is presenting here! The same applies for Hebrews 12:29, where a strong exhortation in verses 25–28 ends with, "for our God is a consuming fire." In the *Mirror Bible* this is now, "His jealousy over us burns like fire," which is true, but hardly what the author wanted to communicate here when he cited these words from Deuteronomy 4: "Take care, lest you forget the covenant of the LORD your God, which he made with you, and make a carved image, the form of anything that the LORD your God has forbidden you. For the LORD your God is a consuming fire, a jealous God" (vv. 23–24). This is then followed by promises of severe judgment on Israel if they turn away from the Lord.

And just as Mick Mooney's wonderful insights are severely damaged by the glaring omissions in his paraphrase, so also Francois du Toit's brilliant and beautiful renderings, which often underscore the ugliness of sin and the high calling of God's people, are greatly undermined by the changes he makes, like in the translation of Romans 14:10–12. In the English Standard Version, it reads, "Why do you pass judgment on your brother? Or you, why do you despise your brother? For we will all stand before the judgment seat of God; for it is written, 'As I live, says the Lord, every knee shall bow to me, and every tongue shall confess to God.' So then each of us will give an account of himself to God." Remarkably, in the *Mirror Bible*, this is rendered:

> What qualifies you to be your brother's judge? On what grounds do you condemn your brother? All of us stand in the footprint of Christ. (We are equally represented in him.) The prophet recorded what he heard God say, "My own life is the guarantee of my conviction, says the Lord, every knee shall freely bow to me in worship, and every tongue shall spontaneously speak from

> the same God-inspired source." Thus the logic of God will find its personal expression in every person.[19]

Say good-bye to our future day of accounting! But what else should we expect from a translation that turns the strong words of Jacob (James) into something very different than what he wrote. In the midst of one of the strongest wake-up calls in the New Testament, Jacob (James) said: "Draw near to God, and he will draw near to you. Cleanse your hands, you sinners, and purify your hearts, you double-minded" (Jacob [James] 4:8). In the *Mirror Bible* this becomes: **"Snuggle up to the warm embrace of God, experience his closeness to you** (In Christ he cancelled every definition of distance or delay.). **The sinner can come with all stains washed from his hands; the double-minded can come with a purified heart"** (du Toit's emphasis).

What a rewriting of the Word—and note how the translator's theology forces him to change the plain sense of the Greek, which specifically speaks of sinning believers needing to draw near to God (since they obviously distanced themselves from Him) and of the promise that God will draw near to them. This cannot be allowed to stand, since "In Christ he cancelled every definition of distance or delay." As for the "snuggle up" rendering, just read the rest of Jacob's [James] letter and ask yourself if he was in a "cuddly" mood—or if he presented God as being "cuddly."

At the end of a useful online article on hell, Paul Ellis wrote, "The condemnation of hell has no place in the gospel of grace."[20] He explained:

> Jesus' gospel was not, "Come to God or you'll burn in hell," but "God's kingdom is at hand and you can participate in it." He was not interested in scaring the hell out of people but inviting all to enter the kingdom of heaven. His invitation still stands.
>
> We haven't been commissioned to preach the bad news of hell but the good news of the kingdom. As Darrin Hufford has said, "God never delights in people getting what they deserve. He is about saving us from what we deserve." That's grace. That's the good news. And that's the message the world most needs to hear.[21]

Then why did Jesus, the ultimate good news preacher (see Mark 1:15),[22] warn His listeners about hell in such vivid terms? Why did He speak to *His disciples* about the future judgment of hellfire in the Sermon on the Mount? Why did He say to His Jewish audience in Luke 13, "Unless you repent, you will all likewise perish" (v. 3)?

What was the purpose of His many parables that warned about future judgment?[23] What was He trying to communicate in His parable of the sheep and the goats, which ends with the words, "And these will go away into eternal punishment, but the righteous into eternal life" (Matt. 25:46)? At the end of the parable of the wheat and the tares, Jesus explained:

> The Son of Man will send his angels, and they will gather out of his kingdom all causes of sin and all law-breakers, and throw them into the fiery furnace. In that place there will be weeping and gnashing of teeth. Then the righteous will shine like the sun in the kingdom of their Father. He who has ears, let him hear.
>
> —MATTHEW 13:41–43

Does this have no place in the gospel of grace? The Book of Acts features a number of sermons that the apostles and others preached to the lost. This is how the first one ends: "And with many other words [Peter] bore witness and continued to exhort them, saying, 'Save yourselves from this crooked generation'" (Acts 2:40). In his next sermon he gave this exhortation: "Moses said, 'The Lord God will raise up for you a prophet like me from your brothers. You shall listen to him in whatever he tells you. And it shall be that every soul who does not listen to that prophet shall be destroyed from the people'" (Acts 3:22–23).

Were these not "grace"-based messages? Did Peter not understand that warnings like this were supposedly out of place in a gospel message? Was he presenting a false view of God?

Paul followed in Peter's footsteps, preaching the forgiveness of sins through Jesus and then warning of the consequences of rejecting the message:

> Let it be known to you therefore, brothers, that through this man forgiveness of sins is proclaimed to you, and by him everyone

> who believes is freed from everything from which you could not be freed by the law of Moses. Beware, therefore, lest what is said in the Prophets should come about: "Look, you scoffers, be astounded and perish; for I am doing a work in your days, a work that you will not believe, even if one tells it to you."
>
> —ACTS 13:38–41

Paul ended his outreach message on Mars Hill in Athens even more strongly, stating, "The times of ignorance God overlooked, but now he commands all people everywhere to repent, because he has fixed a day on which he will judge the world in righteousness by a man whom he has appointed; and of this he has given assurance to all by raising him from the dead" (Acts 17:30–31).

What? Paul preaching a hardcore repentance message?[24] What? Paul warned of the day in which God "will judge the world in righteousness" through Jesus? Perhaps this is also why Paul reasoned with Felix "about righteousness and self-control and the coming judgment" when he spoke with him about "faith in Christ Jesus" (Acts 24:24–25).

Of course the condemnation of hell has a place in the gospel of grace. In fact, it underscores the gracious message of the cross, since we all deserved hell because of our sins, but God showed "his love for us in that while we were still sinners, Christ died for us" (Rom. 5:8). And, as Paul continues, "Since, therefore, we have now been justified by his blood, much more shall we be saved by him from the wrath of God. For if while we were enemies we were reconciled to God by the death of his Son, much more, now that we are reconciled, shall we be saved by his life" (vv. 9–10).

To be sure, we do not threaten believers with hell or tell God's children that He's an angry God who is out to get them. Heaven forbid! But we do need to tell both believers and unbelievers the whole truth about God, and, sadly, the hyper-grace teachers are painting a one-sided picture, even though much of the picture is precious, beautiful, and absolutely essential. There's just more to the picture than they preach and teach.

I believe that many of my friends who emphasize that "God is always in a good mood" want to express some of what A. W. Tozer was trying to convey when he wrote:

> Always remember that God is easy to get along with, and if your heart is right, He is not too concerned with the formula. God is kind and good and gracious, because there are some of us who are just too hard to get along with. If God were as hard to get along with as we are, there would be a perpetual quarrel between our souls and God. God has to be easy to live with, and if He knows you mean right, He will let you make all sorts of mistakes [Tozer is speaking here of not doing things in a proper "religious" order] and will not care.[25]

But that is not all Tozer had to say. He also wrote: "God knows that the most mature of us still need coddling sometimes, and so He is quick to overlook our ignorance, but He is never quick to overlook our sins. The threatening aspect of our lives is sin, and so God is quick to leap on the scene and deal with it."[26]

And how does our sin affect God? Tozer wrote, "A man by his sin may waste himself, which is to waste that which on earth is most like God. This is man's greatest tragedy and God's heaviest grief."[27]

The simple fact that God is love (1 John 4:8) makes clear that He cannot be "happy" all the time or always in a "good mood." As the saintly German Christian leader Basilea Schlink wrote, "Anyone who loves as much as God does, cannot help suffering. And anyone who really loves God will sense that He is suffering."[28]

This is the price of love.

-11-

MARCION REVISITED

Marcion was an influential, heretical church leader who died more than eighteen hundred years ago. Although his name is unknown to most believers today, there are many who follow in his theological footsteps, even if they are not as radical as he was. Marcion taught that the God of the Old Testament was different from the God of the New Testament, and he rejected the Old Testament Scriptures in their entirety along with portions of the New Testament, including most of the four Gospels.

According to the German critical scholar Adolph Von Harnack, who embraced many of Marcion's ideas:

> Completely carried away with the novelty, uniqueness and grandeur of the Pauline Gospel of the grace of God in Christ, Marcion felt that all other conceptions of the Gospel, and especially its union with the Old Testament religion, was opposed to, and a backsliding from the truth. He accordingly supposed that it was necessary to make the sharp antitheses of Paul, law and gospel, wrath and grace, works and faith, flesh and spirit, sin and righteousness, death and life, that is the Pauline criticism of the Old Testament religion, the foundation of his religious views, and to refer them to two principles, the righteous and wrathful god of the Old Testament, who is at the same time identical with the creator of the world, and the God of the Gospel, quite unknown before Christ, who is only love and mercy.[1]

Does this sound familiar? More and more Christian leaders today are making a sharp contrast between the God of the Old Testament and the God of the New Testament, even if they believe, contrary to Marcion, that this was still the same God. And while they would agree that the Old Testament is God's inspired Word, in actual practice, they see little value in the Old Testament for believers today aside from some lessons from history, some character studies, some prophetic promises, some wisdom from Proverbs, and some "positive" psalms. And among modern grace teachers, the primary usage of the Old Testament seems to be one of contrast: we see how good grace is by seeing how bad the Law was. Many of these teachers even claim that the teachings of Jesus were "under the old covenant" and no longer relevant for us. (For more on this, see chapter 13.) It is very serious and potentially dangerous, theologically and spiritually, to dismiss parts of Scripture.

In case you think I'm exaggerating, consider this statement from Andre van der Merwe in his book *GRACE: The Forbidden Gospel*:

> At the risk of sounding critical, it remains a sad reality that the Bible Society chose to combine the Old and New Testaments into one single book. This single decision has caused widespread confusion within the ranks of believers throughout the world. Many of the writings in the Bible before the cross portray God to be a harsh, cruel being, set on destroying and punishing people if they dared to disobey the set of moral standards represented by the 10 Commandments and the other laws.[2]

These are some astounding claims. First, there is no "Bible Society" that made some "decision" to include the Old Testament with the New Testament in our Bibles. The Old Testament was *the* Bible of the first believers, and over a period of time, other books (eventually called the New Testament) were added to it. But the Old Testament was always recognized as the inspired, God-breathed foundation for everything that followed. As it has often been said, the Old Testament is the New Testament concealed; the New Testament is the Old Testament revealed.

Second, a major reason the Old Testament is causing "widespread confusion within the ranks of believers throughout the world" is that they are being taught an unbalanced message of grace. If they were taught correctly, they would love and cherish the Old Testament. Third, the God of the Old Testament is the wonderful Father of Jesus, not some foreign, lesser god (as Marcion believed), and if we see this God as harsh and cruel, then we don't understand who He really is. Fourth, the implication that there was somehow a problem with either the Ten Commandments themselves or the other moral laws themselves is also a false conception. (We'll address this last point in the next chapter.)

Let's take some time and work this through in greater depth, not wanting to lose any of the precious treasures our God has given us in the Old Testament. As Jesus said, "Therefore every scribe who has been trained for the kingdom of heaven is like a master of a house, who brings out of his treasure what is new and what is old" (Matt. 13:52).

We need to remember that the one and only Bible used by the first followers of Jesus was what we now call the Old Testament. This was the Word of God for them, their beloved and holy Scriptures, and they did not have any concept in any way that these Scriptures were outdated, outmoded, or even "old." What was "old" was the *Sinaitic covenant*, which was being replaced by the new (and better) covenant, as prophesied in the Old Testament by Jeremiah (Jer. 31:31–34). But none of Jesus' followers believed that the Hebrew Scriptures were part of an "old" and soon to be replaced Book. Perish the thought. They loved every word of the sacred scriptural scrolls they had, and if you asked them about the "Old Testament," they would have had no idea what you were talking about. All they knew that was this collection of books was the Word of God, the Scriptures, what we now call the Old Testament.[3]

That's why Jesus constantly pointed to the Old Testament witness, telling His fellow Jews that if they believed Moses, they would believe Him (John 5:39–47), and that's why His disciples were reminded of Old Testament verses when they watched His ministry (e.g., John 2:13–17, with reference to Psalm 69:9). And that's why, when Jesus was tempted by Satan in the wilderness, He resisted him by quoting three times from the Book of Deuteronomy (Matt. 4:1–10). (When is the last time you went to Deuteronomy for spiritual nurture and renewal?) And that's why Paul wrote this *about the Hebrew Scriptures*: "All Scripture is breathed out by God and profitable for teaching, for reproof, for correction, and for training in righteousness, that the man of God may be competent, equipped for every good work" (2 Tim. 3:16–17).

Do we believe this today? Do we practice it? Do we use the Old Testament "for teaching, for reproof, for correction, and for training in righteousness, that the man of God may be competent, equipped for every good work"? Could it be that Paul, who had such an incredible revelation of grace, knew something we don't? (Think of *that*: when Paul preached on grace, the Bible he used was the Old Testament!) And could it be that leaders and believers will *not* be fully "competent, equipped for every good work" if they willfully neglect the Old Testament?

But that's not all he said about the Hebrew Bible, called the Tanakh by Jews.[4] According to Paul, the Old Testament was written to give us hope, helping us to persevere: "For whatever was written in former days was written for our instruction, that through endurance and through the encouragement of the Scriptures we might have hope" (Rom. 15:4). Read this once more, substituting the words "the Old Testament" for "the Scriptures," since the only Scriptures his readers had were the Old Testament Scriptures.

You might say, "I accept the fact that we can receive hope by reading the Old Testament, but all those warnings and judgments have no relevance for us today." Are you sure about that? If you are, then you'll have to take on Paul himself. To the Corinthians he wrote,

> For I do not want you to unaware, brothers, that our fathers were all under the cloud, and all passed through the sea, and all were baptized into Moses in the cloud and in the sea, and all ate the same spiritual food, and all drank the same spiritual drink. For they drank from the spiritual Rock that followed them, and the Rock was Christ. Nevertheless, with most of them God was not pleased, for they were overthrown in the wilderness
>
> —1 CORINTHIANS 10:1–5

What does this have to do with New Testament believers? Paul continues:

> *Now these things took place as examples for us, that we might not desire evil as they did.* Do not be idolaters as some of them were;

> as it is written, "The people sat down to eat and drink and rose up to play." We must not indulge in sexual immorality as some of them did, and twenty-three thousand fell in a single day. We must not put Christ to the test, as some of them did and were destroyed by serpents, nor grumble, as some of them did and were destroyed by the Destroyer. *Now these things happened to them as an example, but they were written down for our instruction, on whom the end of the ages has come.* Therefore let anyone who thinks that he stands take heed lest he fall.
>
> —1 CORINTHIANS 10:6–12

This sounds like a serious warning to me! If not, what is Paul saying? What's the use of him writing about how Israel sinned and how God judged His people back then if this has no application for us today? The author of Hebrews actually tells us a number of times that the consequences of our rejecting the gospel are far more severe than were the consequences of Israel's rejecting the Law. (I discuss the relevant verses in chapter 7.) Paul is warning the church: don't do what the Israelites did; otherwise there will be consequences.

Yes, Paul, the ultimate grace preacher, wrote these words in 1 Corinthians 10, and if this doesn't mesh with your understanding of grace, don't try to change Paul. Change your understanding of grace. You don't want grace with human mixture. You want true, pure, unadulterated grace.

The Old Validates the New

Here's another example from 1 Corinthians where Paul uses the Old Testament once again, this time as he explains how seriously we are to take persistent, unrepentant sin within the body. Speaking about a man who was in a relationship with his father's wife, he wrote: "When you are assembled in the name of the Lord Jesus and my spirit is present, with the power of our Lord Jesus, you are to deliver this man to Satan for the destruction of the flesh, so that his spirit may be saved in the day of the Lord" (1 Cor. 5:4–5). This is extreme counsel, but that's how dangerous the spreading of unchecked, unrepentant sin is.

He continued:

> I wrote to you in my letter not to associate with sexually immoral people—not at all meaning the sexually immoral of this world, or the greedy and swindlers, or idolaters, since then you would need to go out of the world. But now I am writing to you not to associate with anyone who bears the name of brother if he is guilty of sexual immorality or greed, or is an idolater, reviler, drunkard, or swindler—not even to eat with such a one. For what have I to do with judging outsiders? Is it not those inside the church whom you are to judge? God judges those outside. "Purge the evil person from among you."
>
> —1 CORINTHIANS 5:9–13

Paul ends this very strong exhortation with a quotation that occurs *nine times* in Deuteronomy: "So you shall purge the evil from your midst" (Deut. 13:5; see also 17:7, 12; 19:19; 21:9, 21; 22:21, 22, 24). In Deuteronomy, it referred to putting to death an unrepentant, sinning Israelite; in 1 Corinthians, it refers to excommunicating an unrepentant, sinning Christian. But in both cases, the danger of sin is underscored and the prescribed treatment is extreme: death under the Mosaic covenant and excommunication (and, in some cases, even turning the person over to Satan!) under the new covenant.[5]

This is the love of God in action, and it is part of the message of grace, which gets polluted when God's people wink at persistent, flouted sin. And notice that Paul didn't have to give some disclaimer to his readers and say, "I apologize for quoting from that dastardly book of Deuteronomy—from the dreaded Law!" Not at all. This was God's holy, beautiful, wonderful Word, and all the writers of the New Testament quoted it as God's Word—not some lesser book about a lesser god, and not just some book (or collection of books) to be used to contrast how bad things were under the law with how good they are under grace.[6]

In fact, often when the apostles wanted to exhort believers about how to live *today*, they quoted without apology from the Old Testament—or, to state this is more accurately, they quoted the Old Testament scriptures as divine words, words of truth and words of life. So when Peter wanted to exhort his readers to be holy in all their conduct, what did he quote? He quoted Leviticus 19:2, "You shall be holy, for I the LORD your God am holy." (See 1 Peter 1:14–16.) Can you imagine a modern grace preacher today exhorting his readers (or congregants) to be holy in their conduct, and as a basis for his exhortation quoting from Leviticus without qualification?[7]

To put this in further perspective and to give you an idea of just how much the Old Testament is intertwined in the New Testament, consider these facts that I previously cited in the fourth volume of my series devoted to answering Jewish objections to Jesus:

> The pages of the New Testament are filled with citations from the Hebrew Scriptures, with as many as 300 direct quotations from the Tanakh and several thousand allusions to the Hebrew Bible in the New Testament. In fact, some scholars claim that *almost one out of three verses* in the New Testament—2,500 out of a total of 8,000 verses—contains an Old Testament quote or general allusion, while, quite solidly, it can be demonstrated that more than ten percent of the New Testament text is made up of citation or direct allusions to the Old Testament. More than ten percent! The book of Revelation, the last book of the New Testament, contains 404 verses, most of which (as many as 331 verses) are drawn from the imagery of the Hebrew Scriptures, although Revelation hardly ever directly quotes a specific verse from the Tanakh. All this indicates how deeply the Hebrew Scriptures are intertwined in the New Covenant Scriptures.[8]

And I repeat: with rare exception, the Old Testament is *not* quoted in order to set up a contrast with the New Testament but rather to validate, authenticate, and explicate what was taking place in the New Testament. That's why Peter, after pointing to the glory of the Transfiguration as evidence that he was not following "cleverly devised myths" about Jesus the Messiah, pointed back to the prophetic scriptures of the Old Testament. It is to these scriptures that "you will do well to pay attention as to a lamp shining in a dark place, until the day dawns and the morning star rises in your hearts" (2 Pet. 1:16–19). Yes, Peter writes, we saw the Lord glorified with our own eyes, but you, along with us, have the prophetic scriptures of the Old Testament. Pay attention to these glorious words!

And if you really want your theology rocked, consider this. When

Paul was contrasting the righteousness of works with the righteousness of faith, he explained the former by quoting from Leviticus, and he explained the latter by quoting from Deuteronomy. (See Romans 10:5–10.)[9] Yes, he used a text in Deuteronomy, not as a contrast but as a platform for declaring the righteousness that comes by faith. In fact, he saw born-again believers in Jesus as part of a spiritual continuum begun by Abraham, who believed the Lord, and it was counted to him as righteousness (Gen. 15:6, quoted in Rom. 4:3). And when Paul declared that "the righteous shall live by faith" in Romans and Galatians (Rom. 1:17; Gal. 3:11), he was quoting Habakkuk 2:4, which was not given as a prophecy of the new covenant but rather as the calling for God's people, beginning with Israel. That's just some of why Paul could write this in Romans 3: "Do we then overthrow the law by this faith? By no means! On the contrary, we uphold the law" (v. 31).

But there's more: some of the greatest revelations of God's mercy, grace, and compassion are found on the pages of the Old Testament, in passages like these:

> The Lord is compassionate and gracious,
> slow to anger, abounding in steadfast love.
> He will not contend forever,
> or nurse His anger for all time.
> He has not dealt with us according to our sins,
> nor has He requited us according to our iniquities.
> For as the heavens are high above the earth,
> so great is His steadfast love toward those who fear Him.
> As east is far from west,
> so far has He removed our sins from us.
> As a father has compassion for his children,
> so the Lord has compassion for those who fear Him.
> For He knows how we are formed;
> He is mindful that we are dust.
>
> —Psalm 103:8–14, NJV

That's why David could proclaim:

> Bless the Lord, O my soul,
> all my being, His holy name.

Bless the Lord, O my soul
  and do not forget all His bounties.
He forgives all your sins,
  heals all your diseases.
He redeems your life from the Pit,
  surrounds you with steadfast love and mercy.
He satisfies you with good things in the prime of life,
  so that your youth is renewed like the eagle's.

—Psalm 103:1–5, NJV

David experienced this revelation of God's grace and goodness under the Sinai covenant! In fact, the word the New Testament uses for "grace" (*charis* in Greek) is the equivalent of the Hebrew word *hen* (with a guttural "h"), and it is used frequently in the Old Testament to describe God's gracious dealings with His people.[10] And I repeat: this was under the Sinai covenant, since it was the same God at work before the cross and after the cross. And this is the God who revealed Himself to Moses on Sinai, saying:

> The Lord, the Lord [in Hebrew, Yahweh, Yahweh], a God merciful and gracious [Hebrew *hanun*], slow to anger, and abounding in steadfast love and faithfulness, keeping steadfast love for thousands, forgiving iniquity and transgression and sin, but who will by no means clear the guilty, visiting the iniquity of the fathers on the children and the children's children, to the third and the fourth generation.
>
> —Exodus 34:6–7

That's why the prophet Micah, whose name is probably short for "Who is like God?" or "Who is like Yahweh?", ended his book with these words:

Who is a God like You,
Forgiving iniquity
And remitting transgression;
Who has not maintained His wrath forever
Against the remnant of His own people,
Because He loves graciousness!
He will take us back in love;

> He will cover up our iniquities,
> You will hurl all our sins
> Into the depths of the sea.
> You will keep faith with Jacob,
> Loyalty to Abraham,
> As You promised on oath to our fathers
> In days gone by.
>
> —Micah 7:17–20, njv

Yes, this was a revelation of God's mercy, grace, and compassion given under the Sinai covenant—and there are scores of other passages that could be quoted to support this. That's why John 1:17 does *not* say, "For the law was given through Moses; *but* grace and truth came through Jesus Christ." No, the word "but" does not occur between these two statements. Rather, John wrote, "For the law was given through Moses; grace and truth came through Jesus Christ." The first was glorious. The second was even more glorious! The first was the foundation. The second built upon it rather than tore it down.

And that's actually what Paul was teaching in 2 Corinthians 3, where he called the Sinai covenant, epitomized in the Ten Commandments written in stone, the "ministry of death" and the "ministry of condemnation" (2 Cor. 3:7, 9). To be sure, the contrast is certainly dramatic, and it does underscore the surpassing glory of the new covenant, which is one of the reasons I love the message of grace so much. But notice what he wrote: the Sinai covenant did come with glory, but that glory is totally surpassed by the glory of the new covenant in Jesus.

The Law Was Not Flawed, We Were

How then could he refer to the Sinai covenant (and note carefully that he did *not* say the whole Old Testament) as the "ministry of death" and the "ministry of condemnation"? It was *not* because the covenant was flawed or, God forbid, the laws were flawed. It was because *we* were flawed, as explained in Hebrews:

> For if that first covenant had been faultless, there would have been no occasion to look for a second. For he finds fault *with them* [meaning the people of Israel] when he says: "Behold, the

> days are coming, declares the Lord, when I will establish a new covenant with the house of Israel and with the house of Judah, not like the covenant that I made with their fathers on the day when I took them by the hand to bring them out of the land of Egypt. For they did not continue in my covenant, and so I showed no concern for them, declares the Lord."
>
> —Hebrews 8:7–9,
> quoting from Jeremiah 31:31–32

Did you catch that? The problem was not with the laws themselves. The problem was with the people, sinful human beings. This is what Paul explained to the Romans (and note carefully the words I have italicized):

> *What then shall we say? That the law is sin? By no means!* Yet if it had not been for the law, I would not have known sin. For I would not have known what it is to covet if the law had not said, "You shall not covet." But sin, seizing an opportunity through the commandment, produced in me all kinds of covetousness. For apart from the law, sin lies dead. I was once alive apart from the law, but when the commandment came, sin came alive and I died. *The very commandment that promised life proved to be death to me.* For sin, seizing an opportunity through the commandment, deceived me and through it killed me. *So the law is holy, and the commandment is holy and righteous and good.*
>
> *Did that which is good, then, bring death to me? By no means!* It was sin, producing death in me through what is good, in order that sin might be shown to be sin, and through the commandment might become sinful beyond measure. *For we know that the law is spiritual, but I am of the flesh, sold under sin.*
>
> —Romans 7:7–14[11]

Let's put this in one sentence. Speaking of the Law (meaning at least the Ten Commandments, if not the whole of the Mosaic Law), Paul said twice that it was holy, twice that it was good, once that it was righteous, once that it was spiritual, and once that it promised life. That is saying a lot! Let's repeat this out loud together: the Law is holy, righteous, good, and spiritual—and it promises life! That's why Moses exhorted the Israelites to "choose life"—and he meant doing so by choosing to obey the Law (Deut. 30:15–20). And that's why God said in Leviticus that life was to be found in keeping the commandments (Lev. 18:5).[12]

To say it again: the problem was not with God's Law. The problem was with us, sinful human beings. The Law itself was perfect, but we were not—far from it!—and so what was intended to bring life became the ministry of death and condemnation. Why? Because it was not written on our hearts but rather on tablets of stone (2 Cor. 3:3–7). Now, in the new covenant, God's laws *are* written on our hearts:

> For this is the covenant that I will make with the house of
>   Israel
>   after those days, declares the Lord:
> I will put my laws into their minds,
>   and write them on their hearts,
> and I will be their God,
>   and they shall be my people.
>
> —HEBREWS 8:10,
> quoting JEREMIAH 31:33

> I will take you from the nations and gather you from all the countries and bring you into your own land. I will sprinkle clean water on you, and you shall be clean from all your uncleannesses, and from all your idols I will cleanse you. And I will give you a new heart, and a new spirit I will put within you. And I will remove the heart of stone from your flesh and give you a heart of flesh. And I will put my Spirit within you, and cause you to walk in my statutes and be careful to obey my rules.
>
> —EZEKIEL 36:24–27

At this point, the words of D. Martyn Lloyd-Jones should make a lot of spiritual sense: "We tend to have a wrong view of law and to think of it as something that is opposed to grace. But it is not. Law is only opposed to grace in the sense that there was once a covenant of law, and we are now under the covenant of grace."[13] Yes, God's Law itself is good, a theme we'll focus on in the next chapter. The problem, again, is the fact that hyper-grace teachers primarily use the Old Testament by way of contrast, failing to plumb its riches, creating false and extreme dichotomies, and ignoring many of the lessons and warnings of the Hebrew Scriptures. After all, we're under grace!

A case in point would be this statement by Ryan Rufus: "The Old Covenant is a standing and working covenant. The New Covenant is a sitting and resting covenant."[14] The fact is, it was David, living under the Sinai covenant, who wrote, "The LORD is my shepherd; I shall not want. He makes me lie down in green pastures. He leads me beside still waters" (Ps. 23:1–2). That sounds like rest to me! And it was Paul, living under the new covenant, who exhorted us to run our race so as to win (1 Cor. 9:24–27; see also chapter 9). That sounds like work!

To be sure, some modern grace teachers, like Andrew Farley, have gone out of their way not to throw the baby out with the bathwater, stating, "I have made the argument that the law has no bearing on the life of the believer. But the Old Testament is a treasure that shouldn't be disregarded."[15]

He continues:

> The Old Testament offers us something we can't get from the New. It provides a thorough background in how God initiated a relationship with humankind and how we did whatever we could to ruin this relationship. The work of Christ has far greater impact against the backdrop of how despicably the human race has acted toward God. How gracious our God has been over the course of human history![16]

And he correctly states that, "To disregard the Old Testament is like covering up a huge portion of a portrait God has been painting for thousands of years." He also notes that "it's important to read and teach from the Old Testament while keeping it in context."[17]

Yet even a careful student of the Word like Pastor Farley overstates the contrasts between the Old and New, writing, "In the Old Testament, we see God punishing the Israelites for their sins. In the New Testament, we see that God punished Jesus for our sins."[18] This is true, but in the New Testament we see God rebuking us and disciplining us for our sins. (See, for example, Hebrews 12:5–13.) And as noted above, we see the authors of the New Testament pointing back to "God punishing the Israelites for their sins" as a warning to us. (See again 1 Corinthians 10:1–11, among other passages.[19])

Farley writes:

> In the Old Testament, we see God withdrawing his presence from his people. In the New Testament, we see that he'll never leave us or forsake us. Even a man after God's own heart, David, pleaded with God not to withdraw his Holy Spirit. David begged, "Do not cast me from your presence or take your Holy Spirit from me" (Psalm 51:11). We don't find such pleas from the apostles under the New.[20]

To be sure, there are many ways that we experience the Holy Spirit today that were beyond what the Old Testament believers experienced (see John 7:39, and John chapters 14–16), but when the writer of Hebrews wrote those precious words, "I will never leave you nor forsake you" (Heb. 13:5), he was quoting from the Old Testament, not from the words of Jesus. (See Deuteronomy 31:6; Joshua 1:5–6). He was obviously quite unaware of the extreme contrast portrayed by hyper-grace teachers.

Let's also not forget that the New Testament believers commonly used the psalms, citing them frequently[21] and singing them as well. (See Ephesians 5:19; Colossians 3:16.) Psalm 51 was used as a great psalm of repentance in the early church; it was even included in some of the ancient liturgy.[22] And Jesus warned that if we denied Him, He would deny us (Matt. 10:32–33), a teaching seconded by Paul (2 Tim. 2:12, "if *we* deny him, he also will deny *us*").[23] So, the New Testament promises reflect the Old Testament promises: the Lord will never leave us or forsake us, but if we turn away from Him, He will turn away from us.[24]

As for the Holy Spirit, the New Testament teaches that we can grieve Him (Eph. 4:30), that He can be outraged (Heb. 10:29, where He is called the Spirit of grace!), and that He can be lied to and tested, with disastrous, deadly consequences (Acts 5:1–10). In fact, as a result of Ananias and Sapphira dropping dead after lying to the Spirit in Acts 5, Luke records, "And great fear came upon the whole church and upon all who heard of these things" (v. 11). The holy God who judged sin in the Old Testament (as He did in Leviticus 10:1–3) was the same holy God who judged sin in the New Testament (along with Acts 5, see Acts 12:20–23). That's why Jesus warned the church of Thyatira that if they continued to tolerate a dangerous false prophetess in their midst, there would be serious consequences:

> I gave her time to repent, but she refuses to repent of her sexual immorality. Behold, I will throw her onto a sickbed, and those who commit adultery with her I will throw into great tribulation, unless they repent of her works, and I will strike her children dead. And all the churches will know that I am he who searches mind and heart, and I will give to each of you according to your works.
>
> —REVELATION 2:21–23

These are the words of Jesus! (Some of the most bizarre "interpretations" of Scripture I've ever seen in my life come from hyper-grace adherents trying to "explain" texts such as Acts 12:20–23, where the angel of the Lord smites Herod, or Revelation 2:21–23, just cited.[25]) And can we forget Paul's warning to the Corinthians? "Do you not know that you are God's temple and that God's Spirit dwells in you? If anyone destroys God's temple, God will destroy him. For God's temple is holy, and you are that temple" (1 Cor. 3:16–17). Even if he is warning both unbelievers and believers here, it is a warning not to play games with the sacred things of God; otherwise God will "destroy" that person.

The real irony, though, in the hyper-grace rejection, neglect, or misuse of the Old Testament is that some of the most wonderful statements about grace are found in the Old Testament, but they are not given first and foremost as promises to the church but rather as promises to Israel. Yet modern grace teachers quote these very verses completely detached from their original context, virtually stealing them from Israel, which is like building the second story of the house while eliminating the first story. I'm thinking of verses such as these:

> Can a woman forget her nursing child, that she should have no compassion on the son of her womb? Even these may forget, yet I

> will not forget you. Behold, I have engraved you on the palms of my hands; your walls are continually before me.
>
> —Isaiah 49:15–16

> "For a brief moment I deserted you, but with great compassion I will gather you. In overflowing anger for a moment I hid my face from you, but with everlasting love I will have compassion on you," says the Lord, your Redeemer. "This is like the days of Noah to me: as I swore that the waters of Noah should no more go over the earth, so I have sworn that I will not be angry with you, and will not rebuke you. For the mountains may depart and the hills be removed, but my steadfast love shall not depart from you, and my covenant of peace shall not be removed," says the Lord, who has compassion on you.
>
> —Isaiah 54:7–10

To repeat, these were promises given by God to ancient Israel, and while they can be applied spiritually to all those in Jesus the Messiah, they are still Israel's treasured possession, all of which means that Marcion was horrifically wrong in rejecting and denigrating the Old Testament. So also are all modern grace teachers and believers who follow the error of his ways, in part or in full. And how interesting it is that, just like Marcion, they do it because they are "completely carried away with the novelty, uniqueness and grandeur of the Pauline Gospel of the grace of God in Christ."[26]

Because of that, they are largely blinded to the revelation of God's grace—and the God of grace—found throughout the Old Testament, reaching its culmination in the person and work of Jesus in the New Testament. This leads to false and destructive caricatures like the one in this ad for a teaching series by Andrew Wommack: "Are you confused about the nature of God? Is He the God of judgment found in the Old Testament, or the God of mercy and grace found in the New Testament?"[27] The spirit of Marcion lives on.

-12-

THE LAW OF THE LORD IS GOOD

ONE OF THE foundational truths of the New Testament is that in Jesus, we are not under law but under grace (Rom. 6:14). At the least, this means that we not under the condemnation of the law (Rom. 8:1–2), we are not under the law as a tutor (or schoolmaster or pedagogue) to lead us to the Messiah (Gal. 3:23–25),[1] and we are not under the law as a system of justification (Rom. 3:20). Instead, we have been pronounced righteous through the blood of Jesus, and we are now empowered by God's grace to live a new life in Him (Rom. 6:4–11). In short, grace did what the law could not (Rom. 8:3–4), and that's why sin is no longer our master (again, Rom. 6:14). Stated succinctly by Joseph Prince, "The law justified no one and condemned the best of us, but grace saves even the worst of us."[2]

Paul stated emphatically that "no one will be declared righteous in [God's] sight by observing the law; rather, through the law we become conscious of sin" (Rom. 3:20, NIV), and he explained that "the law brings wrath, but where there is no law there is no transgression" (Rom. 4:15). He taught that, "The sting of death is sin, and the power of sin is the law" (1 Cor. 15:56), and he warned that, "All who rely on observing the law are under a curse, for it is written: 'Cursed is everyone who does not continue to do everything written in the Book of the Law.' Clearly no one is justified before God by the law, because, 'The righteous will live by faith.' The law is not based on faith; on the contrary, 'The man who does these things will live by them.' Christ redeemed us from the curse of the law by becoming a curse for us, for it is written: 'Cursed is everyone who is hung on a tree'" (Gal. 3:10–13, NIV).

In keeping with these truths, he also wrote, "You who are trying to be justified by law have been alienated from Christ; you have fallen away from grace" (Gal. 5:4, NIV). In contrast, "if you are led by the Spirit, you are not under the law" (Gal. 5:18).

All these verses are quite well known to my friends in the hyper-grace camp, and on a certain level, they cannot be overemphasized. After all, isn't that part of the very essence of the gospel? Let us proclaim these truths from the rooftops!

At the same time, I believe hyper-grace teachers make a common mistake, and that is to think of God's Law itself (or God's laws themselves, or even rules of conduct themselves) as bad or defective or binding. To the contrary, as we saw in the last chapter, Paul was careful to point out that the Law was not sin and that "the law is holy, and the commandment is holy and righteous and good" (Rom. 7:12).

The problem has never been God's perfect and beautiful Law (Torah),[3] nor has the problem been standards and rules. The problem has been human sinfulness, highlighted by the demands of the Sinai covenant. Unfortunately, many modern grace teachers have reacted against the Law (and laws) to the point that they have thrown out the baby with the bathwater.

For example, Andrew Farley makes some excellent observations about the Law, writing:

> The law itself isn't sinful. Law-haters, known as antinomians, have been misinterpreting the Scriptures since the days of the early church. They say that the law is evil. In combating this false doctrine, the apostle Paul notes that the law isn't sin. In fact, he declares it to be holy, righteous, and good: "So then, the law is holy, and the commandment is holy, righteous and good" (Romans 7:12). So there's nothing imperfect about the law itself. It's without blemish.[4]

Precisely so. He continues:

> The law still exists and has a purpose today. But it's not designed for Christians as a tool or guide for daily living. *Its sole purpose is to convict the ungodly of their spiritually dead state.* Understanding the law's place in the world today keeps us from the error of antinomianism ("law hating"). Understanding that

> the law has no place in the life of a Christian keeps us from the error of legalism.[5]

Is this accurate? Well, I very much appreciate some of what Pastor Farley's emphasizes, like this:

> We can dress up, play church, and gain the respect of those around us through the trumpeting of our strict religious rules. But no amount of window dressing can change reality. Sooner or later, life under law will evidence itself. In Christ, we die and are reborn—free from the law. So we don't have to pretend. Playing church leads to *more* sinning every time.[6]

Clearly, he is not advocating loose living or sinful behavior—in fact, he writes against this plainly—but, in common with other modern grace teachers, he denigrates the Law, along with principles of moral living, in a way that God never intended.

Speaking of the "Allure of Rules," he writes, "Principles, rules, and standards—no matter how 'Christian' we believe they are—are poor substitutes for a life animated by God himself." I absolutely agree with this statement. But he adds:

> Paul is addressing the *daily life* of a believer. And he emphatically states that rules and regulations [with reference to Col. 2:20–23] are not the way to go.... Paul dispels the myth that God is pleased with rule-based approaches to "perfecting" ourselves. Paul would ask us the same thing today: "Isn't the presence of the resurrected Christ inside of you enough?"[7]

Yes, I agree that a "rule-based" approach is not the way to "perfect" ourselves, but I would turn around and ask Pastor Farley, whom I believe to be a devoted follower of Jesus, "If Paul believed that the presence of the resurrected Christ inside of us was enough, why did he need to write so many letters telling believers how to live? Why did he need to bring correction? Why did he need to address carnality and doctrinal error? Why did he constantly set forth rules of conduct for believers? Why did he say that God put teachers in the church?" (Why, for that matter, does Pastor Farley need to write a book to tell us that all we need is the resurrected Christ inside of us?)

What Paul *did* reject in Colossians 2:16–23 was an outward attempt to attain inward spirituality, such as urging Gentiles to keep the Sabbath rather than seeing Jesus as the fulfillment of the Sabbath, or engaging in all kinds of self-denial (much like the medieval monks who would flog themselves). Of this Paul wrote, "These rules may seem wise because they require strong devotion, pious self-denial, and severe bodily discipline. But they provide no help in conquering a person's evil desires" (v. 23, NLT).

But in the very next verses, based on our new life in Jesus—we have died and our lives are now hidden in Him, who is seated above, at the right hand of God (Col. 3:1–4)!—Paul lays out specific commands and principles, telling us how to live, beginning with putting to death "what is earthly" in us, speaking of outward sins such as sexual immorality (v. 5). Then he urges us to put away things such as anger, obscene talk, and lying (vv. 8–9), reminding us that we have put off the old self and put on the new man (vv. 10–11). Based on this, he tells us to put on compassion and love, forgiving one another as God forgave us in Jesus (vv. 12–14).

Then, in Colossians 3:18–4:6, Paul gives a series of specific instructions (commands!), including: "Wives, submit to your husbands, as is fitting in the Lord. Husbands, love your wives, and do not be harsh with them. Children, obey your parents in everything, for this pleases the Lord. Fathers, do not provoke your children, lest they become discouraged" (Col. 3:18–21). And on and on it goes, as is common in Paul's letters. In fact, New Testament scholars often refer to these family-related instructions as "Haustafeln," which is German for "house rules" (literally, house tables).[8]

And get this: when Paul laid out these house rules in Ephesians 6, he took things one step further. He quoted one of the Ten Commandments to back up his position! "Children, obey your parents in the Lord, for this is right. 'Honor your father and mother' (this is the first commandment with a promise), 'that it may go well with you and that you may live long in the land'" (Eph. 6:1–3). Yes, for Paul, the Ten Commandments were good, not bad, and encouraging the Gentile believers in Ephesus to live by this commandment was part of life in the Spirit, not condemnation in the flesh.

Ryan Rufus, however, sees things differently. He states emphatically:

> It is only when you believe the law covenant has completely passed away and you have died to it.... God is not putting it on you and does not want you bound by it—it is a ministry of death and He has bought you out of it and resurrected you into the covenant of the Spirit! You are released from the law! You are no longer accountable to the law! God has put His Spirit inside of your hearts and where the Spirit of the Lord is there is liberty! Liberty from that old covenant—you have been liberated from the letter and come into the new way of the Spirit! You can have freedom in that covenant! You don't have to run back to the law! Stay in the Spirit and watch Him transform your life![9]

Once again, there is a lot of truth in what he is saying, but it is grossly overstated, to the point that he adds, "The Bible says that God has put His law on our hearts. He has put His law on our hearts! That's not the Ten Commandments! Goodness gracious—if God did that it would kill us! No, the law God put on our hearts is His nature. It is His perfect nature."[10]

To the contrary, putting the Ten Commandments—or any one of the Ten Commandments—in our hearts would not "kill us." God forbid! What would "kill us" would be writing those words in stone tablets and commanding us to follow them without giving us a new nature. That's the "ministry of condemnation" Paul spoke about in 2 Corinthians 3, the fruit of the Sinai covenant.

But when we are born again, God *does* put His laws into our heart, and it brings life, not death. (To reemphasize the obvious, if putting one of the Ten Commandments into our hearts would kill us, why did Paul *quote* one of the Ten Commandments to the Ephesians, charging them to obey it, with the added encouragement that it was the "first commandment with a promise"—and, as previously stated, say it was a promise of life?)

In his book *The Naked Gospel*, Andrew Farley gave a true and false test, with one of the statements being, "Old Testament law is written on Christians' hearts so we want to obey it."[11] He claimed the answer was false. Unfortunately, he got the answer to his own test wrong.

Speaking of this new heart covenant as it applies to Israel—and so, by spiritual application, to all believers—God promised, "And I will give you a new heart, and a new spirit I will put within you. And I will remove the heart of stone from your flesh and give you a heart of flesh. And I will put my Spirit within you, and cause you to walk in my statutes and be careful to obey my rules" (Ezek. 36:26–27). And note carefully that God giving us a new heart, putting His Spirit within us, and causing us to obey His statutes and rules all go hand in hand.

Sadly, the moment you quote certain passages of Scripture to some "grace"-oriented believers today—verses about how we should live, even from the writings of Paul—they will respond with lines like, "You're not going to put me into bondage again! I'm not going back to your old religious system." Instead, they should say, "Amen! That's my heart! I delight in God's laws and ways!" In contrast, Andre Van der Merwe writes that one of the goals of his book on grace is to "disarm those 'intimidating' verses and perceptions that always seem to put you on the back foot, such as the unforgivable sin, tithing, Job's afflictions, the 10 Commandments, etc."[12]

What is so intimidating about the Ten Commandments for a born-again, Spirit-empowered believer? And take careful note of 1 John 3:4, where John wrote, "Everyone who makes a practice of sinning also practices lawlessness; sin is lawlessness."[13] Commenting on this, Matthew Henry explained:

> Sin is the destitution or privation of correspondence and agreement with the divine law, that law which is the transcript of the divine nature and purity, which contains his will for the government of the world, which is suitable to the rational nature, and enacted for the good of the world, which shows man the way of felicity and peace, and conducts him to the author of his nature and of the law. The current commission of sin now is the rejection of the divine law, and this is the rejection of the divine authority, and consequently of God himself.[14]

In Jeremiah 31:33–34, speaking again of the new heart covenant, God promised that He would put His Law (Hebrew, *torah*) in the hearts of His people, forgiving their iniquity and remembering their sins no more. Interestingly, the Septuagint, the Greek translation of the Old

Testament used widely by the early church, translated this differently, saying that God would put His *laws* (plural) in our hearts, and that's how it is quoted twice in Hebrews: "I will put my laws into their minds, and write them on their hearts" (Heb. 8:10; see also Heb. 10:16).[15] And this is what Paul refers to in Romans 8:1–4, where he explains that Jesus, by His death on the cross, accomplished what the Law could not, so that now "the righteous requirement of the law might be fulfilled in us, who walk not according to the flesh but according to the Spirit" (v. 4).[16]

Simply stated, it is flat-out wrong to say God does not put His laws into our hearts as believers and that commandments and rules are contrary to life in the Spirit. Rather, by the Spirit and by the new birth, it is our nature to keep these laws and commandments as they are expressed throughout the New Testament books. That's why Paul prefaced his moral exhortations to the Thessalonians with the words, "For you know what instructions we gave you through the Lord Jesus" (1 Thess. 4:2), using a Greek word (*paraggelia*) that basically means "a charge, command, or order."

Many leading Thessalonians scholars have commented on this. C. A. Wanamaker explains that:

> In all probability Timothy had brought word to Paul that a problem existed in Thessalonica regarding the stringent sexual code that the missionaries had taught their converts as part of the necessary life-style for those who would please God. This and the problems associated with the *parousia* [Second Coming] treated later in the letter may have been the specific reasons why almost immediately after Timothy's return from Thessalonica the apostle wrote the letter. In this paragraph Paul reinforces the sexual morality that he had originally given his readers by introducing strong sanctions against deviation and by linking the morality he had taught them to their very identity as Christians.[17]

This doesn't exactly sound like the hyper-grace message, but neither does Paul's teaching in 1 Thessalonians 4, for that matter. (See chapter 7.) Professor Wanamaker continues:

> While Paul is said to be the apostle of the "law-free gospel," this can only accurately refer to his rejection of the Jewish law and in particular the cultic and ritual law as a means of salvation.... Paul maintained the ethical law of Judaism as normative for Christians because, as far as he was concerned, it remained the will of God. The reason for this is contained in the expression "your sanctification." Paul understood God to be the holy God of the OT who was set apart from every form of sin and impurity and who demanded similar holiness from the people of Israel through separation (Lv. 11:44f.; 19:2; 21:8). God had not changed, so the same requirement was laid on the new people of God, the Christians.[18]

Did you follow what this learned professor said? Paul was not anti-law per se. He was against the idea that keeping the Jewish Law, with its ritual and temple requirements, would lead to salvation. But Paul absolutely affirmed the ethical standards of the Law and reaffirmed them in his teaching.

And note once more that he did so with authority, as Professor G. L. Green explains:

> The instructions they received were not mere guidelines that could be ignored but, more precisely, "commands" or "orders" (*parangelias*; Acts 5.28; 16.24; 1 Tim. 1.5, 18; and cf. the verb in 4.11; 2 Thess. 3.4, 6, 10, 12). As such, they should not be glibly put aside or ignored according to the whims of those in the church. When an ancient author wanted to speak of an authoritative command that should be obeyed, such as that of a military commander, a philosopher, or a deity, this is a term that was readily at hand. Therefore, when the Thessalonians accepted the apostolic proclamation as the word of God (2.13), they also came under obligation to obey the moral commandments that accompanied it.[19]

May I ask you to read this paragraph again carefully? Contrast Professor Green's accurate commentary with this statement from Andrew Farley:

> Some say, "I don't live under the law of Moses. I know I'm free from those commandments. Instead, I live by 'Christian principles.'"

> This is a fine-sounding variation on what is still a law-based approach. And it's an obstacle to enjoying the dependency-based life. We know that living a "good life" by moral standards is an obstacle to understanding salvation. But choosing "morality" can even prevent a Christian from depending solely on Christ. For Christians, a hidden hindrance to the grace life is a "great" life.[20]

Similarly, Steve McVey writes that it is a lie to believe that we should live by Christian morals since "whether we see people as living morally or immorally, we're viewing life through a lens we aren't intended to use. God hasn't designed life to be lived based on a system of morality. He has a much better plan in mind for us than that."[21] But it is not either life in the Spirit *or* Christian morals. They go hand in hand throughout the New Testament.

It Is Our Privilege to Obey

Could it be that Mick Mooney failed to grasp this truth, which colored his *Grace Paraphrase* and caused him to change some of Paul's commands in Ephesians 5, making them say something very different? Paul wrote, "Wives, submit to your own husbands, as to the Lord.... Now as the church submits to Christ, so also wives should submit in everything to their husbands" (Eph. 5:22, 24). Mooney changes this to, "Wives, believe your husbands when they speak words of loving affection over your life, just as you do with the Lord.... Now just as we, the Church, submit to Christ when he confirms his love for us, so also wives should submit to their husbands and accept their husbands' praises in everything."

So, the call for the wife to submit to her husband is replaced by "believe your husbands when they speak words of loving affection over your life." Then, when the word *submit* is used for both wives and the church, the church is to submit when "he [Christ] confirms his love for us," and the wives are to "accept their husbands' praises in everything."

One gets the impression reading Mooney's paraphrase that the Lord can't simply command us to obey. Rather, we are only to respond when "he confirms his love for us" and lavishes us with praise. As believers, in light of the cross, we never need God to confirm His love for us again, nor does He have to justify His authority over our lives. The love of God was poured out for us at the cross, and we became the Lord's purchased possession (1 Cor. 6:19–20; 7:23). We are His, and it is our joyful privilege to obey Him.

Paul Ellis writes, "A counterfeit gospel will imprison you within the confining walls of rules and regulations, but the true gospel proclaims, 'If the Son sets you free, you will be free indeed' (John 8:36)."[22] Using criteria like this, the Thessalonians could have said to Paul, "Jesus already set us free! Why are you trying to put all your rules and regulations on us?"

I agree with Dr. Ellis that we must abandon "a distorted image of our heavenly Father as a loveless, scorekeeping judge."[23] Absolutely! May that image be banished from our hearts and minds for life, and may it be replaced with a true revelation of the glorious heavenly Father.

Once again, however, hyper-grace teachers create a false dichotomy between a grace-filled relationship with God and an obedient, commandment-keeping relationship with God. Both are part of a Spirit-filled, overcoming, liberated lifestyle, and both are the fruit of love. As Jesus Himself said, "If you love me, you will keep my commandments" (John 14:15), a statement reiterated by John: "Whoever keeps his commandments abides in God, and God in him. And by this we know that he abides in us, by the Spirit whom he has given us" (1 John 3:24; see also 1 John 2:3–4; 3:22; 5:2–3; and note 2 John 6, "And this is love, that we walk according to his commandments"). In fact, Paul himself wrote, "For neither circumcision counts for anything nor uncircumcision, *but keeping the commandments of God*" (1 Cor. 7:19).

You might ask, "But which commandments did he mean? And aren't all the commandments summed up in the command to love one another as Jesus loved us, as Paul taught in Romans 13:8?"

But that is hardly the point at all. The fact is that in the New Testament, Jesus and the apostles were quite free to give commandments—many of them—and keeping those commandments was seen as an act of love, in keeping with life in the Spirit, as opposed to part of a dead, legalistic system from which we should be delivered. (Note also that all of the Ten Commandments, with the exception of the Sabbath command, are reiterated in the Epistles.)

Yet this rejection of laws and commandments to govern how believers live goes very deep, even resulting in some bizarre readings of the Hebrew Scriptures. According to Chuck Crisco, "The Exodus event was an act of divine grace until God offered them a relationship where they would be his special treasure. Death only came after the people demanded a covenant based on performance instead of grace."[24]

Dr. Crisco says the *people demanded* a covenant based on performance instead of grace. I don't know how he draws that conclusion. The Exodus event *begins* with divine commandments (the slaughtering of the lamb and the Passover commands in Exodus 12), and it reaches its climax with this beautiful invitation from Yahweh:

> You yourselves have seen what I did to the Egyptians, and how I bore you on eagles' wings and brought you to myself. Now therefore, *if you will indeed obey my voice and keep my covenant, you shall be my treasured possession among all peoples*, for all the earth is mine; and you shall be to me a kingdom of priests and a holy nation. These are the words that you [Moses] shall speak to the people of Israel. [Note my emphasis here, which you'll soon see is very important.]
>
> —Exodus 19:4–6

God was giving them an invitation to obey Him fully—the people did not demand this—and it was an invitation based on grace, as expressed clearly in Deuteronomy 7:

> It was not because you were more in number than any other people that the Lord set his love on you and chose you, for you were the fewest of all peoples, but *it is because the Lord loves you and is keeping the oath that he swore to your fathers*, that the Lord has brought you out with a mighty hand and redeemed you from the house of slavery, from the hand of Pharaoh king of Egypt. *Know therefore that the Lord your God is God, the faithful God who keeps covenant and steadfast love with those who love him and keep his commandments, to a thousand generations,*

> and repays to their face those who hate him, by destroying them. He will not be slack with one who hates him. He will repay him to his face. You shall therefore be careful to do the commandment and the statutes and the rules that I command you today. And because you listen to these rules and keep and do them, the LORD your God will keep with you the covenant and the steadfast love that he swore to your fathers.
>
> —DEUTERONOMY 7:7–12

God gave Israel His laws because He loved them and because He had given His promise to Abraham, Isaac, and Jacob, and it was all based on His grace, not their merit. Sadly, they could not live up to His high standards, and in that way the Law, which promised life (Deut. 30:15–20), brought death (Rom. 7:10), also paving the way for the new and better covenant, all in the wisdom and plan of God.

Dr. Crisco is not the only one to state that God offered grace to Israel but they demanded a covenant of works (or, in a varied form, that God gave them His laws only because they refused to believe Him). According to Andre van der Merwe, "Eventually, because Israel refused to believe that God was on their side, He gave them the law and all the other commandments to keep, something that didn't require any faith from their side (faith in God's goodness)."[25] (He then cites Exodus 24:7–8, which we'll return to in a moment.) Paul Ellis also writes, "From the beginning, God desired a relationship with us but we preferred rules. God told the Israelites that he wanted them to be his treasured people but they weren't interested. Their attitude was, 'Just tell us what to do and we'll do it.'"[26] (This last sentence is also referring to Exodus 24:7–8.)

Honestly, when I read statements like these, I wonder if we are reading the same Scriptures. (Look again at Dr. Ellis's statement, and then go back and reread Exodus 19:4–6, quoted previously. It is the exact *opposite* of what he writes.)

Where then do these ideas come from? And why is Exodus 24:7–8 so commonly cited in support? That passage tells us that after Moses offered God's commandments to the people and they said they would obey in Exodus 24:3, Moses "took the Book of the Covenant and read it in the hearing of the people. And they said, 'All that the LORD has spoken we will do, and we will be obedient.' And Moses took the blood and threw it on the people and said, 'Behold the blood of the covenant that the LORD has made with you in accordance with all these words'" (vv. 7–8).

So how did so many hyper-grace teachers come to the conclusion that this passage was meant to paint the people of Israel in a negative light, as if they refused God's grace and demanded a works-based covenant? It appears to go back to Joseph Prince, cited by Chuck Crisco in this very context.

In his book *Unmerited Favor* Prince wrote:

> However, the tragedy of all tragedies occurred for the children of Israel when they responded to God after hearing this [referring to the invitation in Exodus 19:4–6] at the foot of Mount Sinai. They were proud and did not want the relationship God had envisioned. They wanted to deal with God at arm's length, through impersonal commandments....
>
> Now, they wanted to exchange the covenant of grace that they had been under for a different kind of covenant. When Moses told them what God had said, they responded arrogantly (which can be seen from the Hebrew syntax), saying in essence, "All that God commands us, we are well able to perform!" In other words, this is what they said to God, "God, don't judge us and bless us anymore based on Your goodness and faithfulness. Assess us based on our merits. Bless us based on our obedience because we are well able to perform whatever You demand of us!"[27]

What? First, I mean no insult to Joseph Prince, but it is flatly untrue that the Hebrew syntax points to an arrogant response by the people of Israel. I can read biblical Hebrew as well as I read English (I've been studying Hebrew seriously since 1973, earning a BA in Hebrew and an MA and PhD in Near Eastern languages and literatures), and I can tell you plainly that God was calling for obedience in response to His gracious offer, and His people then said, "Yes, we accept Your terms! We will obey!" (See Exodus 19:8.)[28] It was a *good* response—the right response—not a bad one.

Second, Pastor Prince can come to these conclusions only by completely ignoring what the biblical text states. As he cites God's invitation in Exodus 19:4–6, he emphasizes in bold these words: **"I bore you on eagles' wings and brought you to Myself.** [The next words are not in bold, so I'll leave them out here.] **...you shall be a special treasure to Me above all people...you shall be to Me a kingdom of priests and a holy nation."**[29]

What are the words he did *not* put in bold? They were the very terms of God's gracious invitation, which I'll put in bold here: **"Now therefore, if you will indeed obey My voice and keep My covenant, then"**—yes, *then*—"you shall be a special treasure to Me above all people.... And you shall be to Me a kingdom of priests and a holy nation."

Isn't this remarkable? The biblical text has been turned completely on its head. The fact is that God gave Israel this covenant as a gift of His love and a revelation of His holy character, but they were unable to keep it because of their sinful flesh. This was part of His plan to expose the depth of our rebellion and to point us to the cross alone for salvation. There's no need to rewrite the Bible in the name of grace.

Pastor Prince also claims that it was only after Israel's alleged "arrogant" response to God that He put a distance between Himself and the people:

> From that moment onwards, God immediately changed His tone with the children of Israel. He distanced Himself from them and told Moses to command the people not to go near Mount Sinai for the mountain was holy. What happened?
>
> Once God's grace was rejected, and the people presumed upon their own righteousness and obedience to respond to Him, God drew back from them. Look at the tone that He used on the Israelites after they chose to come under the covenant of law: "Behold, I come to you in the thick cloud....Whoever touches the mountain shall surely be put to death. Not a hand shall touch him, but he shall surely be stoned or shot with an arrow."[30]

To the contrary, God graciously offered Israel the opportunity to be His special treasure, uniquely entrusted with His holy laws and beautiful commandments, and when they said, "Yes, we will obey," He said, "All right then. I will manifest Myself to the nation, so approach Me with care."

This was the same God who appeared to Moses back in Exodus 3, telling him to take the sandals off his feet because the ground on which he was standing was holy (vv. 1–6). That's why the text says, "And Moses hid his face, for he was afraid to look at God" (v. 6)—and this took place long before Sinai. And right at the time of the Exodus—which, according to Pastor Prince, was during the so-called season of grace—God began to institute detailed laws, such as these (among many others):

> And you shall observe the Feast of Unleavened Bread, for on this very day I brought your hosts out of the land of Egypt. Therefore you shall observe this day, throughout your generations, as a statute forever.... You shall observe this rite as a statute for you and for your sons forever. And when you come to the land that the LORD will give you, as he has promised, you shall keep this service.
>
> —EXODUS 12:17, 24–25

A Wonderful, Righteous Law

I can't tell you how deeply it grieves my spirit when I see the Bible being radically reinterpreted to support a particular doctrine, yet it is on these kinds of faulty foundations that much of the hyper-grace theology is built.

Once again, in stark contrast to the evaluation of these teachers, God told Israel that His laws were a wonderful thing: "For what great nation is there that has a god so near to it as the LORD our God is to us, whenever we call upon him? And what great nation is there, that has statutes and rules so righteous as all this law that I set before you today?" (Deut. 4:7–8). And He followed these words with an exhortation to obey Him carefully. (See the rest of Deuteronomy 4.)

This is why the psalmist could exclaim:

> In the way of your testimonies I delight as much as in all riches. I will meditate on your precepts and fix my eyes on your ways. I will delight in your statutes; I will not forget your word.
>
> —PSALM 119:14–16

Open my eyes, that I may behold wondrous things out of your law.

—Psalm 119:18

Even though princes sit plotting against me, your servant will meditate on your statutes. Your testimonies are my delight; they are my counselors. My soul clings to the dust; give me life according to your word!

—Psalm 119:23–25

I will run in the way of your commandments when you enlarge my heart!

—Psalm 119:32

I will also speak of your testimonies before kings and shall not be put to shame, for I find my delight in your commandments, which I love.

—Psalm 119:46–47

The earth, O Lord, is full of your steadfast love; teach me your statutes!

—Psalm 119:64

The law of your mouth is better to me than thousands of gold and silver pieces.

—Psalm 119:72

Forever, O Lord, your word [meaning God's Law] is firmly fixed in the heavens.

—Psalm 119:89

Oh how I love your law! It is my meditation all the day. Your commandment makes me wiser than my enemies, for it is ever with me. I have more understanding than all my teachers, for your testimonies are my meditation. I understand more than the aged, for I keep your precepts.

—Psalm 119:97–100

How sweet are your words to my taste, sweeter than honey to my mouth! Through your precepts I get understanding; therefore I

> hate every false way. Your word is a lamp to my feet and a light to my path.
>
> —PSALM 119:103–105

> Your testimonies are my heritage forever, for they are the joy of my heart.
>
> —PSALM 119:111

> Therefore I love your commandments above gold, above fine gold.
>
> —PSALM 119:127

> Make your face shine upon your servant, and teach me your statutes. My eyes shed streams of tears, because people do not keep your law.
>
> —PSALM 119:135–136

> Great peace have those who love your law; nothing can make them stumble.
>
> —PSALM 119:165

This is why Psalm 1 states that the man who is truly blessed—like a tree planted by streams of water, always bringing forth fruit in season, whose leaf doesn't wither, succeeding in everything He does—is the man who meditates day and night in God's Law (vv. 2–3). And this is why God told Joshua that the key for him taking the Promised Land was to meditate on the Law day and night so he could obey it. *Then* he would have good success.

And what about Psalm 19? It would be good to read this through a few times out loud:

> The law of the LORD is perfect, reviving the soul; the testimony of the LORD is sure, making wise the simple; the precepts of the LORD are right, rejoicing the heart; the commandment of the LORD is pure, enlightening the eyes; the fear of the LORD is clean, enduring forever; the rules of the LORD are true, and righteous altogether. More to be desired are they than gold, even much fine gold; sweeter also than honey and drippings of the honeycomb. Moreover, by them is your servant warned; in keeping them there is great reward.
>
> —PSALM 19:7–11

How wonderful are God's commandments and laws! That's why traditional Jewish rabbis to this day understand Proverbs 3:18 to be referring to the Torah: "She is a tree of life to those who lay hold of her; those who hold her fast are called blessed."

The problem, to repeat once again, was not with God's wonderful Law. It was with His sinful people. But that should not stop us from rightly using the Law today and from rightly appreciating its power and beauty. In fact, some of the greatest revelations I have received about God's nature, along with the nature of holiness, have come from prayerful study of the Torah. And that's why the Puritans, who constantly celebrated the finished work of the cross and preached salvation by grace alone, so loved God's Law.[31]

And the Puritans believed in preaching the Law to sinners too, convinced that it would help bring them to a place of brokenness and need so they would be ready to receive God's unmerited favor and grace. (Come to think of it, that's what hyper-grace teachers claim Jesus was doing in the Sermon on the Mount, yet few of them preach to the lost like that today.)

Spurgeon once said, "I do not believe that any man can preach the gospel who does not preach the Law," and he issued this warning:

> Lower the Law and you dim the Law of God by which man perceives his guilt! This is a very serious loss to the sinner rather than a gain, for it lessens the likelihood of his conviction and conversion.... I say you have deprived the Gospel of its most able auxiliary [its most powerful weapon] when you have set aside the Law! You have taken away from it the schoolmaster that is to bring men to Christ.... They will never accept Grace till they tremble before a just and holy Law! Therefore the Law serves a most necessary and blessed purpose and it must not be removed from its place.[32]

Pastor Rob Rufus, a modern grace teacher who also makes many balanced statements, some of which I have cited in this book, had this to say about the use of the Law in evangelism:

> If the law is not put in charge with the unsaved, there is nothing the Holy Spirit can use to lead them to Christ, for the only thing

> that will truly lead them to Christ is the Ten Commandments—the law of God! So, the law of God is the essential missing ingredient in evangelism. If unsaved people don't hear the law of God or understand its precepts, they are in danger of coming to Christ without the law and for the wrong reasons. Let me explain—the law itself is powerless to save, but it shows us that we need a Saviour—without this understanding, people might just make an emotional decision not based in seeing their real need. So, in truth, only the law can bring them to Christ.[33]

According to Joseph Prince, this is *not* the way the gospel is to be preached. In fact, he claims that when repentance preachers of past generations got great results through their preaching, it was actually part of the "ministry of condemnation" Paul spoke of in 2 Corinthians 3—a ministry that was glorious but one that ultimately brought death. (Of course, the last thing on Paul's mind when he wrote that part of his letter was anointed repentance preaching!)[34] Prince stated on TV:

> I shared about how some revivals, down through church history, use a lot of law, a lot of condemnation, you know? And even great men of God, men of God that I highly esteem and respect like Finney, like John Sung, you know great men. But they will use the law. They will use the law until you are bleeding from every pore. You know, and people run, people scream to be saved.
>
> These are wonderful men of God, you know? But they will use the law to bring you to a sense of guilt, so that you'll see your need for Jesus, all right?
>
> Now it was glorious meetings, these were glorious meetings. Amen. Bars were shut down, people's lives were transformed, but the Bible says, we ain't seen nothing yet. "Though the ministry of condemnation had glory" [2 Cor. 3:9].
>
> God didn't say you have no glory. Ministry of condemnation has glory. It has glory. But the Bible says the ministry of righteousness exceeds much more in glory.[35]

What's interesting, though, is that if you look at how the gospel is preached in Acts (which provides the best evidence of how Peter and Paul preached to the lost), you'll see that the word *love* doesn't even occur a single time, nor does the word *grace* occur in a single sermon in Acts, and yet Jesus is exalted as Savior in every message and grace is freely preached.[36] And when Peter preached on Pentecost, calling his Jewish listeners to account for the sin of rejecting the Messiah, Acts 2:37 says they "were cut to the heart, and said to Peter and the rest of the apostles, 'Brothers, what shall we do?'"[37] (If you want to know if Peter understood grace—a ridiculous question even to ask—see his words about Jews and Gentiles in Acts 15:11, "But we believe that we will be saved through the grace of the Lord Jesus, just as they will.")

And the same Paul who wrote to the Corinthians that he determined only to preach Christ and Him crucified when he first came to them (see 1 Corinthians 2:2, and compare also Galatians 3:1) is the very person who reasoned with Felix (in a highly questionable marriage) "about righteousness and self-control and the coming judgment" until "Felix was alarmed" (Acts 24:25).[38] And according to Acts 24:24, this is how Paul spoke "about faith in Christ Jesus"!

Is that how we speak about faith in Messiah Jesus today—by reasoning with sinners "about righteousness and self-control and the coming judgment"? Could that be some of the reason that Paul talks first about God's wrath and human sin in Romans (from Romans 1:18 until the end of chapter 3) before talking about justification by faith? Did Paul know something we don't?

Regardless of your method of reaching out to the lost, it is clear that we must recover a love and appreciation for God's Law, along with its New Testament commands for living, if we are to be in harmony with Him. Yes, "by this we know that we love the children of God, when we love God and obey his commandments. For this is the love of God, that we keep his commandments. And his commandments are not burdensome" (1 John 5:2–3).

-13-

WHY ARE WE RUNNING FROM THE WORDS OF JESUS?

WHY IN THE world would a true disciple—a lover of Jesus, a follower of the Son of God—want to reject the words of Jesus? Why would someone who boasts about being "in Christ" have such a problem with the teachings of the Christ? Yet this is a common theme in the hyper-grace movement: "The teachings of Jesus are old covenant, not new covenant. The teachings of Jesus are not for us today."

Quotes like this one are becoming increasingly common in the hyper-grace camp: "Paul preached a different message than Jesus, but for a good reason: They were living under different covenants."[1] And there's this from another modern grace teacher: "Peter, James, John, and Paul wrote epistles about life under the new covenant. Years earlier, Jesus was teaching hopelessness under the old. The audience wasn't the same. The covenant wasn't the same. And the teachings aren't the same."[2] In other words, many of Jesus' teachings are not for believers today!

The following quote, directed against "legalistic" Christians today, manages to not only criticize the Old Testament Law but also to attack the Gospels:

> It is these preachers of law [meaning non-hyper-grace preachers] that love to quote scriptures from the gospels of Matthew, Mark, Luke and John out of context, forgetting that the crowds who Jesus was preaching to were Jews! These Jews had been polluted with hundreds of years of preaching of the Old Testament Law, hearing day after day that it is their obedience to the law [that] will cause them to become righteous and that their level

> of morality and good performance will earn them God's acceptance and blessings.[3]

This is one of the most disturbing—and revealing—aspects of the hyper-grace message. To repeat my initial question: Why in the world would a true disciple want to reject the words of Jesus? Shouldn't we rather be embracing every syllable that came from His lips, the way a person dying of thirst would embrace a cold glass of water?

Andrew Farley writes, "We often attempt to apply directly to our lives every word Jesus said, without considering his audience and purpose. But the context of Jesus' harsh teachings must be seen in the light of the dividing line between the Old and the New. Remember that Christ was born and lived during the Old Covenant (law) era."[4] Accordingly, Pastor Farley would tell us, many of the teachings of Jesus do not apply directly to us today as born-again believers. Indeed, he writes, "The New Testament doesn't actually begin in Matthew 1. In fact, it doesn't begin at any page in the Bible. It begins at the point in history when Jesus' blood was shed."[5] Really?

Pastor Farley writes that it is actually dangerous for believers today to try to directly apply some of the words of Jesus to their lives. To illustrate this point, he recounts how a Christian woman named Barbara, after watching his TV program, began to find liberation from her pattern of self-criticism and discouragement, after which he spent time with her helping her to understand her identity in Christ. She began to feel better about her relationship with the Lord until she read the Sermon on the Mount, at which point she began to struggle again.

Farley then explained to her "the dividing line of Old and New."

> I told her how Jesus' harsh teachings aimed at the religious kill you every time. Barbara began to see the distinction between what Jesus taught to Jews and what God wanted her to enjoy under the New. Her countenance lifted. Once again, truth had done its work.
>
> One thing about distinguishing the Old from the New—it always liberates.[6]

How tragic that a pastor and Bible teacher sees fit to "liberate" a believer by steering her away from the words of Jesus in the Sermon on the Mount![7] Yet this is a common teaching in modern grace circles: they claim that words Jesus spoke before His death on the cross were "old covenant" and only for the Jews who lived that time; they do not apply directly to us.[8] This suggests that:

- We can safely ignore His call to deny ourselves and take up the cross daily.
- We can safely ignore Him telling us that we are salt of the earth and the light of the world.
- We can safely ignore His invitation to leave everything and follow Him.
- We can safely ignore His instructions to turn the other cheek and pray for our persecutors.
- We can safely ignore all the warnings in His parables.
- We can safely ignore His teaching that there will be future rewards based on our obedience.
- We can safely ignore the lofty purity standards of the Sermon on the Mount.
- We can safely ignore His warnings about covetousness and materialism.
- We can safely ignore His urgent words about hell and future punishment.
- We can safely ignore His teaching that if we don't forgive others, our Father won't forgive us.

For a Christian to ignore all this would be spiritual insanity. How could a believer possibly want to ignore the words of our Lord? And isn't denying the relevancy of His words a form of denying Him?

Joseph Prince is quite direct here:

> Whether interpreting the Old Testament, or the words which Jesus spoke in the four gospels (Matthew, Mark, Luke and John), let Jesus and His finished work at the cross be the key to unlocking all the precious gems hidden in God's Word. This

> means that we have to read everything in the context of what He came to do and what He accomplished at the cross for us. For example, some things that Jesus said in the four gospels were spoken before the cross—before He had died for our sins—and some were said after the cross—when He had already won our complete forgiveness and rightfully given us His righteousness. *It is the latter that applies to us (believers under the new covenant) today.*[9]

There you have it. Certain things (or, everything?) Jesus said before He died on the cross don't apply to us today. (Of course, after the cross Jesus made reference to what He taught before the cross, but we'll return to that subject later in this chapter.) And as for Farley's claim that "Jesus' harsh teachings" in the Sermon on the Mount were "aimed at the religious," Matthew 5:1–2 makes it clear that they were for His disciples, and His words formed the very heart and soul of their walk with God for the rest of their lives.

Of course, some modern grace preachers are quick to quote the Lord's words when He rebuked the religious hypocrites (such as Jesus' statements in Matthew 23), applying those rebukes to those who reject their version of the grace message. (See chapter 3.) And some modern grace teachers will find a way to appropriate Jesus' promises, as if they somehow apply to us today. But when it comes to being challenged by His words, they have chosen instead to throw those statements away.

So, all too often, when hyper-grace followers are reminded of Jesus' words that, "Not everyone who says to me, 'Lord, Lord,' will enter the kingdom of heaven, but the one who does the will of my Father who is in heaven" (Matt. 7:21), they simply say, "That doesn't apply to me! I'm under grace."

When Jesus' teaching that "everyone who looks at a woman with lustful intent has already committed adultery with her in his heart" (Matt. 5:28) is brought to their attention, they simply respond, "That's preaching the Law, not grace! That was for the Jews back then. I'm free from sin."

When shown John 15:6, "If anyone does not abide in me he is thrown away like a branch and withers; and the branches are gathered, thrown into the fire, and burned," they answer, "Thank God I'm not under that old performance-based system anymore!"

When exhorted to walk as true disciples because of the Lord's words in Luke 9:23, "If anyone would come after me, let him deny himself and take up his cross daily and follow me," they say, "That is so *old*. I now enjoy an effortless union with Jesus."

And when urged not to be double-minded, because Jesus said, "No one who puts his hand to the plow and looks back is fit for the kingdom of God" (Luke 9:62), they respond, "You are not going to bring me under condemnation to your dead religious system taught by Jesus as a Jew under the Law."

And on and on it goes, sadly and painfully so. In fact, to be consistent in saying that only the words Jesus spoke after the cross apply to us today, modern grace teachers would have to say that John 3:16 is *not* the gospel and is *not* "new covenant." Is this where they really want to go? To discard even some of the words of the Lord Jesus is a truly reckless decision, both practically and theologically.

Spirit and Life

To quote Andrew Farley again in reference to the Sermon on the Mount, "Jesus' harsh teachings aimed at the religious *kill you every time.*"[10] In contrast, Jesus said His words were "*spirit* and *life*," while Peter recognized that Jesus had the words of "*eternal life*" (John 6:63, 68; what's more, John's Gospel was written so that the readers would "believe that Jesus is the Messiah, the Son of God, and that by believing in him [they] will have *life* by the power of his name" [John 20:31, NLT]). Jesus said that "whoever drinks the water that I will give him will never be thirsty again. The water that I will give him will become in him a spring of water welling up to *eternal life*" (John 4:14). And He invited all of us to drink of these life-giving streams: "If anyone thirsts"—that includes you and me!—"let him come to me and drink. Whoever believes in me, as the Scripture has said, 'Out of his heart will flow rivers of *living water*'" (John 7:37–38).

Tragically, Pastor Ryan Rufus wrote:

> Matthew 5:1–7:29 is the 'Sermon on the Mount.' Is this sermon intended for the church? Absolutely not! It's intended for the self-righteous. It's a pre-salvation preach that exposes self-righteous pride and performance and reveals the need for God's righteousness as a gift through faith in order to see the Kingdom and become children of God.
>
> Unless you really understand grace, don't go near the Beatitudes. They will mess you up! Teaching the Beatitudes to Christians produces legalism and religious pride or condemnation in them. We must rightly divide the Word of God to see what Jesus was saying and trying to achieve here.[11]

Jesus said His words were life and brought life—eternal life! Do we believe Ryan Rufus that Christ's words can "mess you up" in the negative sense, or do we believe Jesus? And since Pastor Rufus was talking specifically about the Sermon on the Mount, are we to believe that the Beatitudes, beginning with, "Blessed are the poor in spirit, for theirs is the kingdom of heaven" (Matt. 5:3), will "mess you up"? That His words to His disciples calling them "the salt of the earth" and the "light of the world"—to be known for their compassionate good deeds!—would produce "legalism and religious pride or condemnation"? That the Lord's Prayer and Jesus' encouragement to trust God for all our needs and His exhortation to seek first God's kingdom and His righteousness are somehow a spiritual minefield that we should steer clear of? That His warning about hypocritical judgmentalism; His encouragement to ask, seek, and knock in prayer; and His summary statement that "whatever you wish that others would do to you, do also to them, for this is the Law and the Prophets" (Matt. 7:12) should be avoided until we learn to "rightly divide the Word of God to see what Jesus was saying and trying to achieve"?

Yet Pastor Rufus is so convinced of his position that he devotes a whole chapter to the Sermon on the Mount, concluding with these words:

> The Beatitudes are not for the church but were for unbelieving Israel. The church doesn't need the Sermon on the Mount. If you were to ask Jesus if he intended that sermon to be a standard that the church measures itself against, he would either start

> rolling around on the floor screaming with laughter, or bow his head and weep. This is a pre-salvation message that is delivered to self-righteous people who think that they are doing well with righteousness because they can keep some of the law. Once this message has done its job it has served its purpose and we then move on to the way of the spirit.[12]

Is it any wonder that some hyper-grace Christians have fallen into serious deception? Charles Spurgeon saw things very differently. Referring specifically to Matthew 5:3–12, he wrote:

> The whole of the seven Beatitudes composing this celestial ascent to the House of the Lord conduct Believers to an elevated table-land upon which they dwell alone and are not reckoned among the people. Their holy separation from the world brings upon them persecution for righteousness' sake, but in this they do not lose their happiness, but rather have it increased to them, and confirmed by the double repetition of the benediction![13]

Jeremiah Burroughs, born in 1599, published a 256-page, double-column, small print book just on the Beatitudes, saying about Matthew 5 and the following chapters, "This chapter, with the sixth and seventh chapters, are a sermon that Jesus Christ preached upon the mount, the largest and fullest sermon that we have recorded in the Scripture: the sermon of Christ himself."[14] And when he asked himself what would be the most edifying thing he could preach on to his people, he wrote:

> What can be more suitable for a minister of Christ to preach of, than the sermon of Christ?... For a minister to preach other men's sermons it is negligence, but for him to preach Christ's sermon is faithfulness.... Oh, what attention is called for, while you are hearing this sermon of Christ repeated to you, and opened and applied unto you![15]

According to the respected British leader John R. W. Stott:

> The Sermon on the Mount has a unique fascination. It seems good to present the quintessence of the teaching of Jesus. It makes goodness attractive. It shames our shabby performance. It engenders dreams of a better world.

> As John Donne put it in a sermon preached during Lent 1629, not without a little pardonable hyperbole: "All the articles of our religion, all the canons of our church, all the injunctions of our princes, all the homilies of our fathers, all the body of divinity, is in these three chapters, in this one Sermon on the Mount."[16]

Of the whole Sermon on the Mount, Stott said, "It is the nearest thing to a manifesto that [Jesus] ever uttered, for it is his own description of what he wanted his followers to be and to do."[17] Of the Beatitudes themselves he said, "Their wealth is inexhaustible. We cannot plumb their depths. Truly, 'We are near heaven here.'"[18]

Contrast this again with the verdict of Ryan Rufus:

> The church doesn't need the Sermon on the Mount. If you were to ask Jesus if he intended that sermon to be a standard that the church measures itself against, he would either start rolling around on the floor screaming with laughter, or bow his head and weep. This is a pre-salvation message that is delivered to self-righteous people who think that they are doing well with righteousness because they can keep some of the law.[19]

How terribly this teaching misses the mark. For a deeply spiritual man like Oswald Chambers, the Sermon on the Mount was wonderfully relevant for believers:

> The teaching of the Sermon on the Mount is not—Do your duty, but—Do what is not your duty. It is not your duty to go the second mile, to turn the other cheek, but Jesus says if we are His disciples we shall always do these things. There will be no spirit of—"Oh, well, I cannot do any more, I have been so misrepresented and misunderstood."...Never look for right in the other man, but never cease to be right yourself. We are always looking for justice; the teaching of the Sermon on the Mount is—Never look for justice, but never cease to live it.[20]

The collection of Chambers' teachings on the Sermon on the Mount is actually called *Studies in the Sermon on the Mount: God's Character and the Believer's Conduct*, and it is a rich, penetrating, spiritual feast.[21] Grace lovers such as Spurgeon and Chambers would have been shocked to hear any believer claiming that any of Jesus' words were not relevant to their lives. Perish the thought. Rather, His words are life itself, just as He is life Himself.

Jesus said of Himself during His earthly ministry: "I am the bread of *life*. He who comes to me will never go hungry, and he who believes in me will never be thirsty.... I am *the resurrection and the life*. He who believes in me will *live*, even though he dies; and whoever lives and believes in me will *never die*.... I am the way and the truth and the *life*. No one comes to the Father except through me" (John 6:35; 11:25–26; 14:6, NIV). And to all those who were caught up in religious striving, Jesus said, "Come to me, all you who are weary and burdened, and I will give you rest. Take my yoke upon you and learn from me, for I am gentle and humble in heart, and you will find rest for your souls. For my yoke is easy and my burden is light" (Matt. 11:28–30, NIV); repeat these verses a few times until they sink in.

Is a hyper-grace teacher going to tell me that these are "old covenant" words that applied only to Yeshua's Jewish hearers? Are they not rather words of spirit and life that every true disciple should embrace with heart and soul? Are not all these words for us today? That is the Jesus we love and adore, the Jesus who invited "whosoever" to believe in Him and be saved (John 3:16).

Why wouldn't we sit at His feet, listen to His words afresh, and love and adore Him even more, with amazement and awe? And how do we really know who He is outside of what He communicated while He was here on earth—through His words!—and the example He set with His deeds, culminating in His death and resurrection? What kind of relationship can we have with the Lord if we cut out any of His words to us?

Jesus and Paul Preached the Same Gospel

Let's also remember how Jesus said we were to obtain eternal life. It was to be obtained by faith, as a gift! (See, for example, John 3:16; 4:10; 5:24; 6:47; 12:46.)[22] That sounds like the gospel to me—and that's because it *was* the gospel, meaning, the good news. In fact, that's exactly what Jesus said when He answered the disciples of John: "Go and tell John what you hear and see: the blind receive their sight and the lame walk, lepers are cleansed and the deaf hear, and the dead are raised up, and the poor have good news preached to them. And blessed is the one who is not offended by me" (Matt. 11:4–6).

Jesus came preaching the good news! Jesus came preaching the gospel! The following verses attest to this:

> The Spirit of the Lord is upon me, because he has anointed me to *proclaim good news* to the poor. He has sent me to proclaim liberty to the captives and recovering of sight to the blind, to set at liberty those who are oppressed, to proclaim the year of the Lord's favor.
>
> —LUKE 4:18–19

> And when it was day, he departed and went into a desolate place. And the people sought him and came to him, and would have kept him from leaving them, but he said to them, "I must *preach the good news* of the kingdom of God to the other towns as well; for I was sent for this purpose."
>
> LUKE 4:42–43

> Soon afterward he went on through cities and villages, proclaiming and *bringing the good news* of the kingdom of God.
>
> —LUKE 8:1

> One day, as Jesus was teaching the people in the temple and *preaching the gospel*...
>
> —LUKE 20:1

Note first that these verses use the identical Greek verb—*euangelizō*—used for "preaching the gospel/good news" in Acts,[23] and it is the identical verb that Paul used when he spoke of "preaching the gospel/good news," as in 1 Corinthians 1:17, "For Christ did not send me to baptize but to *preach the gospel*, and not with words of eloquent wisdom, lest the cross of Christ be emptied of its power." Don't believe those who tell you that Jesus preached the Law and Paul preached the gospel. Not so!

In fact, not only is the same *verb* used when both Jesus and Paul talk about "preaching the gospel/good news" (*euangelizō* in Greek), but also the same *noun* is used for "gospel/good news" (*euangellion* in Greek). So Matthew 4:23 reads, "And Jesus went about all Galilee, teaching in their synagogues, and preaching *the gospel* of the kingdom, and healing all manner of sickness and all manner of disease among the people" (KJV). And Romans 1:16 reads, "For I am not ashamed of *the gospel*, for it is the power of God for salvation to everyone who believes, to the Jew first and also to the Greek." Jesus and Paul both preached the gospel!

And note the Lord's words in Matthew 24:14, speaking of the message that would be preached after He died and rose again: "And this *gospel of the kingdom*"—the very message He was preaching—"will be proclaimed throughout the whole world as a testimony to all nations, and then the end will come." Compare that with Paul's words in Acts 20:24–25 (and read this very carefully): "But I do not account my life of any value nor as precious to myself, if only I may finish my course and the ministry that I received from the Lord Jesus, to testify to *the gospel of the grace of God*. And now, behold, I know that none of you among whom I have gone about *proclaiming the kingdom* will see my face again."

Did you catch that? Not only did Jesus and Paul preach the same gospel, but they also associated it with the kingdom of God. In other words, when Paul preached the gospel of grace, he was proclaiming the kingdom, and when Jesus preached the kingdom, He was proclaiming the gospel of grace. As John reminds us—speaking of the earthly ministry of Jesus—"And the Word became flesh and dwelt among us, and we have seen his glory, glory as of the only Son from the Father, full of *grace* and truth" (John 1:14). But there's more: "For from his fullness we have all received, *grace upon grace*" (v. 16). How can hyper-grace teachers tell us that Jesus' faithful earthly followers received law upon law and harsh teaching upon harsh teaching?

Then John writes this, "For the law was given through Moses; grace and truth came through Jesus Christ" (v. 17). Does anything more need to be said? Hyper-grace teachers claim that Jesus taught under the Law to the Jewish people who lived at that time, and only after His death and resurrection was the message of grace release through Peter, Paul, and the other apostles. That is absolutely untrue.[24]

Did Jesus minister as a Law-abiding Jew to His fellow Jews? Of course He did. And He inaugurated the new age, the age of the kingdom, the in-breaking of the rule of God, the year of liberation, the declaration of amnesty. (See Luke 4:16–21.)[25] Then He died on the cross and ratified the covenant with His blood. But be assured that He Himself, in His words and deeds, brought the good news of the kingdom and the revelation of grace.

The Gospels state this emphatically, unless you want to argue that the Gospels don't contain the gospel. John Crowder comes alarmingly close, arguing that: 1) Jesus wasn't a grace preacher but rather a law preacher on steroids; 2) the gospel "is not Matthew, Mark, Luke, or John" (meaning, it is the message about Jesus that is the gospel, not these books themselves); 3) James (Jacob) didn't have the full revelation of the gospel and so his letter is a "transition" book for believing Jews; and 4) only Paul had the full revelation of the gospel.[26]

It's almost as if Jesus saw this hyper-grace teaching coming two thousand years ago and addressed it Himself: "For all the Prophets and the Law prophesied until John" (Matt. 11:13). Or, more fully, "The Law and the Prophets were until John; since then the good news of the kingdom of God is preached, and everyone forces his way into it" (Luke 16:16).[27] There you have it! John says that "the law was given through Moses; grace and truth came through Jesus Christ," and Jesus says that "The Law and the Prophets were until John; since then the good news of the kingdom of God is preached."

The Law came through Moses and was "until John"; the good news (gospel!) of grace came through Jesus, and not just through His death and resurrection. It characterized who He was and was infused in what He said, and those who find "harsh teachings" of the Law and "hopelessness" in His message are missing something glorious, beautiful, and essential. God forbid we ignore, minimize, or deprecate any of the words of Jesus!

And how could anyone suggest that the parable of the prodigal son (part of a threefold parable beginning with the lost sheep and the lost coin) was "law" and not "grace"? That the parable of the good Samaritan in Luke 10 was "law" and not "grace"? That Jesus' forgiving sinners, welcoming outcasts, and seeking and saving the lost were "law" and not "grace"? Such a claim would be preposterous.

According to Steve McVey:

> It is not God's purpose that our lives be built on a system of values. It is His desire that they be built on the person of His Son. Value systems may influence behavior, but God is not interested in systems of living. He is interested in relationships. An intimate relationship with Him will produce a godly lifestyle. A focus on behavior will not create intimacy with God or a godly lifestyle.[28]

In short, McVey says, "As we abide in Christ and allow Him to live His life through us, we live in victory."[29] Absolutely! But where is this most clearly expressed? It is in the words of Jesus in John 15, where He taught us that He was the vine and we were the branches and that, "No branch can bear fruit by itself; it must remain in the vine. Neither can you bear fruit unless you remain in me. I am the vine; you are the branches. If a man remains in me and I in him, he will bear much fruit; apart from me you can do nothing" (vv. 4–5, NIV).

What glorious, grace-filled truths! They are found on the lips of Jesus, spoken during His earthly ministry, and He specifically tied "abiding in the vine" to His words: "If you abide in me, and *my words abide in you*, ask whatever you wish, and it will be done for you" (v. 7). This one verse alone completely demolishes the idea that even some of the words of Jesus do not apply to us as believers today.

Jesus also tied abiding in His love to obeying His commandments:

> By this my Father is glorified, that you bear much fruit and so prove to be my disciples. As the Father has loved me, so have I loved you. Abide in my love. If you keep my commandments, you will abide in my love, just as I have kept my Father's commandments and abide in his love. These things I have spoken to you, that my joy may be in you, and that your joy may be full.
>
> —John 15:8–11

Yes, this is the path to joy! Jesus also said this, "Whoever has my commandments and keeps them, he it is who loves me. And he who loves me will be loved by my Father, and I will love him and manifest myself to him" (John 14:21). Some of you might hear legalism when you read this. I hear life—glorious life!—and intimate fellowship with God.

This is exactly what John wrote decades later (so much for the contrast between the Gospels and the Epistles):

> And by this we know that we have come to know him, if we keep his commandments. Whoever says "I know him" but does not keep his commandments is a liar, and the truth is not in him, but whoever keeps his word, in him truly the love of God is perfected.
>
> —1 JOHN 2:3–5

> Beloved, if our heart does not condemn us, we have confidence before God; and whatever we ask we receive from him, because we keep his commandments and do what pleases him. And this is his commandment, that we believe in the name of his Son Jesus Christ and love one another, just as he has commanded us. Whoever keeps his commandments abides in God, and God in him. And by this we know that he abides in us, by the Spirit whom he has given us.
>
> —1 JOHN 3:21–24

> By this we know that we love the children of God, when we love God and obey his commandments. For this is the love of God, that we keep his commandments. And his commandments are not burdensome.
>
> —1 JOHN 5:2–3

Shades of the words of Jesus in John's Gospel! "But," says someone in the hyper-grace camp, "we're not saying the teachings of Jesus are not good. We're just saying they don't apply to us today, since we're under grace and Jesus was under the Law."

Well, we've already seen how the New Testament utterly demolishes that position. But there's something else that demolishes that position: history and common sense. You see, if the hyper-grace teachers were right about Jesus' words before the cross being meant for Jewish listeners, that would mean that all the teaching Jesus did was just for those Jews who were able to hear Him over a three-year period, having no relevance or application beyond that. That was it! The Sermon on the Mount was just for the disciples who heard Him then, and that's it. The same with all of His parables and lessons and words of faith and promises. They applied just to the thousands who heard Him back then, and that's it. And if we apply His words to ourselves today, we are quoting Him "out of context."

Then why, pray tell, did Matthew, Mark, Luke, and John spend so many years working on their Gospels, meticulously preserving for the first generations of believers the words and deeds of Jesus if they were no longer directly relevant to the church? And why were the Gospels the first books that were recognized as Scripture by these early believers, with the sayings of Jesus widely circulated among them long before Paul wrote his first letter?[30] And why were they read on a weekly basis in some of the early church meetings? Why spend so much time preserving so many teachings if they applied only to those who heard Jesus when He was alive—Jews under the Law—especially if the sole (or primary) purpose of His teachings was to expose the hypocrisy of the religious and the hopelessness of becoming righteous by the deeds of the Law?

And why did Jesus say to His apostles that "the Helper, the Holy Spirit, whom the Father will send in my name, he will teach you all things and bring to your remembrance *all that I have said to you*" (John 14:26)? Why would the Holy Spirit bring His words to their remembrance if they were intended only for those who heard Him speak before the cross?

And what do we do with Jesus' statement, repeated three times in the Gospels, that, "Heaven and earth will pass away, but *my words* will not pass away" (Matt. 24:35; see also Mark 13:31 and Luke 21:33)? What's so important about those words—words that will last beyond the created universe—if they were only intended for the people who heard Him speak for three years, with no lasting application to the billions of people who have read His words since? And why does Acts 1:1 state that "In the first book, O Theophilus, I have dealt with all that Jesus *began to do and teach*" (Acts 1:1) if the Book of Acts does not contain the *continuation* of Jesus' words and deeds through His disciples?

So, to ask again, why do so many in the hyper-grace camp want to reject the words of Jesus? I can only say that His words clearly don't fit their theology. His parables call for accountability and His words demand discipleship, which doesn't fit with the doctrine that "God doesn't require anything from you at all."

Here, then, is a simple rule of thumb for all of us to apply: *If the words of Jesus challenge something I believe or challenge the way I live, the problem is not with Jesus. The problem is with me.* Charles Spurgeon expressed this in broader, scriptural terms when he said, "If there is any verse that you would like left out of the Bible, that is the verse that ought to stick to you, like a blister, until you really attend to its teaching."[31]

How ironic it is that in recent generations believers have so cherished the words of Jesus that they bought red-letter editions of the Bible, where the words of Jesus appear in red. Today, there are hyper-grace preachers who almost want to make His words invisible!

"But," someone says, "is there no difference between believers after the cross and believers before the cross?" That's a great question, and the answer is, yes, there is a great difference between believers before and after the cross. Now, by grace, we have been empowered by God to live out everything that Jesus taught. All of us now have the Holy Spirit living within us, and we have died with Jesus and risen from the dead with Him.[32] Now, all the more, can we experience the fullness and reality of His words. Now we have access to a righteousness that "exceeds that of the scribes and Pharisees" (Matt. 5:20). Now there is greater emphasis on internals than externals.

It would only be appropriate, though, to close this chapter with two important sayings of Jesus, starting with the Great Commission, where Jesus, after His resurrection, commanded His disciples to go and make disciples of the nations. He promised them (and us) that He would be with us to the end of the age as we went throughout the world sharing the good news. "Therefore go," He said, "and make disciples of all nations, baptizing them in the name of the Father and of the Son and of the Holy Spirit, and *teaching them to obey everything I have commanded you*" (Matt. 28:19–20, NIV).

Is that clear enough? The disciples were (and are) to teach others everything Jesus commanded them, and we have His teachings and commands in the Gospels, which are then reflected in the teaching (and responses) in Acts as well as in the later epistles.[33] That means if we leave out the words of Jesus or lessen the importance of His words or find ways to avoid the implications of His words, we cannot be true disciples in the fullest sense of the word, nor can we make true disciples in the fullest sense of the word.

On a practical, ministry level, this is terribly serious. On a heart, intimacy level, it is even more serious, since it speaks of something very wrong in our relationship with our Lord. Why wouldn't we want to sit at His feet and drink in His words?

But Jesus issued a warning too, stating that "whoever is ashamed of me *and of my words*, of him will the Son of Man be ashamed when he comes in his glory and the glory of the Father and of the holy angels" (Luke 9:26).[34] Notice that Jesus associates being ashamed of Him with being ashamed of His words, and when we downplay His words, negate the relevance of His words, and even mock the applicability of His words, at some level we are being ashamed of His words.

Let us rather embrace everything He taught, bringing us to our knees in utter dependence on Him. That is the place of grace.

-14-

THE NEW GNOSTICS

THERE'S A VERY interesting verse in Judah (Jude) where he makes this claim about the false teachers: "It is these who cause divisions, worldly people, devoid of the Spirit" (v. 19). Who exactly was he addressing?

It's not entirely clear, just as the identity of the false teachers that John was addressing in 1 John is not entirely clear,[1] but it's possible that both were combating similar heresies, heresies that eventually developed into Gnosticism.[2] If that's the case, then Judah (Jude) 19 is an especially biting rebuke.

Let me explain. The Gnostics believed that the material world itself was evil to the point that they claimed that the God of the Old Testament was a lesser god, an inferior being who emanated from Yahweh, called the Demiurge. In their minds, pure Spirit could not interact directly with material things, so there had to be an intermediary, secondary god who created the universe. For the Gnostics, then, the God of the Old Testament was not the Father of Jesus,[3] while the Son of God Himself was a spirit being who entered the fleshly body of Jesus at His baptism and then left the physical body before His crucifixion, leaving only a mere human being to be crucified.

The term *Gnosticism* comes from the Greek word for knowledge, *gnosis*, and Gnostics claim to have a special revelation, a deeper and more spiritual understanding of the faith. As noted in the *Dictionary of New Testament Background*, in the view of Gnosticism:

> The material creation, including the body, was regarded as inherently evil. Sparks of divinity, however, had been encapsuled in the bodies of certain pneumatic [i.e., charismatically gifted] or spiritual individuals, who were ignorant of their celestial origins.

> The transcendent God sent down a redeemer, who brought them salvation in the form of secret *gnōsis*. Gnostics hoped to escape from the prison of their bodies at death and to traverse the planetary spheres of hostile demons to be reunited with God.[4]

So, the Gnostics saw themselves as the really spiritual ones and the Christians as the fleshly ones. Judah (Jude) says that the reality is quite the opposite: "It is these who cause divisions, worldly people, devoid of the Spirit." And note carefully what the Greek says: the word for *worldly* is literally "soulish" (*psuchikos*)—which may have been the very way that the Gnostics described the Christians[5]—and the phrase *devoid of the Spirit* is literally "not having spirit," with the word *pneuma*, "spirit," put first for emphasis. Judah (Jude) is saying they are anything but the truly spiritual ones!

New Testament scholar Craig Keener made the important observation that "Gnostics also tended to define sin in various ways, hence some Gnostics believed that they were incapable of committing real sins, although their bodies could engage in behavior non-Gnostic Christians considered sinful."[6] This strikes close to home when it comes to some hyper-grace teaching, especially in its more extreme forms.

But before I go any further, let me be perfectly clear: 1) I do not for a moment consider hyper-grace teachers like Joseph Prince, Clark Whitten, or Andrew Farley (to name just a few) to be modern-day Gnostics. I understand them to be committed brothers in the Lord, despite what I consider to be serious errors in some aspects of their teaching. (I imagine they would feel the same about me.) 2) Within the hyper-grace movement there are some especially dangerous seeds that resemble the ancient Gnostic heresy. 3) Some of those who began in the hyper-grace movement have now fallen into full-blown heresy and deception, much of it resembling ancient Gnosticism.

For these reasons I have named this chapter "The New Gnostics." Are you ready for some real shockers? Then let's continue our study, going from bad teaching to even worse teaching to absolutely horrific teaching.

Scholars have observed that in the Gnostic system, the concept of salvation was more a matter of receiving *special illumination* from

God than a matter of coming into *right relationship* with God. What does this have to do with the modern grace movement? I'm fully aware that hyper-grace leaders like Pastor Prince often state, "Grace is not a theology. It is not a subject matter. It is not a doctrine. It is a person, and his name is Jesus."[7] For my part, I genuinely believe that they mean this, and I'm sure that many of these teachers are truly encountering Jesus through a greater revelation of His grace.

With Peter, I pray that all of us will "grow in the grace and knowledge of our Lord and Savior Jesus Christ" (2 Pet. 3:18), since there is always more for us to grasp in terms of God's amazing grace expressed through His Son. At the same time, I have often observed a non-relational side to some hyper-grace believers, as their walk with God seems to be based more on a theological revelation—often a theoretical one at that, as I'll explain—than on a relationship with the Father.

To cite a case in point, I once interacted with a self-proclaimed hyper-grace preacher, a young pastor who was studying theology at the university level. He had just given me the standard hyper-grace interpretation of 1 John 1:9, explaining that since all his sins had already been forgiven, including his future sins, there was no need for him ever to confess his sins to God. He also made the standard (erroneous) claim that 1 John 1:9 was addressed to Gnostic heretics.[8]

Since he did not seem open to having his theology questioned, I turned to the aspect of his relationship with the Lord, asking him by way of analogy what would happen if he had gotten angry with his wife and spoken harsh words to her, after which he left the house for a few hours. When he returned home, would he just act as if nothing had happened between him and his wife, or would he feel the need to apologize? Would he say, "Honey, please forgive me for the way I treated you. That was totally ugly and completely unjustified, and there's no excuse for my behavior. I apologize from the bottom of my heart and ask you to forgive me."

He immediately said that yes, indeed, he would ask his wife to forgive him. But when I asked him if he would do the same thing if he sinned against the Lord (or recognized that his sin against his wife was also a sin against the Lord), he said absolutely not, explaining that this was the Lord we were talking about, not his wife. That is a very troubling response, even if in his eyes it was very spiritual.

Why do I say this? Well, stop for a moment and ask yourself what kind of *relationship* with the Lord you have—what kind of *fellowship* you are experiencing with Him—if your sins against Him and against others don't grieve you and move you to go to Him in repentance?

I'm not talking about a dead religious ritual here. I'm not talking about legalistic bondage. I'm talking about a living, vibrant relationship, one that can be even deeper than the relationship we enjoy with our own spouses. If this pastor felt the need to get things right with his wife—not out of rote but out of relationship—why wouldn't he feel the need to get things right with God on a relational level? And wasn't there a reason that God compared His relationship to Israel with that of a husband to a wife, while in the New Testament the church is portrayed as the bride of Christ?[9]

Even if I held to a hyper-grace *theology* (which I obviously don't), and even if I believed God had already forgiven my future sins (again, an unscriptural concept), I can't imagine being close to the Lord and loving and cherishing Him, then somehow hardening my heart for a season and acting in ways that I knew displeased Him without wanting to talk with Him about it afterward, confessing my sins and asking His forgiveness. As a reader commented in response to an article I had written on hyper-grace, "Common courtesy tells us to say, 'I'm sorry,' when we do something wrong to someone."

Just think of how Peter felt after betraying Jesus, denying Him three times while Jesus was being interrogated not far away. Luke records that immediately after Peter's third denial, "the Lord turned and looked at Peter. And Peter remembered the saying of the Lord, how he had said to him, 'Before the rooster crows today, you will deny me three times.' And he went out and wept bitterly" (Luke 22:61–62). Do you honestly think that if Peter had believed that Jesus had already forgiven his sins that he would have been less grieved by his actions? That he would not have wept bitterly? The thought is preposterous. Yet it is a thought that would be supported by some hyper-grace teaching.

According to Steve McVey, the concept that "when we do wrong, we are out of fellowship with God" is a lie,[10] yet he rightly defines "fellowship" as "closeness, unity with one another, oneness."[11] If he is correct, this means that a Christian who yields to temptation, goes out and watches violent pornography, then, with those images in his mind, kidnaps a prostitute for a week and has sex with her and beats her up—that this man was in fellowship with God, in "closeness" and "unity" with Him—the whole time he did this. Paul would be horrified at the thought.

Let's remember that the word *koinonia* in Greek can be translated as "communion" or "fellowship," and when Paul wrote to the Corinthians about the sacredness of partaking in Holy Communion, he warned them to flee from idolatry, stating plainly, "You cannot drink the cup of the Lord and the cup of demons. You cannot partake of the table of the Lord and the table of demons" (1 Cor. 10:21). Yet according to Pastor McVey, even while you are drinking the cup of demons and partaking of the table of demons, your communion with the Lord is unbroken. The problems with this thinking cannot be overstated.

Paul also wrote to the Corinthians:

> Do you not know that your bodies are members of Christ? Shall I then take the members of Christ and make them members of a prostitute? Never! Or do you not know that he who is joined to a prostitute becomes one body with her? For as it is written, "The two will become one flesh." But he who is joined to the Lord becomes one spirit with him. Flee from sexual immorality.
>
> —1 Corinthians 6:15–18

Yet Pastor McVey is somehow telling us that while we are joined together with a prostitute, becoming one flesh with her, we are also experiencing fellowship with God. He writes:

> I have one question, though, to show you the problem. How can you be separated or have distance from someone who lives *in you*?
>
> The idea that we're out of fellowship with God when we do wrong is a lie. It's one of those clichés. It sounds good, but it's not biblical. There is nothing you can do to put yourself out of fellowship with God.[12]

Really? And what is his support for the statement, "There is nothing you can do to put yourself out of fellowship with God"? It is based on a spiritual theorem ("How can you be separated or have distance from someone who lives *in you*?") that does not address the *relational* aspect of our walk with God—the thing called "fellowship." And is the God who lives inside of us sometimes grieved over our words, actions, and deeds?

McVey continues:

> Certainly, when we have sinned, whenever we've done wrong, our perception of that fellowship is radically changed. The situation is illustrated well in the story of the prodigal son in Luke 15. When this young prodigal went off into the far country, what was the attitude of the father? Did he stop loving his son? Was he angry with him? Did he feel differently about him? Not at all. There is nothing in the biblical account to even hint at that possibility.[13]

But his illustration about the prodigal son actually proves the opposite of what he intends. You see, the issue here is not whether the Father longs for us or whether He still loves us even when we turn our backs on Him. Of course He does, and of course He is ready to receive us back as His own with great joy, just as Jesus taught in the parable of the prodigal son.

But was the father in *fellowship* with his son when his son left home and plunged into sin? Certainly not. Fellowship was not restored until the son came back home, where he was received with open arms. And so, this was not just a matter of the son's *perception*. This was the reality.

Using logic that sounds almost Gnostic and turning verses on their head, Pastor McVey quotes 1 John 1:5–6, "This is the message we have heard from Him and announce to you, that God is Light, and in Him there is no darkness at all. If we say that we have fellowship with Him and yet walk in the darkness, we lie and do not practice the truth" (NAS).

He then writes:

> God is Light. You are in God. So you are in the light. You can't walk in darkness because God is Light, and in Him is no

> darkness at all. It may look dark to you because sins blind you to the light, but you're still there nonetheless. To say you are "in the dark" or "out of fellowship" with your Father is to not practice (live) the truth.[14]

But John just said the exact opposite of that, and he repeats that theme throughout his letter: "If we say we have fellowship with him while we walk in darkness, we lie and do not practice the truth" (1 John 1:6). What could be clearer? If we choose to walk in darkness, we are *not* having fellowship with God.[15]

Somehow Pastor McVey concludes:

> You are in fellowship with God all the time. Your perception of that may change, but remember: Your feelings are not the standard of truth. The promises of God in Holy Scripture are. I assure you: The idea that we're out of fellowship with God when we do wrong is a lie. Your Father is in fellowship with you *all* the time, and when we understand that truth, it causes us to want to live a lifestyle that glorifies Him.
>
> Fellowship is not about our feelings. It's about how we're related to God because of the finished work of Jesus Christ.[16]

Do you see how this has a Gnostic side to it? The very idea of fellowship or communion speaks of relationship, and it is a relationship that is experienced. The Holy Spirit bears witness with our spirits that we are God's children (Rom. 8:16). God puts the Spirit of His Son into our hearts, by which we cry "Abba, Father" (Gal. 4:6–7). We have the deposit of the Spirit in our lives (Eph. 1:14). These are not just concepts but realities, and they are realities that, on one level or another, we experience, as seen in this blessing that Paul invoked on the Corinthians: "The grace of the Lord Jesus Christ and the love of God and *the fellowship of the Holy Spirit* be with you all" (2 Cor. 13:14). This was not just theoretical.

What Fellowship Has Light With Darkness?

It's one thing to say that even when we don't feel it or even when we have a temporary lapse, we are still children of God, still saints, still beloved, still born from above, still indwelt by the Spirit. It is another thing to say "you are in fellowship with God all the time" and that "there is nothing you can do to put yourself out of fellowship with God." Or, in the words of Andre van der Merwe, "Jesus already paid the full price so that we could have *unbroken fellowship with the Father*. This means that when we make a mistake, *it does not break our fellowship* or right standing with God."[17] Not so! There are absolutely things that we can do that "break our fellowship...with God."[18] (Making "a mistake" is one thing; willfully choosing to live in sin is another.)

In 2 Corinthians 6 Paul wrote:

> Do not be unequally yoked with unbelievers. For what partnership has righteousness with lawlessness? Or what fellowship has light with darkness? What accord has Christ with Belial? Or what portion does a believer share with an unbeliever? What agreement has the temple of God with idols? For we are the temple of the living God.
>
> —2 CORINTHIANS 6:14–16

Note in particular those words, "Or what *fellowship* has light with darkness?" That's why Paul exhorts the believers in Corinth using verses from the Old Testament where the Lord Himself says, "Therefore go out from their midst, and be separate from them, says the Lord, and touch no unclean thing; then I will welcome you" (v. 17).

Yet these hyper-grace teachers are telling us that we can walk in darkness, potentially for protracted periods of time, without walking away from the Lord or experiencing any break in fellowship with Him. That is simply not true. That's why Jesus called the believers in Laodicea to repent, giving them this wonderful promise: "Here I am! I stand at the door and knock. If anyone hears my voice and opens the door, I will come in and eat with him, and he with me" (Rev. 3:20, NIV). He is offering them restored fellowship.[19]

Steve McVey holds to other, non-relational teachings, such as, it is a lie that "God is Disappointed in You When You Do Wrong." He claims that, "This lie is constantly used in the modern church world to motivate and manipulate people to straighten up and act right. It's a guilt-trip ticket passed out by many in religious authority to anybody who is willing to take it."[20] (See chapter 8 for more on this.) I wonder if Pastor McVey believes that the Lord is displeased with those who teach against the hyper-grace message.

Not surprisingly, he also teaches that it is a lie to say that "Your Sins Can Disqualify You from Being Used by God," writing, "There's nothing you've ever done and nothing you could ever do that would keep God from working both in and through your life. The idea that you can commit sins that can disqualify you from being used by God is a lie, and it will keep you in bondage."[21]

Unfortunately, he fails to mention the necessity of repentance—in other words, that we can be restored from our sins and used again by the Lord *if we repent and turn away from those sins*—and he fails to recognize that there are some things we can do that will have lasting consequences in this world, even if God forgives us and restores us in fellowship.

Similarly, Clark Whitten writes, "My bad works don't move God any more than my good works move Him. He simply isn't moved by 'works' of any kind. If you are motivated to do a great work for God, good luck!"[22]

Too bad the writers of the New Testament didn't realize this. They could have saved themselves a lot of ink instead of calling on believers to live right in order to please the Lord. And Jesus could have saved Himself a lot of grief too, especially when addressing the churches in Asia Minor.[23]

It's also a good thing William Carey never heard of this doctrine. He would have never uttered those inspiring words that have ministered to countless millions of Christians: "Expect great things from God; attempt great things for God."[24] And it's a good thing that God never heard of this doctrine, since He will reward us for our deeds of service on that great day.[25]

But all this is only the tip of the iceberg. Much more serious is the notion that, because our spirits are born again and perfect, and because we are spirits who have souls and live in bodies, even if we sin, it's not really us sinning. Yes, I've heard this directly from hyper-grace adherents.

Earlier in this chapter I quoted Professor Craig Keener, who noted that, "Gnostics also tended to define sin in various ways, hence some Gnostics believed that they were incapable of committing real sins, although their bodies could engage in behavior non-Gnostic Christians considered sinful."[26] Do you see how relevant this observation is when it comes to some of these hyper-grace extremes?

Consider what one young man explained in a blog post, which was written to counter my article, "Confronting the Error of Hyper-Grace":

> It isn't a matter of if God sees my sins. I no longer have sins, I am solely identified by God as a perfect spirit though that spirit does live in this temporary "tent" of flesh. God is not blind to how the deeds of my flesh affect myself & others but He does not need to charge me or even my flesh with sin for our relationship to work.[27]

What was the basis for such extreme statements? He referenced these scriptures:

> Hebrews 10:17 says when you enter the New Covenant God promises to "never remember your sins & lawless deeds." Romans 8:9 says, "We are not in the flesh but in the Spirit because the Spirit of God lives in us." 1 John 3:9, 5:18 say a Christian's spirit cannot sin. 2 Corinthians 5:16 says God "no longer identifies anyone according to the flesh." Romans 4:8 says, "The Lord does not take sin into account." 2 Corinthians 5:19 says, "God does not credit people with sin."[28]

In truth, he has miserably misapplied these verses,[29] leading to radical statements like this: "If you can't separate your flesh's actions from your identity you are under the law & don't know what it means to be born again."[30] What a dangerous concept: "God, You know that wasn't really me. It was just my flesh!"

In more moderate tones, yet equally misguided in terms of scriptural truth, a hyper-grace teacher explained to me privately that "sanctified" does not mean being set apart to God by the way we live; it means that God makes us perfect. And while he stated that this didn't mean he never sinned, it did mean that he is not condemned by his sin or under its curse, nor does sin define him in any way. Rather, whatever sins he commits are "confined to the flesh" and will never be laid to his account in any way.[31] So when you and I sin, it's not really us. It's "confined to the flesh" and will never be laid to our account.[32]

Unfortunately, beliefs like this are becoming more mainstream in the modern grace camp, to the point that a friend of mine who had been greatly blessed by the messages at the megachurch he attended became concerned, making an appointment to speak with the executive pastor by phone. (My friend has served as a missionary overseas and has been involved in ministry work for several decades, so he is hardly a novice.) He asked the pastor to respond with a yes or no to the question, "Do you sin?" The pastor answered with "No," going on to explain that he was, essentially, his spirit, and his spirit couldn't sin. Therefore, whatever sins he did commit were not really him!

What about Romans 7, where Paul twice states that if he sins, "it is no longer I who do it, but sin that dwells within me" (Rom. 7:17; see also verse 20)? First, many, if not most, scholars, along with many hyper-grace teachers, believe that Paul is not talking about his life as a believer but rather his experience living under the Law (or the experience of anyone living under the Law).[33] And when Paul made the statement that "it is no longer I who do it, but sin that dwells within me," he was giving a spiritual-psychological analysis rather than talking about whether he was responsible for actions or whether *he* actually sinned. Clearly he acknowledged and took responsibility for his sin. Just reread Romans 7 and notice his use of the words "I" and "me."

Second, hyper-grace teachers emphatically emphasize that we no longer have a sinful nature, based on passages such as Romans 6:6: "We know that our old self was crucified with him in order that the body of sin might be brought to nothing, so that we would no longer be enslaved to sin." One hyper-grace leader even devoted a small book to this specific subject titled, *Do Christians Still Have a Sinful Nature?*[34] And so, based on this, it would make no sense for a born-again believer to say, "When I sin, it's actually sin dwelling in me that's doing the work." (We'll come back to this point shortly.)

Third, and most importantly, God deals with the whole person, not making a division between our spirit and soul and our body when it comes to responsibility for our actions. Just read all the epistles in the New Testament, along with the words of Jesus to the congregations of

Asia Minor in Revelation 2–3. The apostles and Jesus did not say, "We know you dear saints are perfect and sinless, since you are really just spirits living in tents of flesh, but we have a problem with the nasty things your flesh is doing."

Nonsense! Rather, they said, "We are not pleased with the things *you* are doing, so turn away from those things and walk worthy of your high calling as saints." That's why Paul concluded his exhortation in 2 Corinthians 6:14–7:1, cited in part previously and filled with divine promises, with these words: "Therefore, my dear friends, since we have these promises, let us purify ourselves from everything that can defile either body or spirit, and strive to be completely holy, out of reverence for God" (2 Cor. 7:1, CJB).

We Are Not Separate From Our Sinful Flesh

There's an interesting story in the Talmud probably dating to the second century AD, recounting a conversation between a Roman emperor, called Antoninus here, and a rabbinic leader named Yehudah HaNassi (Yehudah the Prince), but referred to simply as "Rabbi" in this account:

> A. Antoninus said to Rabbi, "The body and the soul both can exempt themselves from judgment.
>
> B. "How so? The body will say, 'The soul is the one that has sinned, for from the day that it left me, lo, I am left like a silent stone in the grave.'
>
> C. "And the soul will say, 'The body is the one that sinned. For from the day that I left it, lo, I have been flying about in the air like a bird.'"
>
> D. [Rabbi] said to him, "I shall draw a parable for you. To what may the matter be likened? To the case of a mortal king who had a lovely orchard, and in it were luscious figs. He set in it two watchmen, one crippled and one blind.
>
> E. "Said the cripple to the blind man, 'There are luscious figs that I see in the orchard. Come and carry me, and let us get some to eat. The cripple rode on the blind man and they got the figs and ate them. After a while the king said to them, 'Where are the luscious figs?'

F. "Said the cripple, 'Do I have feet to go to them?'

G. "Said the blind man, 'Do I have eyes to see?'

H. "What did the king do? He had the cripple climb onto the blind man, and he inflicted judgment on them as one.

I. "So the Holy One, blessed be he, brings the soul and places it back in the body and judges them as one, as it is said, 'He shall call to the heavens from above and to the earth, that he may judge his people' (Psa. 50: 4).

J. "'He shall to call to the heavens from above'—this is the soul.

K. "'And to the earth, that he may judge his people'—this is the body."[35]

Putting aside the imaginative (and typically rabbinic) use of Psalm 50, the rabbi's point is well taken: God will judge us as one person, spirit, soul, and body (or, as here, soul and body, referring to our inner being and our outer being, as in 2 Corinthians 4:16).[36] Yet the excuses of the blind man and the lame man in this parable are reminiscent of the concepts circulating in some hyper-grace circles, as in the statement cited above: "I no longer have sins, I am solely identified by God as a perfect spirit though that spirit does live in this temporary 'tent' of flesh."

Also responding to my article "Confronting the Error of Hyper-Grace" was Dr. Paul Ellis, himself a respected hyper-grace teacher and pastor. He wrote: "Dr. Brown asks an important question: 'Does God always love what he sees when he looks at his people?' According to him, the answer is no. God doesn't like what he sees when he looks at us. Our sins grieve him. But here's the thing: *we are not our sins.*"[37]

What should we take that to mean? To give some context to his comments, in my article I had taken exception to Clark Whitten's comments that when God sees us, "He sees us as holy and righteous. He sees us, and He loves what He sees."[38] My issue, of course, was not whether God *loved us*, but rather that, no matter what we did or how we lived, whether God *loved what He saw* (as opposed to loved *who* He saw). In response, Dr. Ellis stated that "we are not our sins."[39]

But what is the point in saying that? Of course "we" are not "our sins." But "we" are quite responsible for "our sins," and those sins affect us, affect those around us, and affect our walk with the Lord.

Once again, using Dr. Ellis's logic, believers throughout the New Testament could respond to rebukes from Paul and other leaders by saying, "Why are you rebuking *us*? We are not our sins!" And an adulterous wife could say to her husband, "Why are you so upset with me? I am not my sins!" Or a disobedient child could say to his parents, "Why are you disciplining me? I am not my sins!" Or a thief could say to a judge, "Why are you sentencing me to jail? I am not my sins!" And from a totally different angle, we could ask the Lord, "Why did Jesus have to die for our sins? After all, we are not our sins!"[40]

Now I do not want to misrepresent Dr. Ellis in any way, since I don't believe he condones sin or winks at sin or thinks lightly of sin. In fact, he is convinced that the gospel of grace is *the* way to overcome sin, as opposed to a guilt-driven, threatening-God approach, and I agree with much of his emphasis. And in his book *The Gospel in Ten Words*, for the second test of an authentic gospel, he asks, "Does this gospel empower me to overcome sin?"[41]

Dr. Ellis also lists these as some of his favorite quotes from Pastor Joseph Prince, and I say amen to every one of them: "The Bible says that sin shall not have dominion over you when you are not under law but under grace. So if you are living in sin, you are definitely not under grace."[42] And, "Grace brings about a restraint that is supernatural."[43] And, "When you fall in love with Jesus, you will fall out of love with sin."[44] Similarly, Ryan Rufus, Clark Whitten, Andrew Farley, and other hyper-grace teachers have stated categorically that grace does not give us a license to sin. That is not in question.

Unfortunately, they send mixed messages with many of their statements, especially when they assure us that nothing we do can possibly separate us from God, break our fellowship with God, or disappoint God, or when they tell us that we never need to confess our sins to God and that the Holy Spirit will never convict us of sin. And what kind of message is sent when some teachers claim that "we" don't sin because our spirits are perfect in God's sight and therefore "we" cannot sin?

Even more dangerous is an increasingly common hyper-grace interpretation of some verses in 1 John 3, where John states that "No one who abides in him keeps on sinning; no one who keeps on sinning has either seen him or known him....No one born of God makes a practice of sinning, for God's seed abides in him, and he cannot keep on sinning because he has been born of God" (1 John 3:6, 9).

Now, what John is saying is fairly straightforward, even if it is challenging: if someone is living in persistent, habitual, unrepentant sin,[45] that person cannot be a believer, since a true believer is born of God and has God's seed in his or her heart. Some hyper-faith adherents turn this completely on its head, using the following "logic": "Well, I know I'm a believer, but I'm also practicing sin, and since a believer cannot be practicing sin, and I am really a perfect spirit, indwelt by God, I'm not really sinning!" Talk about a Gnostic-like deception!

On a spiritual level, it parallels a teaching found in some Word of Faith circles in which you are not allowed to say you are sick, since it is believed that you are already healed by Jesus' stripes (as opposed to believing that your healing is paid for and can be received by faith). So the doctor might say you have bronchitis, the blood tests may confirm that you have bronchitis, and the pain in your throat assures you that you have bronchitis, but according to this teaching, these are all just "lying symptoms." You are already healed.

In the same way, some hyper-grace believers claim that they do not sin since their spirits are fully redeemed and they are spirits living in a body, so whatever sins they do commit are not really sins. The extreme Word of Faith person says, "I'm not sick," as he coughs and hacks, and the extreme hyper-grace person says, "I don't sin," as he lies and lusts.

Commenting on 1 John 1, Andrew Farley wrote:

> Why is John now concerned about those who claim they're sinless? Do you know any true believers today who say they've never sinned? Of course not! What do you have to do to become a believer in Christ? Admit you're a sinner! Someone who claims they have never sinned is not a Christian. So here John is concerned for unbelievers.[46]

We saw in chapter 5 that John was, in fact, writing to believers, not unbelievers, but in answer to Andrew Farley's question, I now know some hyper-grace believers who claim *they no longer sin*—ever. This is a deadly deception.

According to 1 John 1:8, "If we say we have no sin, we deceive ourselves, and the truth is not in us." Explaining this, Greek scholar Kenneth Wuest writes:

> Here John again combats the Gnostic heresy which held that we do not have any principle of sin within us, since matter is evil and the soul is not contaminated by sinful flesh.... Here we have the heresy of the eradication of the totally depraved nature during the earthly life of the Christian. The heresy of perfectionism and of the eradication of the evil nature is the present day form of this problem of the indwelling sinful nature.[47]

John Crowder teaches the opposite, stating, "I no longer even have an independent self that is capable of pleasing God. It is no longer *I* but Christ.... There is no separate, individual *you*. Christ has *replaced* you.... Saved people don't sin."[48] Or in the words of Andre Rabe, "Can we say that we are without sin? Yes!"[49]

Consequently, some hyper-grace teachers claim we can live a "temptation-free" existence, which makes verses such as 1 Corinthians 10:13 virtually meaningless. There Paul writes, "No temptation has overtaken you that is not common to man. God is faithful, and he will not let you be tempted beyond your ability, but with the temptation he will also provide the way of escape, that you may be able to endure it." If these teachers were right, Paul should have simply written, "Just follow my lead, and you'll never be tempted again!"[50]

But Crowder goes even further, claiming that the believer has no sinful nature, and the only reason we struggle with sin is because we believe the lie that we are still partly sinner and partly saint.[51]

Similarly, Benjamin Dunn writes: "The 'old life' has been destroyed. You can dig as much as you want, but you will find no remnants of this 'old life' buried in the Gospel! This makes joy and happiness come effortlessly for the believer."[52] Yes, "Because of this God-flood [with reference to Ephesians 3:19 in the Amplified Bible], the former heart is eclipsed to absolutely nothing more than a memory."[53] Really?

This is similar to what Ryan Rufus has preached:

> There is no sin nature in there. There is nothing of the old creation that lives inside of your new creation spirit. There is no sin or unrighteousness. Your spirit has received full perfection! Full holiness! God is not trying to give you anything else—He has already given you fullness!...All of the fullness of God lives inside of you![54]

How then do we still manage to sin? And why do we still have to resist temptation? According to John Crowder, if we are still struggling with sin, then we have never been saved or, if we are saved, we have not yet heard the revelation that we are now totally free from sin.[55] Is there no denial of reality taking place here?

I agree that in Jesus, we have died to sin and we can no longer live in it. And I agree that in Jesus, we have taken on a new nature and we are not who we used to be. But the Word makes clear and our experiences confirm that "we" are human beings, living in these bodies (which are part of us!), needing to renew our minds in the midst of a fallen world and with a real devil who wants to attack and destroy and deceive. Because of this, "we" must resist sin, from the inside and the outside.

According to Chuck Crisco, "The revolutionary truth is that as a believer you have a new identity: *whatever is true of Jesus is now true of you.* 1 John 4:17 says it like this: 'As He is, so are we in this world....' [I] have taken on Christ's identity. *Whatever is true of Jesus is now true of me!* This is the gospel!... *Whatever is true of Jesus is true of me.* Therefore, since God is love, then so am I."[56]

You can readily see where this kind of thinking leads. Why not say: "Since God is perfect, I am perfect"? "Since God is sinless, I am sinless"? "Since God is all powerful, I am all powerful"? "Since God is King and Lord, I am King and Lord"? Why not? As Andre Rabe claims, "God doesn't just think thoughts about you....You are His thoughts in physical form."[57]

But there's more still. Ben Dunn actually claims that "Christ not only set us free from sin but also its effects and its consequences....We should no longer be limited by the curse and Fall of Man."[58] If that is the case, why do we still die? Why is it even possible for us to get sick? Do you see how detached from reality this becomes?

And yet there is even more. Some hyper-grace adherents have gone completely off the deep end, actually claiming to have "redeemed" profanity and other fleshly behaviors. One young man, who actually has a small but devoted following, claimed in March 2013 that "Joel's Army conquered all swear words and can use them all as blessings with a clean conscience! Enjoy!"[59]

Under an online post with the title "Formerly Known as Cuss Words" (after which he lists them), he writes, "These words belong to the Army of God now!" This is followed by one of the most despicable sentences I have ever read in my life, mixing together foul profanity with the Holy Spirit. Then he writes, "LOL all forms are being taken by the Holy Spirit."

On March 22, 2013, he posted on Facebook, "Only the brave, only the free, [severe profanity] perfected liberty. [Mild profanity.] The river will continue to flow mightily through the free and the brave to the point of washing away all curses from every culture on earth."

On March 26, 2013, he posted, "The only cult on earth is the mass majority with unrenewed minds. See Romans 8. They fight like goats against the people with renewed minds."

Yes, all of us who reject gross deception like this are part of a cult, making up the mass majority with unrenewed minds, fighting like goats against the people with renewed minds like this young man. And so, because God's grace is so powerful and they have been made perfectly holy, even sin is no longer sin. It probably won't be long before they claim that sexual immorality and drunkenness have been redeemed too (if they haven't already).

Yet I've seen older, experienced believers interacting on some of these Facebook pages, discussing holiness and grace and trashing "religion," as if this "redeeming profanity" nonsense was actually serious. Judah's (Jude's) words are ringing true once again, as he also warned about the false teachers in his day "who pervert the grace of our God into sensuality and deny our only Master and Lord, Jesus Christ" (Judah [Jude] 4). Or as rendered in the New American Standard Bible, "who turn the grace of our God into licentiousness and deny our only Master and Lord, Jesus Christ." God's grace can be abused!

This is the same perverted mentality that inspired this Facebook post by a so-called "gay Christian": "It's so funny how all of our gay Christian friends love going to nude beaches. LOL. It kinda shows how we are throwing off the chains of religious oppression upon another area of sexuality."[60]

Without a doubt, the vast, vast majority of hyper-grace teachers would categorically reject unscriptural garbage like this, and for good reason. At the same time, I have watched hyper-grace adherents go off the deep end because of the very errors that are mixed into the modern grace message, and for them it is a logical progression.

That's why it is so critical that we hold to biblical grace alone—to grace without mixture, grace without addition, grace without exaggeration, grace without dilution. Grace is such a glorious, powerful, life-changing truth that tampering with it can prove deadly.

-15-

THE FINISHED WORK OF THE CROSS

MORE THAN SIXTY years ago Arthur Pink sounded a strong alarm in his message "The Gospel of Satan." He wrote:

> Again; thousands are deceived into supposing that they have "accepted Christ" as their "personal Saviour," who have not first received Him as their LORD. The Son of God did not come here to save His people in their sin, but "from their sins" (Matthew 1:21). To be saved from sins, is to be saved from ignoring and despising the authority of God, it is to abandon the course of self-will and self-pleasing, it is to "forsake our way" (Isa. 55:7). It is to surrender to God's authority, to yield to His dominion, to give ourselves over to be ruled by Him. The one who has never taken Christ's "yoke" upon him, who is not truly and diligently seeking to please Him in all the details of life, and yet supposes that he is "resting on the Finished Work of Christ" is deluded by the Devil.[1]

Pink was addressing a teaching current in his day that claimed believers had no obligation to live as disciples once they were "saved," since Jesus already did all the work on the cross. After all, if Jesus announced "it is finished" right before He died, then there's nothing left for us to do other than believe. As Mick Mooney wrote in his book *Look! The Finished Work of Jesus*, "We only need to believe upon Jesus for whom he truly is and our works obligation to God is perfectly fulfilled."[2] Shades of the very error Arthur Pink was confronting!

Of course, it is true that the "work" of salvation that God requires is to believe in His Son (see John 6:28–29), but it is absolutely false to claim that by believing in Jesus "our works obligation to God is perfectly fulfilled." Joseph Prince puts the idea this way, "Live life knowing that there is nothing for you to do—only **believe**! It is finished!"[3]

To be sure, there are glorious truths that Mooney and Prince convey in their writings, and we do well to meditate on those truths. At the same time, as we have seen, those truths are often stated in exaggerated and misleading form. And so, contrary to the claim that "our works obligation to God is perfectly fulfilled" once we believe, Paul wrote that "we are his workmanship, *created in Christ Jesus for good works*, which God prepared beforehand, that we should walk in them" (Eph. 2:10). That certainly sounds like an obligation![4] (Note also that Paul wrote this in a context extolling salvation by grace through faith and not by works; see Ephesians 2:8–9). And Jacob (James) minced no words, emphasizing that "as the body apart from the spirit is dead, so also faith apart from works is dead" (Jacob [James] 2:26).

The Lord has purchased us with His blood, and He expects much from us: "Or do you not know that your body is a temple of the Holy Spirit within you, whom you have from God? You are not your own, for you were bought with a price. So glorify God in your body" (1 Cor. 6:19–20). And even though it is Jesus working in us, God requires our participation, calling us to "work out [our] own salvation with fear and trembling, for it is God who works in [us], both to will and to work for his good pleasure" (Phil. 2:12–13).

To be candid, though, I'm not at all surprised that some teachers go too far when they teach about grace and "the finished work on the cross." After all, what Jesus accomplished on the cross is so magnificent and comprehensive that it is easy to overstate the effects of His "finished work." And it's easy to see how some would argue that if Jesus did it all and if the work of salvation is completely "finished," there's nothing for us to add to it. In fact, you can easily make the claim that if you have to add anything to what Jesus did—including your faith—then the work is not really finished, a line of thinking that I believe leads to even more serious error in interpreting Scripture.

This is the very teaching now advocated by pastors Philip Gulley and James Mulholland, who believe that if the message of grace is really true and Jesus really paid for the sins of the world on the cross, then every person will be saved. They write (speaking with one voice as "I"):

> For many years God had been eroding my obsessive devotion to judgment, punishment, and wrath. God had used countless

> experiences to wear away my inadequate understanding of his grace. The life and stories of Jesus had slowly undercut theological formulas I'd accepted uncritically....
>
> Now I have a new formula. It too is simple and clear. It is the most compelling truth I've ever known. It is changing my life. It is changing how I talk about God. It is changing how I think about myself. It is changing how I treat other people. It brings me untold joy, peace, and hope. This truth is the best news I've ever heard, ever believed, and ever shared.
>
> *I believe God will save every person.*
>
> Now by salvation, I mean much more than a ticket to heaven. I mean much more than being cleansed of our sins and rescued from hell's fire. I mean even more than being raised from the grave and granted eternal life. By salvation, I mean being freed of every obstacle to intimacy with God. We will know as we are known and love as we are loved.[5]

Doesn't this sound familiar? These pastors claim to have received a new understanding of grace that changed their lives and filled them with joy and peace and hope, and they are convinced this message is scriptural and must be restored to the church.[6] This sounds like the new "grace reformation," except it goes one big step further.

But it is a step that is understandable, as incorrect as it is. As I pointed out in chapter 2, John Crowder has written, "The gospel is simply too good to be true. If the message you've heard is not too good to be true, then it probably isn't. The gospel is too easy. Too marvelous. Too extraordinary. Too scandalously good to be true."[7]

Based on this logic, you could easily argue that if there's a hell or future judgment for anyone at all, then the message is *not* "too good to be true" and grace is *not* really grace. And based on this line of reasoning, you could easily claim that there is not an aspect of God's creation that cannot be redeemed by the love of the Father and the blood of Jesus Christ—meaning that even Satan and his demons could be saved—a concept that, as I mentioned in chapter 2, has already been proposed.

Pastor Rob Bell has embraced a similar line of thinking about the redemption of all mankind, based on the "finished work" of the cross. He writes:

> It begins with the sure and certain truth that we are loved.
> That in spite of whatever has gone horribly wrong deep in our hearts
> and has spread to every corner of the world,
> in spite of our sins,
> failures, rebellion,
> and hard hearts,
> in spite of what's been done to us or what we've done, God has made peace with us.
> Done. Complete.
> As Jesus said, "It is finished."[8]

These serious misinterpretations of Scripture in the name of grace should make us stop and think for a moment, since it's all too common for our friends in the hyper-grace movement to accuse others of "not having the grace revelation" or "not understanding the finished work of the cross," like the pastor who posted that my "theology lacks an understanding of what Jesus accomplished for us."[9] Perhaps it's not a lack of understanding of the finished work of the cross. Perhaps it's a true reading of the Scriptures and an accurate appreciation of what Jesus accomplished for us.

In his book *Unmerited Favor*, Joseph Prince made reference to the "finished work" more than forty times, writing, "Unfortunately, there are some believers who are cheapening grace and the finished work of Jesus because of their wrong beliefs."[10] And while I agree with so much of what he wrote about "the finished work of the cross" (along with so much of what Mick Mooney wrote), I can't help but point out, once again, that truth is being exaggerated and, I believe, even mixed with error.

According to Andrew Wommack, "Jesus hasn't saved, healed, delivered, or prospered a single person in the last 2,000 years. What God has provided by grace 2,000 years ago now becomes a reality when mixed with faith. Faith appropriates what God has already provided."[11] Similarly, one of my missionary friends in Italy sent me detailed notes from a sermon by a hyper-grace preacher there who proclaimed that there are some prayers that do not have to be prayed in the light of the finished work of the cross, including:

- "Lord, forgive me for I am sorry."
- "Lord, bless Jimmy today."
- "Lord, save Auntie Jean."
- "Lord, heal Uncle Bob."

Yes, these hyper-grace teachers believe that God has already saved, forgiven, and healed the whole world, since Jesus already paid for our complete redemption. The only thing lacking is our faith, and once we believe, then we are saved, forgiven, and healed. As for Jesus, He hasn't done any saving or healing or prospering of anyone in two thousand years. He finished the work on the cross.

This, of course, is absolutely untrue, but it's just another indication of how far off the deep end we can go when we misunderstand grace and misrepresent the finished work of the cross. (For those needing proof that this teaching is untrue, here are a few verses that speak of God saving or healing or forgiving after the cross: Acts 9:34; Titus 3:5–7; Hebrews 7:25; Jacob [James] 5:15; 1 John 5:16.)

"It Is Finished"

What then did Jesus mean when He uttered the words "It is finished" in John 19:30? The phrase actually translates one word in Greek, *tetelestai*, from the root *teleō*, which means "to finish, fulfill." And note this carefully: this specific form of the verb, *tetelestai*, is found only *twice* in the entire New Testament, both times in John 19. In fact, the two occurrences of *tetelestai* are found within three verses of each other: "After this, Jesus, knowing that all *was now finished*, said (to fulfill the Scripture), 'I thirst.'….When Jesus had received the sour wine, he said, '*It is finished*,' and he bowed his head and gave up his spirit" (vv. 28, 30).

Do you see that? Although the verb *teleō* occurs twenty-eight times in the New Testament, the form *tetelestai* is found only twice, and those two occurrences are in the same context, right next to each other, making the meaning perfectly clear. Jesus was saying, "Mission accomplished! Everything that had to be done has been done! It is finished!"

G. R. Beasley-Murray explains this in his commentary on John:

> After drinking the wine, Jesus uttered his last word known to the Evangelist, τετέλεσται [*tetelestai*]. The rendering, "It is finished!" conveys only half the meaning. For the verb τελέω [*teleō*] fundamentally denotes "to carry out" the will of somebody, whether of oneself or another, and so to fulfill obligations or carry out religious acts. "It is *accomplished!*" renders that aspect of the word. Doubtless both meanings of the term, the temporal and the theological, are intended here. "So the last word of Jesus interprets his suffering and dying as the crowning conclusion and high point of the work that he has performed in obedience—the obedience of the Son finds here its most radical expression—and enables the believing eye to see the glorifying of the Son through the Father."[12]

Similarly, leading New Testament scholar D. A. Carson writes:

> The verb *teleō* from which this form derives denotes the carrying out of a task, and in religious contexts bears the overtone of fulfilling one's religious obligations. Accordingly, in the light of the impending cross, Jesus could earlier cry, "I have brought you glory on earth by completing (*teleiōsas*; *i.e.* by accomplishing) the work you gave me to do" (17:4). Having loved his own who were in the world, he loved them *eis telos*—not only "to the end"' but to the full extent mandated by his mission. And so, on the brink of death, Jesus cries out, *It is accomplished!*[13]

Another great New Testament and Greek scholar, B. F. Westcott, has this to say:

> [*It is finished*] Comp. *v.* 28. The earthly life had been carried to its issue. Every essential point in the prophetic portraiture of Messiah had been realized (Acts 13:29). The last suffering for sin had been endured. The "end" of all had been gained. Nothing was left undone or unborne. The absence of a definite subject forces the reader to call up each work which was now brought to an end. Comp. Luke 18:31, 22:37, and the phrase of St Paul, 2 Tim. 4:7.[14]

Similarly, Marcus Dods wrote:

> The cry, τετέλεσται [*tetelestai*], "it is finished," was not the gasp of a worn-out life, but the deliberate utterance of a clear consciousness that His work was finished, and all God's purpose accomplished (17:4), that all had now been done that could be done to make God known to men, and to identify Him with men.[15]

Yes, the divine mission has been accomplished! Jesus has done it! Every sin has been paid for, every evil deed judged, and the full and total price of our redemption purchased at the cross. That is the power of the blood of Jesus. That is the glory of the Son of God. That is the depth of the Father's love—and it was all for you and for me so that forever we could be with Him and even share in His nature. Who could imagine such a story of love?

There's really no need to read other meanings into "It is finished," such as: "When Christ died, He said 'it is finished', meaning the old covenant was now fulfilled and done away with."[16] Or, Jesus spoke in Hebrew on the cross, and when He said, "It is finished," it was actually the Hebrew word *nishlam*, which means 'Paid in full.'"[17] Regardless of whether there is any truth to these claims (Jesus certainly spoke in either Aramaic or Hebrew on the cross, not Greek),[18] neither of them convey what John intended to communicate. Jesus perfectly lived the life He had to live and perfectly died the death He had to die. It is finished! It is with good reason that John G. Lake (1870–1935) said, "In all of your preaching and teaching you must always leave people with the consciousness of the triumph of Christ." Yes! Amen!

Somehow that is enough for some hyper-grace teachers, and, as we saw earlier in this chapter, grace truths *can* be exaggerated, as is done by Rob Bell and others who teach forms of universal (or ultimate) reconciliation, the notion that every human being will ultimately be saved. And while it is true that the great majority of modern grace teachers have not embraced this error about "the finished work of the cross," I believe they have embraced other errors—claiming that there's nothing God requires of us as believers, or that there's no way we can displease or disappoint Him, or that He doesn't call us to grow in holiness, because Jesus has done it all.

The interesting thing is that there's nothing new about this teaching, even though some of the hyper-grace teachers claim to have discovered a new revelation, something that has been unknown since the days of Paul. To the contrary, this same teaching has surfaced numerous times through the centuries, only to be corrected by the Word, then to reappear as a "new revelation" decades later. Arthur Pink dealt with it a number of times in his writings.[19] J. C. Ryle dealt with it in his book on *Holiness*.[20] Charles Spurgeon dealt with it under the heading of "imputed sanctification," claiming that this line of thinking was already addressed by John Gill, who died in 1771.[21] And it has appeared in different forms before and since the days of Spurgeon, Ryle, and Pink. As Ecclesiastes said long ago, "there is nothing new under the sun" (Eccles. 1:9).

Purchased at the Cross

But we've focused on the faulty teaching long enough. It's time we put all our focus on the cross, where Jesus the Messiah "suffered once for sins, the righteous for the unrighteous, that he might bring us to God, being put to death in the flesh but made alive in the spirit," where God "made him to be sin who knew no sin, so that in him we might become the righteousness of God," where the Father canceled "the record of debt that stood against us with its legal demands. This he set aside, nailing it to the cross" (1 Pet. 3:18; 2 Cor. 5:21; Col. 2:14).[22]

It was at the cross that the Lord "disarmed the [demonic] rulers and authorities and put them to open shame," triumphing over them through Yeshua's death and resurrection (Col. 2:15). And it was there at the cross that Jesus "himself bore our sins in his body on the tree, that we might die to sin and live to righteousness. By his wounds [we] have been healed. For [we] were straying like sheep, but have now returned to the Shepherd and Overseer of [our] souls" (1 Pet. 2:24–25).

The story really is too good to be true, and to exaggerate it is to cheapen it. As Paul wrote two thousand years ago:

> For while we were still weak, at the right time Christ died for the ungodly. For one will scarcely die for a righteous person—though perhaps for a good person one would dare even to die—but God

> shows his love for us in that while we were still sinners, Christ died for us. Since, therefore, we have now been justified by his blood, much more shall we be saved by him from the wrath of God. For if while we were enemies we were reconciled to God by the death of his Son, much more, now that we are reconciled, shall we be saved by his life.
>
> —Romans 5:6–10

And note those words "much more"! Paul goes on to say:

> But the free gift is not like the trespass. For if many died through one man's trespass, *much more* have the grace of God and the free gift by the grace of that one man Jesus Christ abounded for many.... For if, because of one man's trespass, death reigned through that one man, *much more* will those who receive the abundance of grace and the free gift of righteousness reign in life through the one man Jesus Christ.
>
> —Romans 5:15, 17

Everything about the cross shouts, "Much more!" Everything about God's love cries out, "Much more!" Surely that "much more" is more than enough for us!

We sinned. He died.

We were guilty. He was punished.

We deserved death. He gave his life.

We rejected Him. He accepted us.

We drove the nails in His hands. Those nails saved our souls!

And now, in Him, we have everything we need. And now, through Him, we can do the Father's bidding. And now, with Him, we can go and change the world. Isn't this more than enough?

Our sins have been dealt with once and for all at the cross, and we need never look for another sacrifice or offering for our guilt. When we fall short, we look back to the cross, and the same blood that saved us cleanses us afresh, and we go forward, free from condemnation and guilt, living lives that please the Lord.

And there's something else that we now understand. When He died, we died with Him, and we too have been raised in newness of life, considering ourselves dead to sin and alive to God (Rom. 6:6–12). That is the power of the gospel!

And when Jesus ascended to the right hand of the Father, He sent the Spirit down to us, now to dwell within us, to guide us and instruct us, turning us from error and leading us into truth, communing with us in holy fellowship and empowering us for holy service. This is the all-complete, all-comprehensive grace of God, and all of it was purchased at the cross, where the Savior of the world perfectly accomplished the Father's mission, declaring, "It is finished!"

Because of that:

> His divine power has granted to us all things that pertain to life and godliness, through the knowledge of him who called us to his own glory and excellence, by which he has granted to us his precious and very great promises, so that through them you may become partakers of the divine nature, having escaped from the corruption that is in the world because of sinful desire.
>
> —2 PETER 1:3–4

What a glorious calling! He has now promised that nothing in the universe can separate us from His love and that He Himself will keep us strong to the end, as we "continue in the faith, stable and steadfast, not shifting from the hope of the gospel that [we] heard" (Col. 1:23), confident that the God "who began a good work in [us] will bring it to completion at the day of Jesus Christ" (Phil. 1:6), and putting our trust in the one "who is able to keep [us] from stumbling and to present [us] blameless before the presence of his glory with great joy, to the only God, our Savior, through Jesus Christ our Lord, be glory, majesty, dominion, and authority, before all time and now and forever. Amen" (Judah [Jude] 24–25).

Is this not enough? Is this not much more than enough?

That's why for the next trillion years, just as eternity is getting started, we will glory more and more in the finished work of the cross, finally understanding just what Paul meant when he said, "But far be it from me to boast except in the cross of our Lord Jesus Christ, by which the world has been crucified to me, and I to the world" (Gal. 6:14). May this be our boast as well.

-Appendix-

ONCE SAVED, ALWAYS SAVED?

Within evangelical circles there are three main beliefs concerning the possibility of a child of God forfeiting his or her salvation, and countless thousands of pages have been written debating the question. How can we sort things out here in a few short pages?

Let's look first at the three main evangelical views:

1. The teaching commonly known as "once saved, always saved" (OSAS) states that once you are truly saved, no matter how you live or what you do, even denying Jesus and turning your back on Him, you cannot lose your salvation. Although your sin might shorten your life or lessen your future rewards, you will still be eternally saved.
2. The teaching called "perseverance of the saints" states that a true believer will not ultimately turn away from the Lord, and therefore if you claim to be born again and die in sin, denying the Lord, you were never truly saved.
3. The final teaching doesn't have one specific name associated with it, but it states that a true believer can choose to apostatize, reject God's grace, and forfeit salvation. Although we are secure in Jesus, if we ultimately reject Him, we lose our secure standing.

Those holding to the first viewpoint refer to verses such as Romans 8:28–39, which state that nothing that can separate us from God's love, or John 10:26–29, which state that Jesus' sheep have eternal life and no one can pluck them out of His hand. Those holding to the second viewpoint emphasize those same verses but also point to verses such as 1 John 2:19, which states that those who left the church were never really part of it, or 1 John 3:6, which states that those who continue to live in sin have never really known the Lord. Those holding to the third viewpoint look to verses such as Colossians 1:21–23, which state that our salvation is assured if we persevere in faith to the end, or 2 Peter 2:20–22, which state that it would be better never to have known the Lord than to know Him and then turn away from Him.

For the most part, hyper-grace teachers emphatically hold to the doctrine of "once saved, always saved" (viewpoint #1), although some seem to hold to the doctrine of "perseverance of the saints" (viewpoint #2), making comments such as, "True Christians are one spirit with Christ and could never reject Him. It is simply impossible!...Any person who can reject Christ, stop believing, or plunge into a life of rebellion against God without remorse, was simply never born again—regardless of testimony to the contrary. True Christians cannot deny Jesus, and true unbelievers cannot remain with Him."[1]

Of course, there is an irony when hyper-grace teachers hold to views like this, since it ultimately puts the emphasis back on the believer's "performance." In other words, "If I claim to be a believer and I'm living right, then I'm saved, but if I claim to be a believer and have turned away from God, I guess I was never saved." This is obviously the last thing intended by my hyper-grace colleagues, but again, it is the logical conclusion to statements like the one just quoted.

How then do we sort things out? It's really very simple. *God's promises are to believers—to those who want to follow the Lord and whose lives belong to Him—not to rebels who have chosen sin and rejected His Lordship.* Put another way, there is not a single promise anywhere in the Bible that God will bless us with eternal life if we ultimately reject Him and choose rebellion, and we give people false assurance when we make that claim. (In other words, viewpoint #1 is not true.)[2]

Find me one verse anywhere in the Bible—just one—that gives assurance of eternal life and blessing to an unrepentant rebel who is living in willful, persistent sin, denying the Lord in an ongoing, hardened way, and I will invite you to join me on national radio or TV and tell the whole world that I was wrong. Just one verse!

Without a doubt, you'll find many verses promising mercy and forgiveness to those who turn back (thank God!), and you'll find many verses assuring us of God's keeping power, but note clearly that the promises are given to Jesus' sheep—to those who know His voice and follow Him (see John 10:27)—rather than to those who reject His voice and walk away from Him. In short, viewpoints #2 or #3 could be right, but #1 cannot.

So, on a practical level it comes down to this: if you have put your trust in the Lord and desire to serve Him, He has given you absolute assurance that He will never leave or forsake you, that He will keep you safe to the end, and that no one and nothing can separate you from His love. Rest secure in Him! He is the Author and Finisher of your faith!

But if you believe that since you were once saved, even if you reject Him and live in unrepentant sin you are still saved, then you have deceived yourself and are in danger of falling under God's judgment (that's why Jesus and Paul often warned us not to be deceived).[3] If you walked away from the Lord, either you were never saved or you have forfeited your salvation, so turn back to Him now, knowing that He is quick to forgive, that He loves to show mercy, and that He can restore you to Himself with life, hope, and purpose through Jesus. To repeat: the promise of eternal life is only to Jesus' sheep, those who know His voice and follow Him.

But why would we ever want to walk away from Him? Everything we need is found in Him, and in Him alone is life—true, abundant life—so drink deeply of His incredible love and be assured that He who began the good work in you will bring it to completion (Phil. 1:6). And if you find yourself playing games with sin and growing distant from the Lord, get sober, get serious, and turn back to the cross. The cleansing blood of Jesus will never lose its power.

NOTES

Preface

1. Philip Yancey, *What's So Amazing About Grace?* (Grand Rapids, MI: Zondervan, 1997), 45.

2. As cited in Michael L. Brown, *Go and Sin No More: A Call to Holiness* (Concord, NC: EqualTime Books, 1998, 2013), 205. Used by permission.

3. See my article "Recovering the Lost Letter of Jacob," CharismaNews .com, March 11, 2013, http://www.charismanews.com/opinion/38591 -recovering-the-lost-letter-of-jacob (accessed August 27, 2013).

1—Why I Love the Message of Grace

1. See Paul C. Vitz, *Faith of the Fatherless: The Psychology of Atheism* (Dallas: Spence Publishing Company, 1999); John P. Koster Jr., *The Atheist Syndrome* (Brentwood, TN: Wolgemuth & Hyatt, 1989).

2. I shared these insights in my book *Go and Sin No More*, in the chapter "It's All About Grace," as well as in the chapters "No Condemnation," "The Letter Kills," and "God's Cure for Dirty Feet." Over the years I have been blessed to hear from readers who were delivered from legalism, discovered God's grace, and even returned to the Lord after previously falling away because of what they perceived to be legalistic, graceless Christianity. If you want to know if I truly understand the liberating power of grace, I would encourage you to read *Go and Sin No More* and draw your own conclusions.

2—Is There a New Grace Reformation?

1. Clark Whitten, *Pure Grace: The Life Changing Power of Uncontaminated Grace* (Shippensburg, PA: Destiny Image, 2012), 25–26. Used by permission.

2. Ibid., 29.

3. Ibid., 28, my emphasis.

4. Robert. A. J. Gagnon, "Cheap Grace Masquerading as Pure Grace: The Unfortunate Gospel of Rev. Clark Whitten—Alan Chambers' Mentor, Pastor, and Chair of His Board," RobGagnon.net, September 8, 2012, http://www.robgagnon.net/Clark%20Whitten%20Critique.htm (accessed August 27, 2013).

5. John Crowder, *Mystical Union* (Santa Cruz, CA: Sons of Thunder, 2010), 17. Although some hyper-grace leaders would consider Crowder to be somewhat fringe in his views, he is actually widely received in many hyper-grace circles (as witnessed by the fact that he is cited as an endorser to a number of books cited in this study), and his views, while more extreme at times, are quite representative. He also works together with a number of key hyper-grace teachers.

6. Ibid., 94, his emphasis.
7. Ibid. 24.
8. Andre Van der Merwe, *GRACE, the Forbidden Gospel: Jesus Tore the Veil. Religion Sewed It Back Up* (Bloomington, IN: WestBow, 2011), xi. Used by permission.
9. Ibid., xvii.
10. Ibid., from the book's endorsements.
11. Ibid., from the book's endorsements.
12. Ibid., 88.
13. In *Destined to Reign: The Secret to Effortless Success, Wholeness and Victorious Living* (Tulsa, OK: Harrison House, 2007), Joseph Prince refers to this "Gospel Revolution" approximately eight times; see, e.g., viii, 317. Used by permission.
14. Whitten, *Pure Grace,* from the book's endorsements.
15. Van der Merwe, *GRACE*, xx.
16. Charles Spurgeon, "The Doctrines of Grace Do Not Lead to Sin," sermon preached August 19, 1883, The Spurgeon Archive, http://www.spurgeon.org/sermons/1735.htm (accessed August 27, 2013).
17. Michael L. Brown, *Revolution in the Church* (Grand Rapids, MI: Chosen Books, 2002). Used by permission.
18. For Luther's anti-Semitic writings, see Michael L. Brown, *Our Hands Are Stained With Blood: The Tragic Story of the "Church" and the Jewish People* (Shippensburg, PA: Destiny Image, 1992). Used by permission.
19. Paul Ellis, *The Gospel in Ten Words* (n.p.: KingsPress, 2012), 28. Used by permission.
20. Stephen J. Lawson, *The Unwavering Resolve of Jonathan Edwards* (Lake Mary, FL: Reformation Trust, 2008), xi.
21. Ibid., xiii.
22. Ibid., xi.
23. Romell D. Weekly, *The Rebuttal: A Biblical Response Exposing the Deceptive Logic of Anti-Gay Theology* (n.p.: Judah First Publishing, 2011), book dedication.
24. M. W. Sphero, *The Gay Faith: Christ, Scripture, and Sexuality* (New Orleans: Herms Press, 2011), 6.
25. Ibid., 27; for many more examples, see my forthcoming book, *Can You Be Gay and Christian?* (Lake Mary, FL: FrontLine, 2014).
26. Sphero, *The Gay Faith*, 45–46.
27. Crowder, *Mystical Union*, 154.
28. Philip Gulley and James Mulholland, *If Grace Is True: Why God Will Save Every Person* (New York: Harper Collins, 2009).

3—Name-Calling, Judgmentalism, and Divisiveness in the Name of Grace

1. Rob Rufus, *Living in the Grace of God* (United Kingdom: Authentic Media, 2007), 14. Viewed at Google Books.
2. Ibid.

3. Whitten, *Pure Grace*, 121.

4. Of course, traditional Jews believe that the Pharisees have been given a bad name in the New Testament, and to this day religious Jews look back at the Pharisees with great respect, believing them to have been very spiritual, devoted men. To square this with the New Testament data, we can point out that: 1) not all Pharisees were hypocrites; and 2) Jesus could see into people's hearts, and He would expose hypocrisy in many of our lives, even though we would look good on the outside.

5. Whitten, *Pure Grace*, 96.

6. Ibid., 106.

7. Ibid., 111.

8. Ibid., 118.

9. Ibid., 20.

10. Rufus, *Living in the Grace of God*, 6.

11. Whitten, *Pure Grace*, 147, my emphasis.

12. Comment by Joel232 on March 27, 2013, to my article "A Dangerous and Deadly Deception, at http://www.charismanews.com/opinion/38821-a-dangerous-and-deadly-deception. I cite this because it is typical.

13. For my use of the term "religious establishment," see my book *Revolution in the Church*, especially pages 182–203.

14. Whitten, *Pure Grace*, 23, my emphasis.

15. David Fish, in communication with the author via e-mail, March 21, 2013. Used with permission.

16. Ellis, *The Gospel in Ten Words*, 147.

17. Ibid.

18. Ibid., 140, 143–144.

19. Comment #14, March 14, 2013, to Michael L. Brown, "A Compromised Gospel Produces Compromised Fruit," *Ministry Today*, March 12, 2013, http://ministrytodaymag.com/index.php/ministry-news/main/19922-the-fruit-of-a-compromised-gospel (accessed September 3, 2013).

20. Steve McVey, *52 Lies Heard in Church Every Sunday:...And Why the Truth Is So Much Better* (Eugene, OR: Harvest House Publishers, 2011), 47. Used by permission. Once again, I agree with much of what he writes in his books, but the powerful truths he presents are also mixed with what I believe are serious misreadings of Scripture; see further discussion in chapters 6 and 14.

21. Prince, *Destined to Reign*, 83.

22. Jeff Turner and Sound of Awakening Ministries, April 4, 2013, https://m.facebook.com/272360779549171/timeline/story?ut=2&hash=-3189933460533376153&wstart=0&wend=1367391599&ustart&__user=1065236126 (accessed September 3, 2013). He notes that "remarks from men like Michael Brown, and Mike Bickle, I just want to say that the claim that this message of Grace is dangerous, and leading folks into sin are completely and totally ridiculous."

23. Comment dated February 23, 2013, to "Grace Stories," EscapetoReality.org, http://escapetoreality.org/resources/grace-stories/#comment-11183 (accessed September 3, 2013).

24. David Fish, "An Open Letter to the 'Finished Works' Movement," *Revival Culture* (blog), January 23, 2013, http://revivalculture.wordpress.com/2013/01/23/an-open-letter-to-the-finished-works-movement/ (accessed September 3, 2013).

25. John Crowder, Facebook post, March 23, 2013, https://www.facebook.com/thenewmystics?fref=ts (accessed September 3, 2013).

26. Van der Merwe, *GRACE*, 27.

27. D. Martyn Lloyd-Jones, *Romans: Exposition of Chapter 6: The New Man* (Carlisle, PA: Banner of Truth, 1972), 8–9.

28. For the record, I have been accused of giving people a license to sin—by preaching biblical grace and assurance—by various groups inside and outside the body, including cult members, religious Jews, and other believers. So I could just as well use these same quotes from Lloyd-Jones and Spurgeon to justify my position. What then would that prove? Obviously nothing. The fact is that we cannot prove the rightness of our doctrines by the false accusations that come against them. We must appeal to what God has said in His Word.

29. Facebook.com, Robert A. Gagnon, https://www.facebook.com/robert.a.gagnon.56?fref=ts&ref=br_tf (accessed September 30, 2013).

30. Van der Merwe, *GRACE*, 27.

31. Prince, *Destined to Reign*, 20, his emphasis.

32. Crowder, *Mystical Union*, 9, his emphasis.

33. Ibid., 10.

4—Has God Already Forgiven Our Future Sins?

1. Ryan Rufus, "Totally Forgiven! Totally United! Totally Filled!", sermon preached at the Grace and Glory Conference, 2011, transcript, "Ryan Rufus on Mortifying Sin," *Ryan Rufus* (blog), June 10, 2011, http://ryanrufus.blogspot.com/2011_06_01_archive.html (accessed September 3, 2013); audio available at http://www.citychurchinternational.net/2011.html (accessed September 3, 2013). Used by permission.

2. Joseph Prince, *Unmerited Favor* (Lake Mary, FL: Charisma House, 2010), 195. Used by permission.

3. Prince, *Destined to Reign*, 107.

4. Rufus, "Totally Forgiven! Totally United! Totally Filled!"

5. Ibid. To be clear, Pastor Rufus also states, "Get your eyes off your sins and get your eyes onto Christ! The more you do that, the more you will overcome sin in your life." So he strongly encourages God's people to overcome sin by grace.

6. Ibid.

7. In Francois Du Toit's *Mirror Bible* (Kindle Edition; n.p.: Mirror Word Publishing, 2012), Hebrews 10:17 is rendered, "This is final: I have deleted

the record of your sins and misdeeds. I no longer recall them," followed by this parenthetical explanation: "Nothing in God's reference of man, reminds him of sin."

8. As quoted earlier, Pastor Prince dismisses this concept, saying, "God's forgiveness is not given in installments."

9. For the meaning of 2 Corinthians 5:18–20, see chapter 7, note 27.

10. Mark 1:4–5; see also Luke 3:7–14 for details of what transpired at John's baptism.

11. When I asked one hyper-grace preacher how he explained the words of Jesus to the churches in Revelation 2–3, he replied, "If you base your theology on the Book of Revelation, you'll end up in a mess!"

12. A pastor in California discussed this issue with a former youth leader in his church who had embraced the hyper-grace message. The young man explained to him—completely contrary to context and logic—that the forgiveness spoken of in Jacob (James) 5:15 was actually from man (as if anticipating verse 16) rather than from God! This, again, is an example of what happens when we interpret the Word through our theology rather than our theology through the Word.

13. On his hyper-grace blog, Simon Yap argues that Hebrews 12:1 does not say that we have to deal with sins that entangle us. He writes, "Dear friends, many quote that Hebrews 12 talks about sin that entangles us and as such the Father disciplines us. I am sorry it is wrong, it says 'the sin' and it is not sin. This sin that easily entangles us is the same sin in Hebrews 10:26. It is the sin of thinking Jesus' blood is not enough to satisfy God of your sins past, present & future. It is called the sin of unbelief. That is why he asks us to continue to look at Jesus, the author and perfecter of our faith." [Simon Yap, "What Is the Sin That Easily Entangle Us?", *His Grace Is Enough* (blog), May 5, 2011, http://hischarisisenough.wordpress.com/2011/05/05/what-is-the-sin-that-easily-entangle-us-hebrews-121/ (accessed September 3, 2013).] He also quotes John MacArthur to support his view, but MacArthur hardly supports his claims, as he mentions "sins" along with the sin of unbelief. Rather, the text in Hebrews is pointing to sin generically, as in the ESV's "and sin which clings so closely." But even based on Yap's wrong reading, we still have to deal with sin, namely, the sin of unbelief. Yap, however, seems to believe that if the sin we are committing is failing to embrace the hyper-grace message, then somehow it alters what the Scripture is saying. In keeping with this, he claims that the only way we can grieve the Spirit is "by speaking words and messages that teach God has only partially forgiven you of your sins"! [Simon Yap, "Grieving the Holy Spirit," *His Grace Is Enough* (blog), November 15, 2012, http://hischarisisenough.wordpress.com/2012/11/15/grieving-the-holy-spirit/ (accessed September 3, 2013).] Once again, though, I should note that he does *not* in any way condone living in sin and strongly preaches that true grace causes us to turn from sin.

14. William Lane, *Hebrews 9–13*, Word Biblical Commentary (Dallas: Word, 1991), 261.

15. Ibid., 261; according to F. F. Bruce, *The Epistle to the Hebrews*, New International Commentary on the New Testament, revised (Grand Rapids, MI: Eerdmans, 1990), 236: "If the old sacrificial order had possessed true cleansing efficacy—that is to say, if it had been able to cleanse the conscience—then the worshipers would have enjoyed unrestricted communion with God.... The implication of our author's argument is that the true inward cleansing is permanently effective and therefore unrepeatable.... The sense is much the same as that of our Lord's words to Peter in John 13:10: 'He that is bathed does not need to wash, except for his feet, but he is clean all over.'" According to Gareth Lee Cockerill, *The Epistle to the Hebrews*, New International Commentary on the New Testament, revised (Grand Rapids, MI: Eerdmans, 2012), 431: "The sacrifices of the Mosaic system left worshipers 'conscious' not merely of guilt but of sin, and especially of its pollution that demanded cleansing."

16. "Jesus Paid It All" by Elvina M. Hall. Public domain.

5—Should Believers Confess Their Sins to God?

1. Ellis, *The Gospel in Ten Words*, 28.
2. Rufus, "Totally Forgiven! Totally United! Totally Filled!"
3. Ibid.
4. Ibid.
5. Andre Rabe, *Metanoia (Clarity)* (Kindle Edition; n.p.: Amazon Digital Services, 2012), Kindle locations 272–273. Used by permission.
6. Rufus, "Totally Forgiven! Totally United! Totally Filled!"
7. Ibid.
8. Ironically, Clark Whitten writes that, "True biblical repentance is relational in nature," emphasizing how it is an interchange between a loving, caring Father and His devoted child, both of whom are completely open with each other (see *Pure Grace*, 101). Yet he strongly advocates *against* believers confessing their sins to God.
9. See, for example, Whitten, *Pure Grace*, 94.
10. Andrew Farley, *The Naked Gospel* (Grand Rapids, MI: Zondervan, 2009), 151–153. Used by permission.
11. Van der Merwe, *GRACE*, 144.
12. Prince, *Unmerited Favor*, 189.
13. Chuck Crisco, *Extraordinary Gospel: Experience the Goodness of God* (originally published as *God Is in a Good Mood*) (Travelers Rest, SC: True Potential Publishing, 2013), 104, n. 15.
14. Cited in Colin G. Kruse, *The Letters of John*, The Pillar New Testament Commentary (Grand Rapids, MI: Eerdmans, 2000), 26.
15. D. A. Carson, R. T. France, J. A. Motyer, and G. J. Wenham, consulting eds., *The New Bible Commentary* (Downers Grove, IL: IVP Press, 1996), introduction to 1 John.
16. Stephen S. Smalley, *1, 2, 3 John*, Word Biblical Commentary (Dallas: Word, 1989), xxv.

17. For an older but still important introduction to Gnosticism, see Kurt Rudolph, *Gnosis: The Nature and History of Gnosticism*, Eng. translation (New York: HarperCollins, 1987). For a convenient collection of texts, see Bentley Latyon, *The Gnostic Scriptures: A New Translation With Annotations and Introductions*, Anchor Bible Reference Library (New York: Doubleday, 1987). For questions about how much can be said with certainty about "the Gnostics," see Michael Allen Williams, *Rethinking "Gnosticism": An Argument for Dismantling a Dubious Category* (Princeton, NJ: Princeton University Press, 1996).

18. Craig S. Keener, *IVP Bible Background Commentary: New Testament* (Downers Grove, IL: IVP Academic, 1994), 735–736.

19. Ibid., my emphasis.

20. Farley's attempt to argue that this does not apply to believers is very weak (see *Naked Gospel*, 151–152), even claiming (totally erroneously) that "John uses *we* to politely combat Gnostic heresy" (Ibid., 152, his emphasis). Hardly!

21. Amazingly I have even seen hyper-grace teachers try to claim that the people addressed as "we" vs. "them" changed partway through the letter!

22. C. Haas, M. D. Jonge, and J. L. Swellengrebel, *A Handbook on the Letters of John*, UBS Handbook Series (New York: United Bible Societies, 1994), 30.

23. Robert J. Utley, *The Beloved Disciple's Memoirs and Letters: The Gospel of John, I, II, and III John*, Study Guide Commentary Series (Marshall, Texas: Bible Lessons International, 1999), 199.

24. Kruse, *The Letters of John*, 68.

25. This is his complete note: "If we confess (ἐαν ὁμολογωμεν [*ean homologōmen*]). Third-class condition again with ἐαν [*ean*] and present active subjunctive of ὁμολογεω [*homologeō*], 'if we keep on confessing.'" [A. T. Robertson, *Word Pictures in the New Testament*, vol. 6 (Grand Rapids, MI: Baker Books 1960), 208.]

26. R. C. H. Lenski, *The Interpretation of the Epistles of St. Peter, St. John and St. Jude* (Minneapolis, MN: Augsburg, 1966), 392.

27. Kenneth S. Wuest, *Wuest's Word Studies From the Greek New Testament: For the English Reader* (Grand Rapids, MI: Eerdmans, 1997), s.v. "1 John 1:9."

28. Colin Dye, "Should We Confess Our Sins?", January 4, 2012, http://www.colindye.com/2012/01/04/should-we-confess-our-sins/ (accessed September 3, 2013).

29. Ibid.

30. Farley, in *The Naked Gospel*, 149–150, denigrates this kind of thinking, writing: "And they use terms such as *judicial*, *patriarchal*, and *forensic* as they delicately dance around the reality of once-for-all forgiveness and push the idea of a two-tiered forgiveness system in which eternally God is satisfied, but right now we somehow maintain our own daily cleansing through a confession ritual" (his emphasis). He further denigrates this concept in

this online post, writing, "It's all make-believe. It is literally fabricated terminology that turns the work of the Cross into something less powerful than the blood of bulls and goats in the Old Testament." [Andrew Farley, "Positional Forgiveness versus Relational Forgiveness?", *What I'm Really Saying!* (blog), June 13, 2013, http://www.patheos.com/blogs/andrewfarley/2013/06/positional-forgiveness-versus-relational-forgiveness/ (accessed September 3, 2013).

31. Charles Spurgeon, *Morning and Evening* (n.p.: Hendrickson Publishers, 1990), "February 18, evening," 99. Viewed at Google Books. Andre van der Merwe, in *GRACE*, page 105, asks: "When we mess up, do we run to Him feeling guilty and condemned like a murderer about to be condemned to retribution? Or do we ask Him for wisdom in overcoming the habits of our unrenewed minds, knowing we stand completely forgiven and holy in His sight?" Of course, he has made a very good point but, I believe, mixed it with some faulty teaching.

32. Ellis, *The Gospel in Ten Words*, 28.

33. Ibid., 30.

34. Utley, *The Beloved Disciple's Memoirs and Letters*, 199.

35. Kruse, *The Letters of John*, 64–65.

36. For more on 1 Corinthians 6:9–11, see chapter 7, "Sanctified or Not?"

37. This section on John 13 was adapted from chapter 9 of my book *Go and Sin No More*, entitled "God's Cure for Dirty Feet," 166–169.

38. David and Nancy Ravenhill, "Rooting Out Fuzzy Theology Behind the Hyper-Grace Message," CharismaNews.com, April 13, 2013, http://www.charismanews.com/opinion/39015-rooting-out-fuzzy-theology-behind-the-hyper-grace-message (accessed September 3, 2013). Used by permission.

39. Historically, confession of sin among believers has been a constant in times of revival, and it is noteworthy that the famous Welsh Revival of 1904–1905 began after Evan Roberts preached a simple message with four main points: (1) confess all known sin to God; (2) deal with and get rid of any "doubtful" area of your life; (3) be ready to obey the Holy Spirit instantly; and (4) confess Christ publicly.

6—The Holy Spirit, Conviction of Sin, and Repentance

1. McVey, *52 Lies Heard in Church Every Sunday*, 39.

2. "In Evil I Took Long Delight" by John Newton. Public domain.

3. Charles Haddon Spurgeon, *The Autobiography of Charles H. Spurgeon: 1834–1854*, compiled by Susannah Spurgeon and W. J. Harrald (Chicago: Curts and Jennings, 1898), 76. Viewed at Google Books.

4. James A. Stewart, *Evangelism*, 4th ed. (Asheville, NC: Revival Literature, n.d.), 15–16.

5. Paul Ellis, "'Confronting the Error of Hyper-Grace,' a Response to Michael Brown," *Escape to Reality* (blog), February 22, 2013, http://escapetoreality.org/2013/02/22/error-of-hyper-grace-michael-brown/ (accessed September 3, 2013).

6. Cited in Colin C. Whitaker, *Great Revivals* (Springfield, MO: Gospel Publishing House, 1984), 158.

7. Cited in Arnold Dallimore, *Spurgeon: A New Biography* (Carlisle, PA: Banner of Truth, 1988), 14.

8. Cited in Winkie Pratney, Steve Hill, and Tamara Winslow, eds., *The Revival Study Bible* (Singapore: Armour Publishing, 2010), 152.

9. Rabe, *Metanoia*, Kindle locations 159–161. Of course, he mischaracterizes the traditional view of repentance as well. How many true believers actually think that God is reluctant to forgive us and we need to twist His arm?

10. For an examination of the meaning of 2 Corinthians 5:18–20, see chapter 7.

11. McVey, *52 Lies Heard in Church Every Sunday*, 39.

12. Ibid., 42.

13. See also Acts 3:19; 5:31; 10:43; 13:38; 26:18.

14. Michael L. Brown, *It's Time to Rock the Boat: A Call to God's People to Rise Up and Preach a Confrontational Gospel* (Shippensburg, PA: Destiny Image, 1993), 4–5. Used by permission. I'm fully aware that not everyone experiences deep conviction before they are saved, but if there is no consciousness of sin and no awareness of the need of a Savior, it is right to wonder how deep the conversion experience really was.

15. For more on this topic, see *It's Time to Rock the Boat*, 75–82, and Michael L. Brown, *A Time for Holy Fire: Preparing the Way for Divine Visitation*, 3rd ed. (Concord, NC: FIRE Publishing, 2008), 107–120. Used by permission.

16. Prince, *Destined to Reign*, 135.

17. Whitten, *Pure Grace*, 107.

18. Brown, *Go and Sin No More*, 131.

19. Charles Hodge, *Systematic Theology*, vol. 1, Christian Classics Ethereal Library, http://www.ccel.org/ccel/hodge/theology1.iii.i.vi.html (accessed September 3, 2013).

20. Prince, *Destined to Reign*, 134.

21. Also in *Destined to Reign*, 151, Prince writes, "Remind yourself that the Holy Spirit was sent to convict you of your righteousness apart from works." Similar statements, apparently going back to Prince, are commonly found in hyper-grace circles. For a clear and relevant study, see Roger Sapp, *Grace in the Gospels 3: Understanding a Healthy Consciousness of Sin* (Springtown, TX: All Nations Publications, 2013).

22. John Sheasby, with Ken Gire, *The Birthright: Out of the Servants' Quarters Into the Father's House* (Grand Rapids, MI: Zondervan, 2010), 94.

23. Rabe, *Metanoia*, Kindle locations 199–201.

24. Rufus, *Living in the Grace of God*, Kindle locations 772–775.

25. McVey, *52 Lies Heard in Church Every Sunday*, 116.

26. Notice that what happens to the prodigal son is characterized as "repenting" in the earlier parts of this parable (lost sheep, lost coin, lost son); see Luke 15:7, 10.

27. Whitten, *Pure Grace*, 20. Even if we don't concur with every part of this description, to call it "heathenish" is completely over the top.

28. McVey, *52 Lies Heard in Church Every Sunday*, 116.

29. Prince, *Destined to Reign*, 233.

30. Crisco, *Extraordinary Gospel*, 96. I could have easily multiplied additional citations from other hyper-grace authors.

31. Richard Chenevix Trench, *Synonyms of the New Testament* (London: Macmillan and Company, 1880), 260. Viewed at Google Books.

32. Whitten, *Pure Grace*, 102.

33. Ibid., 100.

34. Crisco, *Extraordinary Gospel*, 97.

35. Note, however, that Romans 2:4 is sometimes misapplied. Paul wrote there to a nonbeliever, "Or do you presume on the riches of his kindness and forbearance and patience, not knowing that God's kindness is meant to lead you to repentance?" Don't be haughty and self-righteous just because you haven't experienced God's judgment yet. He is patient and kind with you, giving you time to repent. That, of course, is different from the concept that God only leads sinners to Himself through a kind message.

36. Rabe, *Metanoia*, Kindle locations 97–122, provides a few examples of this meaning, including Hebrews 12:17 (see the New International Version; to render here with "change of mind" is possible but far from certain). And again, there is no dispute that in some contexts, especially outside the New Testament, *metanoia* simply means a change of mind, as confirmed in any dictionary of classical Greek. Rabe quotes 1 John 5:20, which does *not* contain *metanoia*, then writes: "The truth about God and man is revealed in Christ. The good news presents man with a whole new way of understanding God and himself. *Metanoia*, in the context of the gospel, is to come to our senses, to change our thinking in accordance with this revelation." It is quite revealing that he fails to provide clear examples where the word simply has this meaning in the New Testament, and more revealing is that he ignores the passages where it clearly cannot have this meaning.

37. Walter Bauer, Frederick William Danker, et. al., eds., *A Greek-English Lexicon of the New Testament and Other Early Christian Literature*, third ed. (Chicago: University of Chicago Press, 2001), 640–641.

38. Timothy Friberg, Barbara Friberg, and Neva F. Miller, *The Analytical Greek Lexicon* (Victoria, British Columbia: Trafford Publishing, 2005), ad loc.

39. J. P. Louw and Eugene A. Nida, *Greek-English Lexicon of the New Testament: Based on Semantic Domains* (New York: United Bible Societies, 1989), 510.

40. Joseph Thayer, *Thayer's Greek-English Lexicon of the New Testament* (Grand Rapids, MI: Zondervan, 1974), 405.

41. Ibid., 405–406.

42. J. Behm, in Gerhard Kittel and Gerhard Friedrich, eds., *Theological Dictionary of the New Testament*, English trans. (Grand Rapids, MI: Eerdmans, 1967), 4:1000.

43. Robertson, *Word Pictures in the New Testament*, 3:34.

44. J. Goetzmann, in Colin Brown, ed., *New International Dictionary of New Testament Theology* (Grand Rapids, MI: Zondervan, 1986), 1:358.

45. H. R. Balz and G. Schneider, eds., *Exegetical Dictionary of the New Testament*, English trans. (Grand Rapids, MI: Eerdmans, 1990–1993), 2:416.

46. Ibid.

47. Whitten, *Pure Grace*, 99.

48. Michael L. Brown, *The End of the American Gospel Enterprise* (Shippensburg, PA: Destiny Image, 1989), 23–24. Used by permission.

49. Brown, *It's Time to Rock the Boat*, 33.

50. Balz and Schneider, *Exegetical Dictionary of the New Testament*, 2:416.

51. Brown, *It's Time to Rock the Boat*, 33.

52. Ibid., 34–36.

53. Ellis, "'Confronting the Error of Hyper-Grace,' a Response to Michael Brown"; see also *The Gospel in Ten Words*, 30, where Dr. Ellis claims that, "Repentance for forgiveness is what John the Baptist preached. It's forgiveness conditional on you turning from sin. It's a verb for a verb. But this is not what Jesus is saying here [in Luke 24:47]. He doesn't use verbs for repentance and forgiveness but nouns. He's saying, 'From now on, forgiveness is not something God does, it's something he's done.'" All of these points—from Dr. Ellis's website and from his book, both cited here—are easily refuted. First, verses like Zechariah 1:3–4 are just two among many that speak of an Old Testament call to turn back to God; second, the verses just cited from Revelation (9:20–21; 16:9–11), make clear that in the New Testament repentance included *turning away from sin*. Second, John the Baptist did not use "a verb for a verb" (see Matt. 3:8, 11; Mark 1:4; Luke 3:3, 8, all of which refer to John and all of which use the noun *metanoia*, repentance; and Mark 1:4 and Luke 3:3, also the noun *aphesis*, forgiveness; this alone makes Dr. Ellis's statement completely inaccurate); and in the Book of Acts, the verb "repent" is used, followed by a promise of forgiveness, as in Acts 2:38—once again, the exact opposite of what Dr. Ellis writes.

7—Sanctified or Not?

1. Crowder, *Mystical Union*, 42, his emphasis. Accordingly, the second chapter of this book is titled, "Sanctification Is Not a Process."

2. Whitten, *Pure Grace*, 166, my emphasis.

3. Ibid., 28.

4. Rufus, "Totally Forgiven! Totally United! Totally Filled!" For a clarification of his views, even recognizing some ways in which sanctification is a process, see Ryan Rufus, *Sanctification by Grace* (Hong Kong: New Nature Publications, 2011). Used by permission.

5. As quoted in Simon Yap, "D. L. Moody and Joseph Prince," *His Grace Is Enough* (blog), May 17, 2011, http://hischarisisenough.wordpress.com/2011/05/17/d-l-moody-preacher-of-radical-grace/ (accessed September 4, 2013). Note that Colossians 2:10 is commonly misunderstood in hyper-grace circles. The KJV says, "And ye are complete in him," but a more accurate translation would be, "you have been filled in him" (ESV) or "you have been given fullness in Christ" (NIV). As for those translations that use "complete" (NAS), the intended meaning is that we have everything we need in Jesus, as opposed to being "perfect" already.

6. Ibid.

7. Prince, *Unmerited Favor*, 198.

8. Crowder, *Mystical Union*, 13.

9. Ibid., 36–37, 47.

10. According to Spurgeon, "If you take away the grace of God from the gospel you have extracted from it its very life-blood, and there is nothing left worth preaching, worth believing, or worth contending for. Grace is the soul of the gospel: without it the gospel is dead. Grace is the music of the gospel: without it the gospel is silent as to all comfort." [Charles Spurgeon, "The Doctrines of Grace Do Not Lead to Sin," sermon preached at Exeter-Hall on August 19, 1833, Metropolitan Tabernacle Pulpit, http://www.spurgeon.org/sermons/1735.htm (accessed September 4, 2013).

11. As we'll see in chapter 15, this is actually not a new teaching.

12. See my book *Go and Sin No More*, 137–145.

13. Ibid., 137, emphasis in the original.

14. See Romans 1:7; 15:25, 31; 1 Corinthians 16:15; 2 Corinthians 1:1; Ephesians 1:1, 18; 3:18; 5:3; Philippians 1:1; Colossians 1:2, 26; 2 Thessalonians 1:10; Hebrews 6:10; Judah (Jude) 3; Revelation 11:18.

15. Theologians often call this "realized eschatology."

16. Dr. Bob Gladstone, in communication with the author, June 7, 2013.

17. John H. Stoll, "The Three Elements of Sanctification," in *The Biblical Principles for Christian Maturity* (n.p.: BMH Books, 1996), http://www.leaderu.com/offices/stoll/maturity/chap20.html (accessed September 4, 2013).

18. Crowder, *Mystical Union*, 17; cited also in chapter 2.

19. Ibid., 50.

20. Raymond E. Brown, *The Epistles of John*, Anchor Bible Commentaries (Garden City, NY: Doubleday, 1995), 431.

21. Technically, these are in the aorist tense in the Greek, which speaks of past, completed action.

22. See also Hebrews 2:11; 13:12.

23. Rabe, *Metanoia*, Kindle locations 189–191.

24. Second Corinthians 5:18-20 states, "All this is from God, who through Christ reconciled us to himself and gave us the ministry of reconciliation; that is, in Christ God was reconciling the world to himself, not counting their trespasses against them, and entrusting to us the message of reconciliation. Therefore, we are ambassadors for Christ, God making

his appeal through us. We implore you on behalf of Christ, be reconciled to God." One key portion of this text is paraphrased in *The Message* to say, "God put the world square with himself through the Messiah, giving the world a fresh start by offering forgiveness of sins. God has given us the task of telling everyone what he is doing." So, has God already forgiven the sins of the entire world through Jesus—meaning, pronounced their sins forgiven? Paul is saying that in the cross, rather than God condemning the world, He is shouting, "Your sins have been paid in full!" However, until sinners turn to the Lord in repentance and faith, they are still in their sins and under the judgment of their sins.

25. As one hyper-grace teacher puts it, you start your race at the finish line. While I understand the point, it actually contradicts many biblical statements.

26. C. A. Wanamaker, *The Epistles to the Thessalonians: A Commentary on the Greek Text*, New International Greek Testament Commentary (Grand Rapids, MI: Eerdmans, 1990), 150–151.

27. F. F. Bruce, *1 and 2 Thessalonians*, Word Biblical Commentary (Dallas: Word, 1998), 82. In contrast, according to the author, the word *hagiōsunē*, which is used in 1 Thessalonians 3:13, means "the state of being holy."

28. Crowder, *Mystical Union*, 42.

29. According to Bruce, "This wishprayer is in essence a repetition in different words of that in 3:11–13, the climax of which is the prayer that the Thessalonians' hearts may be established 'unblamable in holiness' at the Parousia [Second Coming]." [Bruce, *1 and 2 Thessalonians*, 129.] Crowder in *Mystical Union* (see page 94) argues against the common evangelical understanding of this verse, in my judgment, completely without success.

30. Leon Morris, *The Epistle to the Romans*, The Pillar New Testament Commentary (Grand Rapids, MI: Eerdmans, 1988), 265.

31. Robertson, *Word Pictures*, to Romans 6:19, my emphasis.

32. Bruce, *The Epistle to the Hebrews*, 243. He continues, "It is a sanctification which has taken place once for all; in this sense it is as unrepeatable as the sacrifice which effects it."

33. Robertson, *Word Pictures*, to Hebrews 2:11.

34. Let's look once again at what Professor Cockerill has to say: "Christ came to make the existing people of God [meaning the Jewish people] 'holy' by cleansing them from the pollution and the dominion of sin so that they would have true access to God. This cleansing is 'once for all' in that it is completely adequate without need of supplement or repetition. Those who embrace what Christ has done through faithful obedience continue in this cleansing as part of the persevering people of God. However, as the pastor [meaning, the author of Hebrews] makes abundantly clear, the full sufficiency of this cleansing work is no guarantee of, but the strongest motivation for, perseverance. Repudiation of Christ through faithlessness and disobedience results in severance from his sanctified people. Thus the

author expresses his pastoral concern by repeatedly urging his hearers to persevere by making use of the cleansing work of Christ to continue in faithful obedience (10:19–31). By his obedience Christ makes their obedience possible." [Cockerill, *The Epistle to the Hebrews*, 445.]

35. In full, he wrote (Lane, *Hebrews 9–13*, note cc to 10:14), "The careful use of tenses in v 14 is remarkable. A suggestive contrast is involved. The pf tense of τετελείωκεν defines a work that is finished on its author's side, but that is progressively realized in the process depicted by the present ptcp. The force of τοὺς ἁγιαζομένους is purely durative, 'those who are in the process of sanctification' (cf. Grothe, "Was Jesus the Priestly Messiah?" 165, n. 145)." Francois du Toit, in his *Mirror Bible*, renders this differently, seeking to justify this with the accompanying note (his emphasis): **"By that one perfect sacrifice he has perfectly sanctified sinful man forever.** (The word, *hagiazomenous*, means sanctify, the present participle describes an action thought of as simultaneous with the action of the main verb, 'perfectly;' *teteleioken*, in the Perfect Tense denotes an action which is completed in the past, but the effects of which are regarded as continuing into the present [see Heb. 2:11]. For he who sanctifies and those who are sanctified have all one origin.)" It is with good grammatical reason that translators and commentators do *not* understand *hagiazomenous* here as "has…sanctified." Quite simply, the Greek would have required a different form of *hagiazo* to connote finished, past activity, and as noted by M. Zerwick and M. Grosvenor in *A Grammatical Analysis of the Greek New Testament* (Rome: Biblical Institute Press, 1974), 676, the form of the word here denotes "a continuous process."

36. Whitten, *Pure Grace*, 166.

37. Bruce, *The Epistle to the Hebrews*, 22.

38. Thomas D. Lea, *Hebrews, James*, Holman New Testament Commentary (Nashville: Broadman & Holman, 1999), 184–185.

39. Cockerill, *The Epistle to the Hebrews*, 451–452.

40. As quoted by Paul Ellingworth, *The Epistle to the Hebrews: A Commentary on the Greek Text*, New International Greek Testament Commentary (Grand Rapids, MI: Eerdmans, 1993), 511.

41. R. C. H. Lenski, *The Interpretation of the Epistle to the Hebrews and of the Epistle of James* (Columbus, OH: Lutheran Book Concern, 1938), 357.

42. Whitten, *Pure Grace*, 14, his emphasis.

43. I owe this insight to David Ravenhill; see his article titled "Would You Recognize the Deception of Hyper-Grace?", CharismaNews.com, May 18, 2013, http://www.charismanews.com/opinion/39494-would-you-recognize-the-deception-of-hyper-grace (accessed September 5, 2013).

8—Find Out What Pleases the Lord

1. Whitten, *Pure Grace*, 53.

2. Rufus, "Totally Forgiven! Totally United! Totally Filled!" I want to reiterate that Ryan Rufus is *not* sanctioning or encouraging sin in any way,

as he makes clear in many of his sermons and writings; his father, Pastor Rob Rufus, writes in *Living in the Grace of God*, "Grace is not a license to live disobediently. Living in grace gives us the capacity to obey God" (Kindle location 125).

3. Rufus, "Totally Forgiven! Totally United! Totally Filled!"
4. Ibid.
5. Whitten, *Pure Grace*, 40.
6. Ellis, *The Gospel in Ten Words*, 112.
7. Crowder, *Mystical Union*, 9, his emphasis.
8. Farley, *The Naked Gospel*, 81.
9. McVey, *52 Lies Heard in Church Every Sunday*, 85, his emphasis.
10. Prince, *Unmerited Favor*, 43, his emphasis.
11. Andrew Wommack, *Grace: The Power of the Gospel* (Tulsa, OK: Harrison House, 2007), 197, his emphasis.
12. Some scholars debate whether the words "in Ephesus" were part of the original letter, but that is entirely beside the point here; I encourage you to see the standard commentaries on Ephesians for more details.
13. I. D. E. Thomas, compiler, *The Golden Treasury of Puritan Quotations* (Chicago: Moody Press, 1975), 140.
14. Oswald Chambers, *My Utmost Devotional Bible* (Nashville: Thomas Nelson, 1997), 126.
15. Louw and Nida, *Greek-English Lexicon of the New Testament: Based on Semantic Domains*, 600. Bauer, Danker, et. al., *A Greek-English Lexicon of the New Testament and Other Early Christian Literature*, 805, explains the Greek word used here (*perisseuō*) as, "cause to abound, make extremely rich."
16. In Ephesians alone, Paul uses "in Him" in 1:4, 9, 10; 2:15; 4:21; and 6:20.
17. William W. Klein, "Ephesians," in Tremper Longman III and David E. Garland, eds., *The Expositor's Bible Commentary, Revised Edition* (Grand Rapids, MI: Zondervan, 2006), 12:55.
18. On the defilement of the inner being ("the heart"), see Matthew 15:15–19.
19. Although I'm completely sure that God cares for each of His children deeply, far more than we could imagine, I'm also sure that much of our contemporary gospel preaching and ministry has played right into our society's mentality that "It's all about me." And so we preach a message that seeks to make God acceptable to lost sinners rather than one that seeks to make lost sinners acceptable to God. And even within the body, we often follow this same mentality, putting so much emphasis on "how the message makes me feel" as opposed to asking, "How does my lifestyle make God feel?" I addressed this at length in *It's Time to Rock the Boat*, published in 1993, but I did so often before that and have since.
20. Prince, *Destined to Reign*, 187; others have followed Prince here, without citing his exact words.
21. It's clear that Paul is addressing believers here, especially in 1 Corinthians 11:28, since he tells these people to partake of Communion after they do examine themselves.

22. The end of 1 John 4:17, "as he [Jesus] is so also are we in this world," is often understood by modern grace teachers to mean that we are just like God in terms of holiness, purity, and perfection already in this world. But that cannot be what John is saying, since he already wrote in 1 John 3:2, "Beloved, we are God's children now, and what we will be has not yet appeared; but we know that when he appears we shall be like him, because we shall see him as he is." So, clearly (and obviously!) we are not yet fully "as he is." This is reinforced in the next verse, which reminds us that, "Everyone who has this hope in him purifies himself, just as he is pure" (1 John 3:3, NIV). So, we still must purify ourselves in light of the coming of the perfectly pure one. Although commentators debate the meaning of 1 John 4:17, one common interpretation is that we have the same standing with God in this world that Jesus does in heaven, which gives us confidence in the Day of Judgment. (The whole verse reads, "By this is love perfected with us, so that we may have confidence for the day of judgment, because as he is so also are we in this world.")

23. Although some have claimed that the Laodiceans were not believers, there is no question that they were, since the *ekklesia* ("church"; "congregation") of the New Testament has exclusive reference to believers.

24. Crowder, *Mystical Union*, 9.

25. Clark Whitten uses these terms in *Pure Grace*, but I'm not sure if they are original to him. A Google search on June 2, 2013, for both "behavior modification" and "sin management" yielded 1,080 hits, primarily to hyper-grace-related links.

9—Is Spirituality Effortless?

1. Crowder, *Mystical Union*, 9.
2. Ibid., 39.
3. Ibid., 140.
4. John Henry Jowett, "The Disciple's Sacrifice," in *Passion for Souls*, as quoted in Brown, *Time for Holy Fire*, 198–199.
5. John Sheasby, *The Birthright* (Grand Rapids, MI: Zondervan, 2010), 102.
6. Prince, *Unmerited Favor*, 56–57.
7. Ibid., xiii.
8. Ibid.
9. Ibid., 145.
10. In order to get out of the obvious call to *do* something in response to the call to repentance, one hyper-grace teacher claims that in the days of our first love, we basically did nothing, meaning that everything just flowed naturally out of love for God. The opposite is true: because of our great love for Him, we delighted in spending quality time with Him, among other things. That is certainly part of the "doing" to which Jesus refers.
11. Benjamin Dunn, *The Happy Gospel: Effortless Union With a Happy God* (Shippensburg, PA: Destiny Image, 2011), used by permission; Andrew

Wommack, *Effortless Change: The Word Is the Seed That Can Change Your Life* (Tulsa, OK: Harrison House, 2011).

12. Prince, *Unmerited Favor*, 216.
13. Ibid., 7.
14. Ibid., 145.
15. Ibid., xii, his emphasis.
16. Ibid., x.
17. Ibid., 310.
18. Ibid., 341, my emphasis.
19. "I Am Thine, O Lord" by Fanny J. Crosby. Public domain.
20. Dunn, *The Happy Gospel*, 138, my emphasis; see also chapter 12.
21. Ibid., 165.
22. Ibid., 136–137, his emphasis.
23. Ibid., 141, his emphasis.
24. Wommack, *Effortless Change*, Kindle locations 39–40.
25. Ibid., Kindle location 375.
26. Ibid., Kindle location 53.
27. Ibid., Kindle locations 1252–1253.
28. Julian Wilson, *Wigglesworth the Complete Story* (Franklin, TN: Authentic Publishers, 2004), 109.
29. Smith Wigglesworth, "Paul's Vision and the Baptism of the Holy Ghost," *Pentecostal Evangel*, April 21, 1928, 6, viewed at http://ifphc.org/pdf/PentecostalEvangel/1920-1929/1928/1928_04_21.pdf (accessed September 5, 2013).
30. In a very fair review of Joseph Prince's *Destined to Reign*, George P. Wood notes that, "Paul is not against works or self-effort per se, he is against their being used as the ground of justification. Paul's vision of sanctification is not 'effortless,' in other words. Thus, for example, in Ephesians 4:17–32, Paul exhorts the Ephesians to 'put off your old self,' 'be made new in the attitude of your minds,' and 'put on the new self.' This requires effort. It may even require hard work." [George P. Wood, "Review of *Destined to Reign* by Joseph Prince," April 30, 2012, http://georgepwood.com/2012/04/30/review-of-destined-to-reign-by-joseph-prince/ (accessed September 5, 2013).] He rightly notes, "But the motivation for this effort is not the hope of gaining God's favor. God's favor has already been bestowed. That is, as it were, the diamond of insight in Prince's book. Whatever work the Christian performs is motivated precisely by the knowledge that one *already* has God's favor. Work, then, is not the ground of justification. Rather, work—the work of holiness—is the expression of having been justified" (his emphasis).
31. For the strange interpretation put on this text by Simon Yap, see chapter 4, note 13.
32. J. C. Ryle, *Holiness: Its Nature, Hindrances, Difficulties, and Roots*, reprint (Lafayette, IN: Sovereign Grace Publishers, 2001), vii.
33. Ibid., viii–ix.

34. Ibid., 19.
35. Ibid., 36.

10—Is God Always in a Good Mood?

1. Erika, "Late Nights," *The Downpour* (blog), February 8, 2011, http://hereinredding.tumblr.com/ (accessed September 6, 2011).
2. This post is no longer available online.
3. Theologians often speak about divine "impassibility," meaning their belief that God's "emotional" state is unchanging and unchangeable, and that all the descriptions in Scripture about His grief, joy, and anger are simply figures of speech. But then in what way are we made in His image? And didn't Jesus reflect God's heart when He was on the earth?
4. Crisco, *Extraordinary Gospel*, 23.
5. Dunn, *Happy Gospel*, 39.
6. See Sam Storms, *The Singing God: Feel the Passion God Has for You…Just the Way You Are* (Lake Mary, FL: Charisma House, 2013).
7. This post is no longer available online.
8. Chuck Crisco, *God Is in a Good Mood* (n.p.: Simply B, 2011), Kindle location, 131; Crisco, *Extraordinary Gospel*, 23.
9. For a challenging study, see Kazo Kitamori, *Theology and the Pain of God*, Eng. translation (Richmond, VA: John Knox Press, 1965).
10. See the powerful imagery in chapters like Jeremiah 2 and Ezekiel 16 and 23.
11. Crisco, *Extraordinary Gospel*, 46.
12. See Romans 1:18; 2:5 [2 times], 8; 3:5; 4:15; 5:9; 9:22 [2 times]; 12:19; 13:4; Ephesians 2:3; 5:6; Colossians 3:6; 1 Thessalonians 1:10; 2:16; and 5:9, and note that these are only references to God's wrath (*orgē* in Greek).
13. Mick Mooney, *The Gospel Cannot Be Chained: A Grace Paraphrase of Paul's Four Prison Letters* (n.p.: Lightview Media, 2012), Kindle locations 265–267.
14. Ibid., Kindle locations 276–279.
15. Ibid., Kindle locations 853–856.
16. Yes, Jesus did take our punishment on the cross, but this is *not* what Paul is saying here.
17. Mick Mooney, *Look! The Finished Work of Jesus: A Message of God's Radical Love for You* (n.p.: Searching for Grace, 2010).
18. The translation note to these verses explains, "The phrase, *uious tēs apeitheias*, translates as unbelief produces a breed of people; not sons of disobedience as most translations read here! The word, *orgē*, means excitement of mind, from the word, *oregomai*, meaning to stretch one's self out in order to touch or to grasp something, to reach after or desire something."
19. The lengthy translation note to Romans 14:11 in no way justifies his rendering and, in fact, does not even attempt to justify the more extreme changes he makes. On the other hand, he does not eliminate the reference to "grieving" the Spirit, as Mooney did, in Ephesians 4:31, rendering

with, "The Holy Spirit is your signet ring from God to confirm that you are redeemed to live your life in the light of day; any conduct that belongs to the night grieves him."

20. Paul Ellis, "What About Hell? 10 Things to Know," *Escape to Reality* (blog), April 23, 2013, http://escapetoreality.org/2013/04/23/what-about-hell/ (accessed September 6, 2013).

21. Ibid.

22. For more on this, see chapter 13.

23. See, for example, Matthew 13:24–30, 36–43; 22:1–14; 25:1–46.

24. For the meaning of "repent," see chapter 5.

25. A. W. Tozer, *And He Dwelt Among Us: Teachings From the Gospel of John* (Ventura, CA: Regal, 2009), 150.

26. Ibid.

27. As quoted in Francis Chan, *Crazy Love: Overwhelmed by a Relentless God* (Colorado Springs, CO: David C. Cook, 2013), 53.

28. *Sown in Weakness, Raised in Glory: From the Spiritual Legacy of Mother Basilea Schlink*, (Darmstadt, Germany: Evangelical Sisterhood of Mary, 2004), 82.

11—Marcion Revisited

1. Adolf Von Harnack, *History of Dogma*, vol. 1, Eng. tr., repr. (Gloucester, MA: Peter Smith, 1976), 268. For a useful, beginner-level summary of Marcion's beliefs and activities, see http://earliestchristianity.wordpress.com/2010/08/02/marcion-a-beginners-guide/ (accessed September 6, 2013).

2. Van der Merwe, *GRACE*, 28.

3. Note that when Paul speaks of "the old covenant" in 2 Corinthians 3:14, he is not referring to the Old Testament as a whole but rather the Sinai Covenant as laid out in the Torah, although it's easy to see how readers today might miss that, especially since the KJV uses "the old testament" here.

4. The word *Tanakh* is an acronym standing for three words: *Torah* (the Pentateuch), *Nevi'im* (Prophets, pronounced *n'-vee-eem*), and *Ketuvim* (Writings, pronounced *k'-tu-veem*). For more on this, see Michael L. Brown, *60 Questions Christians Ask About Jewish Beliefs and Practices* (Grand Rapids: Chosen, 2011). Used by permission.

5. I appreciate that Rob Rufus writes, "If, after receiving grace, people still sin continually and refuse to be disciplined, then the process of biblical judgment must come. There is a place for that, but it is a rare extreme case. We must keep uppermost in our minds the truth that the church is a community of grace." [Rufus, *Living in the Grace of God*, Kindle locations 712–714.]

6. Joseph Prince wrote in *Destined to Reign* (122–123), "I have been accused of being an antinomian (someone who is against the law of Moses). The truth is I have the highest regard for the law. And it is precisely because

I have the highest regard for the law that I know that no man can keep the law.... It is us grace preachers who have the highest regard for the law!... I am for the law, for the purpose for which God gave the law... God did not give the law for us to keep. He gave the law to bring man to the end of himself, so that he would see his need for a Saviour." I do appreciate his perspective, but there is far more to God's Law and its purposes in our lives than Pastor Prince recognizes here.

7. Some scholars believe that 1 Peter was written to Jewish believers, but either way, they were new covenant, born-again believers, and therefore the same argument that I raise here would apply.

8. Michael L. Brown, *Answering Jewish Objections to Jesus*, vol. 4, *New Testament Objections* (Grand Rapids, MI: Baker, 2006), 3, emphasis added here. Used by permission.

9. Andrew Wommack in *Grace: The Power of the Gospel* (page 181) notes that, "As Paul continued to write about righteousness, he began quoting Old Testament scripture about the law [citing Romans 10:5].... This is talking about a person who is legalistic and trusting their own goodness as the foundation of their relationship with God." However, he fails to note that Paul's quotation about the righteousness that comes by faith in Romans 10:6–7 (he writes, "Instead of demanding you to come up to Him, He's already come down to you," 183) is also taken from Old Testament Law. This obviously paints an incomplete picture.

10. *Charis* occurs 77 times in the Old Testament (in the Septuagint) and 155 times in the New Testament (none in Matthew and Mark).

11. For discussion of Romans 7 and its applicability (or lack thereof) to believers today, see Brown, *Go and Sin No More*, 265–283.

12. Jesus actually reiterated this concept as well; see Mark 10:17–22, and note that when Jesus exposed the rich young ruler's materialism, He did it out of love: "And Jesus, looking at him, loved him, and said to him, 'You lack one thing: go, sell all that you have and give to the poor, and you will have treasure in heaven; and come, follow me.' Disheartened by the saying, he went away sorrowful, for he had great possessions" (vv. 21–22).

13. D. Martyn Lloyd-Jones, *Studies in the Sermon on the Mount*, repr. (Grand Rapids, MI: Eerdmans, 2000), 196.

14. Rufus, "Totally Forgiven! Totally United! Totally Filled!"

15. Farley, *The Naked Gospel*, 68.

16. Ibid., 68–69.

17. Ibid., 69.

18. Ibid.

19. Again, I appreciate Rob Rufus's comments in *Living in the Grace of God* (Kindle locations 845–858): "For the person who is in Christ, the wrath of God's punishment has burnt itself out on the innocent head of Jesus Christ and there is only God's loving discipline left—discipline that will bring us to maturity in Jesus. Consequently, the safest place to be in the

universe is in Christ." He then lays out the differences between punishment and discipline, closing with, "Discipline produces security."

20. Farley, *The Naked Gospel*, 69.

21. In the New Testament, Deuteronomy is the most frequently quoted book from the Pentateuch, Isaiah the most frequently quoted book from the prophetic and historical writings, and Psalms the most frequently quoted book from the poetry and wisdom literature.

22. See Quentin F. Wesselschmidt, ed., *Psalms 51–150*, Ancient Christian Commentary on Scripture (Downers Grove, IL: InterVarsity Press, 2007), 1–12; see also Yale University, "Introduction to Medieval Christian Liturgy, II.3 The Liturgy of the Hours," http://www.yale.edu/adhoc/research_resources/liturgy/hours.html (accessed September 9, 2013).

23. I discuss the next verse, "If we are faithless, he remains faithful—for he cannot deny himself" (2 Tim. 2:13), in the appendix, "Once Saved, Always Saved?"

24. Again, see the appendix for more on this.

25. For one among many, see Paul Ellis, "Who Killed Herod?", *Escape to Reality* (blog), March 1, 2011, http://escapetoreality.org/2011/03/01/who-killed-herod/ (accessed September 9, 2013).

26. Von Harnack, *History of Dogma*, 268.

27. This is from the ad for Andrew Wommack's audio teaching series "The True Nature of God" found in the back of his book *Grace: The Power of the Gospel.*

12—The Law of the Lord Is Good

1. The Greek word used here is *paidagōgos*, defined in Bauer, et. al., eds., *A Greek-English Lexicon of the New Testament and Other Early Christian Literature* (page 748) as originally "a slave" (lit. "boy-leader") "whose duty it was to superintend the conduct of the boys in the family to which he was attached and to conduct them to and from school and to superintend his conduct."

2. Prince, *Destined to Reign*, 124. See also Tony Cook, *Grace: The DNA of God* (Tulsa, OK: Harrison House, 2011).

3. The Hebrew word *torah* means "instruction, teaching, law," and it is often used in contexts in the Old Testament where the emphasis is clearly on "instruction" as opposed to "law," because of which it is often translated with "Teaching" in the New Jewish Version (see, for example, Joshua 1:8, "Let not this Book of the Teaching cease from your lips…").

4. Farley, *The Naked Gospel*, 60.

5. Ibid., 61–62, my emphasis.

6. Ibid., 64, his emphasis.

7. Ibid., 58–59. Farley goes on to make the following statement, which is in keeping with many others, but I find it odd and unscriptural: "While some view Christianity as a behavior improvement program, the Eden story

reveals that a desire for behavior improvement was the cause of spiritual death" (Ibid., 72). Was it really?

8. For a convenient online source about Haustafeln, see Chaplain Mike, "The NT Haustafeln (House-Tables)," August 20, 2011, http://www.internetmonk.com/archive/the-nt-haustafeln (accessed September 9, 2013).

9. Rufus, "Totally Forgiven! Totally United! Totally Filled!"

10. Ibid.

11. Farley, *The Naked Gospel*, 27.

12. Van der Merwe, *GRACE*, x.

13. The word translated "lawlessness" is *anomia*, from the Greek word for "law," *nomos*, plus the negating *a* (as in apathy, the absence of *pathos*, or atheism, not believing in God, *theos* in Greek). So, since *anomia* refers to "lawlessness," by extension, it also means "wickedness, iniquity."

14. Matthew Henry, *Matthew Henry's Commentary on the Whole Bible*, repr. (Peabody, MA: Hendrickson, 2009), s.v. "1 John 3:4."

15. Somehow, Andre van der Merwe in his book *GRACE* (page 17) can state that, "The laws referred to in this verse [Heb. 8:10] are not the 10 Commandments either, since we are living under a new and better covenant and not under the Old Covenant anymore." Again, however, the issue was the *nature* of the covenant, not the *laws* of the covenant. Van der Merwe, however, is clear to add: "If we now tell people that they should live up to the demands of this Old Covenant System, it means that we are actually putting death on them. To conclude, if people think that we are saying they can just go out and live in full blown depravity, licentiousness and immorality, simply running like animals after the desires of their flesh, *then they are wrong*. If God has removed our old sinful nature with its lustful desires, why would we want to live in it any longer?" So, the problem with van der Merwe's message is not that he wants to give believers a license to sin, but rather that he does not explain that God would write His moral laws on our hearts.

16. Not surprisingly, hyper-grace teachers commonly claim that this refers to God's life inside of us, as opposed to God's Law.

17. Wanamaker, *The Epistles to the Thessalonians*, 150.

18. Ibid.

19. Gene L. Green, *The Letters to the Thessalonians*, The Pillar New Testament Commentary (Grand Rapids, MI: Eerdmans, 2002), 186.

20. Farley, *The Naked Gospel*, 58.

21. McVey, *52 Lies Heard in Church Every Sunday*, 153.

22. Ellis, *The Gospel in Ten Words*, 147.

23. Ibid., 70–71.

24. Crisco, *Extraordinary Gospel*, 19.

25. Van der Merwe, *GRACE*, 3.

26. Ellis, *The Gospel in Ten Words*, 20.

27. Prince, *Unmerited Favor*, 111–112.

28. The Hebrew is simply, "Everything Yahweh spoke we will do."

29. Prince, *Unmerited Favor*, 111.

30. Ibid., 112, citing Exodus 19:12–13.

31. In the foreword to David Wilkerson's book *It Is Finished: Finding Lasting Victory Over Sin* (Bloomington, MN: Chosen, 2013; originally published as *The New Covenant Unveiled*), Gary Wilkerson, David's son, relates how his father grew up in a legalistic religious background, because of which he often felt he was falling short in God's sight. To remedy this, he would study the writings of the Puritans because they had such a great revelation of the finished work of the cross!

32. Charles Spurgeon, "The Perpetuity of the Law of God," sermon no. 1660, delivered on May 21, 1882, at Metropolitan Tabernacle, Newington, http://www.spurgeongems.org/vols28-30/chs1660.pdf (accessed September 9, 2013).

33. Rufus, *Living in the Grace of God*, Kindle locations 1057–1062. He wisely adds: "It's true to say, though, that some people accept Christ before they feel the full weight of their sin; also, Jesus reveals himself to those from different religious backgrounds (and none) who have never understood the law. As they grow in their understanding, they then begin to 'see.' But we have to be aware that there are those who are, in effect, false converts who have never come to their Saviour in reality because they have never truly seen their need of salvation."

34. Paul himself preached a strong repentance message in Acts! See Acts 17:30, where he calls all people everywhere to repent from idolatry; Acts 20:21, where he describes his gospel message as repentance toward God and faith in Jesus; and Acts 26:20, where Paul said he called his hearers to repent and turn to God and prove their repentance by their deeds.

35. Joseph Prince, *Destined to Reign* television program, December 3, 2010, http://livedash.ark.com/transcript/joseph_prince__destined_to_reign/4284/ABCFP/Friday_December_03_2010/527844/ (accessed November 1, 2013).

36. The absence of the word *love* in Acts (alone the only such instance in the New Testament) was pointed out to me by Pete Mullins, pastor of Coweta Community Church in Newnan, Georgia; in Acts 7:10, 46, the word *charis* is used in Stephen's sermon, but in the sense of "favor" (received by Moses in Acts 7:10 and David in Acts 7:46). As for no form of the word *love* in Greek being found in Acts, the word for "beloved" in Acts 15:25 is *agapētos* in Greek, but this simply means "dear" (as in "dear friends") and is not, quite obviously, related to the love of God in a gospel message.

37. The Greek for "cut to the heart" is very wrong, rendered as "pricked in their heart" (KJV), "pierced to the heart" (NAS), "stung in their hearts" (CJB), and "acutely distressed" (NET).

38. Note that Felix's wife Drusilla, who was Jewish and was his third wife, "was Herod Agrippa I's youngest daughter and Agrippa II's sister. She married the king of a small region in Syria, but at the age of sixteen divorced him at Felix's instigation to marry him instead. Although it violated normal

Roman policy for a governor to marry a woman from his province, Felix had much power as long as his brother Pallas remained in favor in Rome" (Keener, *IVP Bible Background Commentary: New Testament*, 396). Richard N. Longenecker, in "Acts" in *The Expositor's Bible Commentary, Revised Edition* (10:1064), notes that, "The relationship between Felix and his young wife seems to have been based on greed, lust, and expectations of grandeur. Yet they apparently still had some qualms of conscience and therefore took the opportunity to send for Paul and hear his message." If they had no qualms of conscience and were simply curious, they certainly left the meeting with Paul having some qualms! "And as [Paul] reasoned about righteousness and self-control and the coming judgment, Felix was alarmed [or, frightened] and said, 'Go away for the present. When I get an opportunity I will summon you'" (Acts 24:25).

13—Why Are We Running From the Words of Jesus?

1. Van der Merwe, *GRACE*, ix. For another typical example, see Mike Kapler and Joel Brueske, "How Much of What Jesus Said Is for Us Today?", *Growing in Grace* (podcast), August 1, 2013, http://www.growingingrace.org/2013/08/how-much-of-what-jesus-said-is-for-us.html (accessed September 9, 2013).

2. Farley, *The Naked Gospel*, 86.

3. Van der Merwe, *Grace*, 40. Notice that he says the Jews of Jesus' day were "polluted with hundreds of years of preaching of the Old Testament Law." How can one be polluted by the preaching of God's holy, beautiful, glorious Law? See chapter 12 for more on this.

4. Farley, *The Naked Gospel*, 84.

5. Ibid., 80.

6. Ibid., 87.

7. Pastor Farley has clarified his views in his blog, writing, "Jesus *sometimes* taught his hearers about the true spirit of the Law and revealed a truly impossible standard of perfection (anger equals murder, looking with lust equals adultery, cut off your hand, pluck out your eye, be perfect, forgive others to be forgiven by God, sell everything, etc.). Recognizing this plain and obvious purpose of some of Jesus' teachings is not even remotely the same as disregarding what Jesus said before the cross. Before the cross, Jesus clearly taught many, many things that are applicable to the church today—the Vine and the Branches, the Holy Spirit, the Kingdom, just to name a few among *many*." [Andrew Farley, "What I'm Really Saying!", Patheos.com, June 6, 2013, http://www.patheos.com/blogs/andrewfarley/2013/06/what-im-really-saying/ (accessed September 9, 2013).

8. Examples of this are found throughout the messages and writings of hyper-grace teachers.

9. JosephPrince.com, "What Does It Mean to 'Rightly Divide the Word,' and How Are We to Do It?", FAQ: Questions About the Bible, May 20, 2011, http://support.josephprince.org/index.php?/Knowledgebase/Article/

View/122/22/i-what-does-it-mean-to-rightly-divide-the-word-and-how-do-we-do-it (accessed September 9, 2013), my emphasis.

10. Farley, *The Naked Gospel*, 87, my emphasis.

11. Ryan Rufus, *Extra Virgin Grace* (n.p.: New Nature Publications, 2011), Kindle locations 1064–1069. Used by permission.

12. Ibid., Kindle locations 1278–1282.

13. Charles Spurgeon, "The Beatitudes," sermon no. 3155, SpurgeonGems.org, http://www.spurgeongems.org/vols55-57/chs3155.pdf (accessed September 9, 2013).

14. Jeremiah Burroughs, *The Saints' Happiness: Sermons on the Beatitudes*, repr. (Sanford, FL: Soli Deo Gloria Publications, 1988), 1.

15. Ibid.

16. John R. W. Stott, *The Message of the Sermon on the Mount (Matthew 5–7)* (Downers Grove, IL: InterVarsity Press, 1993), 9.

17. Ibid., 15.

18. Ibid., 30, citing F. F. Bruce.

19. Rufus, *Extra Virgin Grace*, Kindle locations 1278–1282.

20. Oswald Chambers, "The Account With Persecution," in *My Utmost for His Highest* (Uhrichsville, OH: Barbour Publishing, Inc., 1935, 1963), July 14.

21. It has been reprinted by different publishers over the decades.

22. For more on Jesus's encounter with the rich young ruler, see chapter 11, note 12.

23. Acts 5:42; 8:4, 12, 25, 35, 40; 10:36; 11:20; 13:32; 14:7, 15, 21; 15:35; 16:10; 17:18.

24. It is absolutely true that "God sent forth his Son, born of woman, born under the law, to redeem those who were under the law, so that we might receive adoption as sons" (Gal. 4:4–5). But as the New Testament plainly teaches, He then brought the message of the good news of God's grace and announced the in-breaking of God's kingdom. And there is no doubt that certain teachings had immediate application to His Jewish hearers, such as Matthew 5:41, "And if anyone forces you to go one mile, go with him two miles," which referred to a Roman soldier ordering someone living in Roman-occupied territory to carry his arms for one mile, but the *application* of His words to any number of situations is self-evident.

25. For the massive implications of this, see Michael L. Brown, *Israel's Divine Healer*, Studies in Old Testament Biblical Theology (Grand Rapids, MI: Zondervan, 1995), 215–218. Used by permission.

26. Crowder, *Mystical Union*, 79–80.

27. As noted in the *Theological Dictionary of the New Testament* (1:613), "Jesus speaks here as He who inaugurates the new epoch which replaces and transcends all that has gone before, the Law, the prophets and the Baptist." See also I. H. Marshall, *The Gospel of Luke: A Commentary on the Greek Text*, New International Greek Testament Commentary (Grand Rapids, MI: Eerdmans, 1978), 628–629, "A new era has begun ἀπὸ τότε [*apo tote*], i.e. from the time of John.... The facts that Luke presents John as a preacher of

good news in 3:18 (cf. 1:77), and that he regards the ministry of John as the beginning of the gospel (Acts 1:22)."

28. Steve McVey, *Grace Walk: What You've Always Wanted in the Christian Life* (Eugene, OR: Harvest House, 1995), 105; while I totally affirm that everything flows out of our abiding in the vine in intimacy with Jesus, I do not see this in opposition to having divine values written on our hearts, as noted in the last chapter.

29. Ibid., 97.

30. See Richard Bauckham, *Jesus and the Eyewitnesses: The Gospels as Eyewitness Testimony* (Grand Rapids, MI: Eerdmans, 2006).

31. Charles Spurgeon, *Sermons on the Miracles* (n.p.: Marshall, Morgan and Scott, n.d.), 92. Viewed at Google Books.

32. My colleague Bob Gladstone has pointed out that in the Sermon on the Mount, it is the joyful life ("blessed!") received as a result of living by the Beatitudes that empowers the disciple to live out the rest of the sermon (Matt. 5–7).

33. I read one argument that when Jesus made reference to "all that I commanded you" in Matthew 28:20, He was actually speaking of His post-resurrection commands. Not only is there no evidence for this, but it makes void all the words of Jesus before the cross (which are essential for making disciples) and replaces them with a handful of teachings or commands after the resurrection. It is also refuted by the Greek, which speaks of commands given at a previous time.

34. This clearly goes beyond the warning to "this…generation" in Mark 8:38.

14—The New Gnostics

1. See chapter 5.

2. As we noted in chapter 5, there was most likely no such thing as Gnosticism when these letters were written, but the seeds of that false teaching appear to have existed already in the last third of the first century AD.

3. See chapter 11.

4. Edwin M. Yamauchi, "Gnosticism," in Craig A. Evans and Stanley E. Porter, eds., *Dictionary of New Testament Background* (Downers Grove, IL: InterVarsity Press, 2000), 416.

5. According to Richard J. Bauckham, "This is especially suitable for the interpretation of the false teachers as Gnostics; they classify themselves as pneumatics and the ordinary Christians as psychics [meaning, soulish]." See Richard J. Bauckham, *2 Peter, Jude*, Word Biblical Commentary (Dallas: Word, 1983), 105.

6. Keener, *The IVP Bible Background Commentary: New Testament*, 736.

7. Prince, *Destined to Reign*, 24.

8. First John 1:9 reads, "If we confess our sins, he is faithful and just to forgive us our sins and to cleanse us from all unrighteousness." We discussed this text at length in chapter 5.

9. See, for example, Jeremiah 3:1 and Ephesians 5:22–32. Let's also remember that the Jewish people have often read the Song of Solomon as the love song between God and Israel while Christians have often read it as the love song between Jesus and the church.

10. McVey, 52 *Lies Heard in Church Every Sunday*, 73.

11. Ibid., 75.

12. Ibid., 73, his emphasis.

13. Ibid.

14. Ibid., 76.

15. See 1 John 1:6; 2:3–6, 9–11, 28 (verse 28 indicates that "abiding in Him" is not guaranteed); 3:6, 14–15; 5:2.

16. McVey, 52 *Lies Heard in Church Every Sunday*, 76.

17. Van der Merwe, *GRACE*, 105.

18. For the question of whether we can lose our salvation, see the appendix.

19. This one verse answers the challenge presented forcefully (and with question as to motive) by Pastor Whitten: "Many think and teach that while sin doesn't destroy my relationship with God as a believer, it does damage my fellowship with God implying God punishes or disciplines me for sin by withdrawing His fellowship. Some mental gymnastics are required to arrive at this conclusion, but keeping people under the thumb of God is necessary to make them behave and, after all, behavior control is the goal. The threat of God withholding fellowship while remaining in relationship is another nonbiblical concept. It is a lie. Show me where the New Testament even hints at such a thing. The opposite is true." See *Pure Grace*, 21–22.

20. McVey, 52 *Lies Heard in Church Every Sunday*, 85.

21. Ibid., 139, 144.

22. Whitten, *Pure Grace*, 20.

23. See chapters 6 and 8.

24. As quoted in *The Baptist World Alliance: Second Congress, Philadelphia, June 19–25, 1911*, (Philadelphia: Harper and Brother Company, 1911), 130. Viewed at Google Books.

25. See the parables in Matthew 25, and note also Daniel 12:2–3; Matthew 10:41–42; 1 Corinthians 3:11–15; 2 Corinthians 5:10; 2 Timothy 4:8; 2 John 1:8; Revelation 11:18.

26. Keener, *The IVP Bible Background Commentary: New Testament*, 736.

27. Michael Reyes, "'Hyper-Grace' Is True!", *Loved by God, Loving Others* (blog), February 19, 2013, http://love-god-love-others.blogspot.com/2013/02/hyper-grace-is-true.html (accessed September 10, 2013).

28. Ibid.

29. For example, in 2 Corinthians 5:16, Paul is explaining that he no longer evaluates people based on fleshly, worldly standards, although he once did.

30. Reyes, "'Hyper-Grace' Is True!"

31. He based part of this on a misunderstanding of Hebrews 10:14, treated at length in chapter 7. And note that "sanctified" does *not* mean "being made totally perfect," as he stated to me. This teacher also explained his belief that, while only God can sanctify, we must still be transformed by the renewing of our minds. But if being sanctified means being made perfect, as he claims, then why do we need to be transformed? From what to what?

32. Even those who believe in once saved, always saved and hold that sin will not be held to their account (this includes some hyper-grace teachers) still recognize that sin is very destructive and dangerous for us as believers, with serious consequences.

33. Again, for discussion of Romans 7 and its applicability (or lack thereof) to believers today, see Brown, *Go and Sin No More*, 265–283.

34. Ryan Rufus, *Do Christians Still Have a Sinful Nature?* (n.p.: New Nature Publications, 2011). Used by permission. To be clear once more, Pastor Rufus preaches strongly against sin in the book, even though he believes strongly in once saved, always saved.

35. Sanhedrin 91a–b, as rendered in outline form by Jacob Neusner, *The Babylonian Talmud: Translation and Commentary* (Peabody, MA: Hendrickson, 2007, electronic edition).

36. Most theologians speak of human beings as dichotomous (body and soul; outer man and inner man) vs. trichotomous (body, soul, spirit), but either way, it is clear that that the inner being can be subdivided (at least functionally speaking) into spirit and soul or even heart and mind.

37. Ellis, "'Confronting the Error of Hyper-Grace,' a Response to Michael Brown."

38. See chapter 8 for more on this.

39. Clark Whitten writes, "Can you see the reality that you are not your sin? Your identity is in Christ and your relationship with Him...not your fleshly behavior? How can this shift in perspective, or a deepening of this perspective, revolutionize your walk? To know that there is absolutely NO shame for those who are in Christ Jesus? None, nada, zero...forever...and ever. That in all your fears and failures, you can talk with Him and He will always be right there willing and waiting to love you?" [Clark Whitten, "Team Grace Message for May 29, 2013," Pure Grace Online, http://puregraceonline.com/team-grace-message-for-may-29-2013/ (accessed September 10, 2013)] I absolutely affirm the last sentence of this paragraph, but it is all too easy to come to wrong conclusions—and open the door to wrong living—based on the first two sentences.

40. A hyper-grace teacher explained to me his belief that Paul was speaking by faith when he said to the Corinthians, "This is what you were" [speaking of being fornicators or adulterers or drunkards or practicing homosexuals] "but you've been washed, sanctified and justified" (1 Cor. 6:11), since, this teacher claimed, the Corinthians were *still living in these very sins* when he wrote to them. To the contrary, Paul is saying that some

of the believers *used to live like this* but they didn't any longer. So, without any textual evidence, this teacher claims that Paul was making a faith statement about people who were not actually changed, claiming they already were changed. This reminds me of one Word of Faith Bible school that had to tell its prospective students not to use "faith" answers when they applied (some applicants actually changed their past by "faith," claiming, for example, that they hadn't done drugs for the last five years though they had done drugs in the last five months; others gave "faith" answers about their personal finances and even wrote "faith" checks!).

41. Ellis, *The Gospel in Ten Words*, 143.

42. Prince, *Destined to Reign*, 167.

43. Prince, *Unmerited Favor*, 147.

44. This saying from Pastor Prince is widely quoted, and justifiably so.

45. The Greek verbs certainly cannot mean anything less than this.

46. Farley, *The Naked Gospel*, 151.

47. Wuest, *Wuest's Word Studies from the Greek New Testament: For the English Reader, ad loc.* The original was formatted in italics. He continues, "'Sin' here is singular in number and is used without the definite article, all pointing to the fact that the nature is referred to, not acts of sin. Here we have the denial of the indwelling, totally depraved nature passed down the race from Adam.... The Christian who believes his evil nature has been completely eradicated is deceiving himself, nobody else. All others can see sin stick out all over his experience. And that sin must come from the indwelling sinful nature. John says that the truth is not in that person. In the case of the Gnostics, that statement must be taken in an absolute sense. They were unsaved. In the case of a misinformed and mistaken present-day Christian, the statement will have to be qualified to mean that the truth of the indwelling sinful nature is not in him. The context would require this interpretation."

48. Crowder, *Mystical Union*, 54. This, of course, is based on Crowder's understanding of Galatians 2:20, claiming that our positional standing in the Lord actually equals our total and complete identity even at the present time; see chapter 7.

49. Rabe, *Metanoia*, Kindle location 229. It is remarkable to see how he quotes 1 John 1 to come to the opposite conclusion of what John was saying.

50. For other relevant verses, see the discussion in chapter 9.

51. See Crowder, *Mystical Union*.

52. Dunn, *The Happy Gospel*, 156.

53. Ibid. In order to justify some of his exaggerated and, I believe, erroneous claims, he uses bizarre and impossibly wrong interpretations of Scripture. For instance, in Genesis 4:7, God says to Cain, "If you do well, will you not be accepted? And if you do not do well, sin is crouching at the door. Its desire is for you, but you must rule over it." He interprets the text as follows: "The Lord here is actually saying to Cain, 'If you did not do well, in that you did not offer the sacrifice I required, a sin-offering (Christ

the lamb) is lying on all fours waiting at the entrance of your door, ready to be sacrificed.'" (See *The Happy Gospel*, page 145.) This is flatly untrue according to Scripture, despite the citations he provides to attempt to justify this. For those familiar with the term *eisegesis*, reading one's ideas into the text, this would be a good example, even if an extreme one.

54. Rufus, "Totally Forgiven! Totally United! Totally Filled!" In *Do Christians Have a Sinful Nature?* (Kindle location 80) he states that the belief that Christians still have to struggle with a sinful nature is "heresy and an affront to the cross!" Even if you agree with him that believers no longer have a sinful nature, to call this "heresy" would mean that some of the finest Christian leaders in history (and until this day) were heretics.

55. See chapter 7.

56. Crisco, *Extraordinary Gospel*, 155, 157, 167, my emphasis added. For the meaning of 1 John 4:17, see chapter 8, note 22.

57. Rabe, *Metanoia*, Kindle location 293.

58. Dunn, *Happy Gospel*, 67. In support, he quotes the Amplified Bible's rendering of Isaiah 53:11, "shall…My Servant, justify many and make many righteous (upright and in right standing with God), for He shall bear their iniquities and their guilt [with the consequences, says the Lord]." Unfortunately, the Amplified Bible simply adds the words in brackets; the Hebrew doesn't say this.

59. I will not provide links because they are too profane.

60. Post sent to the author via e-mail on June 9, 2013.

15—The Finished Work of the Cross

1. A. W. Pink, "The Gospel of Satan," http://www.pbministries.org/books/pink/Miscellaneous/gospel_of_satan.htm (accessed September 10, 2013). He raised similar warnings about a misuse of "the finished work of the cross" in a number of his other writings.

2. Mooney, *Look! The Finished Work of Jesus*, 43.

3. Joseph Prince, "It Is Finished!", July 1, 2012, devotional, his emphasis, http://www.josephprinceonline.com/2012/07/it-is-finished/ (accessed September 10, 2013). This was the full paragraph: "My friend, the work is finished. The victory is won. Our enemies have been made His footstool. Our blessings have been bought by His blood! Live life knowing that there is nothing for you to do—only believe! It is finished!"

4. For other calls to good works in the New Testament, see, e.g., Matthew 5:16; Titus 2:7, 14; 3:8, 14; Hebrews 10:24.

5. Gulley and Mulholland, *If Grace Is True*, 7–8.

6. The authors also claim that their beliefs are grounded both in the Scriptures and the early church.

7. Crowder, *Mystical Union*, 154.

8. Rob Bell, *Love Wins: A Book About Heaven, Hell, and the Fate of Every Person Who Ever Lived* (New York: Harper Collins, 2012), 172.

9. Bill Snell, "Grace Is Neither 'Hyper" nor 'Dangerous,'" GraceOrlando .com, March 26, 2013, http://www.graceorlando.com/grace-is-neither-hyper -nor-dangerous/ (accessed September 10, 2013). The post by Pastor Bill Snell, who serves with Pastor Clark Whitten, mentions that, "It is important to know that Dr. Brown has not seen fit to contact us, nor has he bothered to dialogue with us in anyway before making his slanderous statements." In point of fact, I was attempting to make contact with them at that very time, and Pastor Snell and I subsequently interacted at length by phone and e-mail in a very cordial, mutually respectful way, both with the goal of seeing Jesus exalted and God's people transformed. The article remains unchanged, however, at the time of this writing.

10. Prince, *Unmerited Favor*, 182.

11. Andrew Wommack, "Living in the Balance of Grace and Faith," Andrew Wommack Ministries, http://www.awmi.net/extra/article/living_balance (accessed September 10, 2013).

12. G. R. Beasley-Murray, *John*, Word Biblical Commentary (Dallas: Word, 2002), 352–353, citing Dauer, *Passionsgeschichte*, 20.

13. D. A. Carson, *The Gospel According to John*, The Pillar New Testament Commentary (Grand Rapids, MI: Eerdmans, 1991), 621.

14. B. F. Westcott, *The Gospel According to St. John Introduction and Notes on the Authorized Version* (London: J. Murray, 1908), 277–278.

15. Marcus Dods, *The Gospel of St. John* (New York: George H. Doran Company, 1910), 859.

16. Michael Donahoe, comment to article "The Old Testament Law…FULFILLED," January 26, 2012, http://www.newcovenantgrace.com/old-testament-law-fulfilled/ (accessed September 10, 2013).

17. For example, see *For His Glory* newsletter, September 2011, http://www.forhisglory.org/NewsLetters/201109/Newsletter.pdf (accessed September 10, 2013). I agree with the general message of this web page; it is just inaccurate in its statement that "It is finished" primarily means "paid in full." Of course, Jesus spoke either Aramaic or Hebrew on the cross, not Greek, but John is communicating a specific point in the use of the Greek in John 19:27, 30.

18. See previous note.

19. See note 1 for this chapter.

20. Ryle, *Holiness: Its Nature, Hindrances, Difficulties, and Roots.*

21. Charles Spurgeon, "Threefold Sanctification," sermon no. 434, delivered February 9, 1862, at the Metropolitan Tabernacle, Newington, http://www.spurgeongems.org/vols7-9/chs434.pdf (accessed September 11, 2013). According to Spurgeon, "We are justified through the Imputed Righteousness of Christ, but as to being imputedly *sanctified*, no one who understands the use of language can so speak! The term is inaccurate and unscriptural.…It is a fact that for the sake of what Jesus Christ did, God's people, though in themselves but *partially* sanctified as being yet subject to sin, are for Christ's sake treated and regarded as if they were perfectly

holy. But this, according to theological definitions, is rather Justification than Sanctification; it must, however, be admitted that the Scripture sometimes uses the word 'sanctification' in such a manner as to make it tantamount to justification. This, however, we can clearly see, that God's people have access with boldness to the Lord, because they are regarded through Christ as though they were perfectly holy. Oh, Brethren, think of this for a moment! A holy God cannot have dealings with unholy men. A holy God—and is not Christ Jesus God?—cannot have communion with unholiness, and yet you and I are unholy! How, then, does Christ receive us to His bosom? How does His Father walk with us and find Himself agreed? Because He views us, not in ourselves, but in our great federal Head, the Second Adam" (his emphasis). Yet Spurgeon wrote this, which would be affirmed by many hyper-grace teachers, while rejecting the notion that our sanctification was already total and complete. This, again, is our *positional* sanctification.

22. The word *sin* in 2 Corinthians 5:21 could also mean "sin offering," as seen in the Complete Jewish Bible's rendering: "God made this sinless man be a sin offering on our behalf, so that in union with him we might fully share in God's righteousness."

Appendix—Once Saved, Always Saved?

1. Whitten, *Pure Grace*, 130.

2. One caller to my radio show suggested that 2 Timothy 2:13 answered this challenge, as it says, "If we are faithless, he remains faithful—for he cannot deny himself." But I pointed out to him that this verse follows 2 Timothy 2:12, "If we endure, we will also reign with him; if we deny him, he also will deny us." As Greek scholar William D. Mounce explained in *Pastoral Epistles*, Word Biblical Commentary (Dallas: Word, 2000), 519, "Paul concludes with a magnificent hymn, which regardless of origin speaks directly to Timothy and his historical situation and includes a strong eschatological emphasis. (1) Conversion: those who have died with Christ in their conversion/baptism will live with Christ in their post-conversion life (sanctification). (2) Perseverance: if during their lives as believers they continue to be faithful to God and persevere, then they will surely reign with Christ in heaven. (3) Apostasy: however, if some deny Christ, if through their lives they deny knowing him by their word and deed, then before the judgment seat Christ will also deny knowing them. (4) Faithlessness: however, if a believer fails to persevere fully but yet stops short of apostasy, God will remain true to his character, true to his promises, and therefore will remain faithful to that person (immutability of God)." Similarly, J. N. D. Kelly states in *The Pastoral Epistles*, Black's New Testament Commentary (London: Continuum, 1963), 180: "But what **if we** actually **disown him**? The stern answer, based on Christ's own warning (Mt. 10:33), is that he **will also disown us**. The reference is again to the Last Judgment, when the Lord will refuse to recognize those who have denied him. [v. 13] The

hymn then envisages a further possibility—**if we prove faithless**. Some interpret this (Gk. *apistoumen*) as equivalent to 'if we abandon faith in him', i.e. apostatize. But this is to repeat the thought of the preceding sentence; it also ignores the fact that the verb is in the present (of continuous action?), not in the future, like **disown**. Hence the paraphrase 'if we fail to live up to our profession', or 'if we sin and prove unstable in trials and temptations', seems to bring out the meaning better. The rejoinder which in strict logic we expect is, 'he too will be faithless', but the paradox of the divine love does not permit that. Triumphantly the truth comes out: **he remains faithful**." I mention this here because this is the closest anyone has ever come to answering this challenge, but of course, this verse too does *not* teach that no matter how you live or what you do, you cannot forfeit your salvation.

3. See, for example, Matthew 24:4–5 and 1 Corinthians 6:9–10.